T0000699

Rodale Classics

The Rodale Book of Composting

Simple Methods to Improve Your Soil,
Recycle Waste, Grow Healthier Plants,
and Create an Earth-Friendly Garden

Grace Gershuny & Deborah L. Martin, Editors

RODALE.

Copyright © 1979, 1992 by Rodale, Inc.
Copyright © 2018 by Hearst Magazines, Inc.

All rights reserved.

Published in the United States by Rodale Books, an imprint of the Crown Publishing Group,
a division of Penguin Random House LLC, New York.
crownpublishing.com
rodalebooks.com

RODALE and the Plant colophon are registered trademarks of Penguin Random House LLC.

Originally published as *The Rodale Guide to Composting* in 1979 and subsequently
in a revised edition as *The Rodale Book of Composting* in 1992.

"Compost in a Bag" on page 164 is adapted from *The National Gardening Association Guide
to Kid's Gardening* by Lynn Ocone with Eve Pranis, copyright © 1990 National Gardening
Association, Inc. Reprinted by permission of John Wiley & Sons, Inc. "Creating a Small-Scale
Ecosystem" on page 42 is adapted from an article in *Green Scene: The Magazine of the
Pennsylvania Horticultural Society*, copyright © 1990 Pennsylvania Horticultural Society,
325 Walnut Street, Philadelphia, PA 19106.

Library of Congress Cataloging-in-Publication Data is available upon request.

ISBN 978-1-63565-102-7

Ebook ISBN 978-1-63565-103-4

Printed in the United States of America

Book design by Joanna Williams
Photographs by Rodale Images
Illustrations by John Carlance and Jerry O'Brien

5 7 9 10 8 6

Second Revised Edition

The Rodale Book of Composting

CONTENTS

Introduction vii

1 Composting throughout
   History... 1

2 The Benefits of Compost.................................. 8

3 Life inside a Compost Heap............................. 26

4 Compost and Plant Health 45

5 The Frontiers of Composting 64

6 Materials for Composting................................ 81

7 Using Manure.. 133

8 Methods 143

9 Composting with Earthworms...................... 182

10 Compost Structures 195

11 Shredders and Other Equipment.................. 214

12 Using Compost.. 228

13 Large-Scale Composting............................... 242

Appendix: Resources and Information...281

Index..285

INTRODUCTION

In a recent visit to the Bronx Zoo, I learned to my surprise that composting, far from being an ingenious human invention, is actually known to be performed instinctively by a species of animal. The Australian brushturkey (*Alectura lathami*) is a common, widespread species of mound-building bird native to eastern Australia. The males of this species build mounds of fresh organic material in which multiple females, attracted by the industriousness displayed and ready to mate, lay their enormous eggs. The heat of the decomposing organic material then serves to incubate the eggs, as the diligent male monitors the temperature by sticking his beak into the mound and adjusts it by adding or removing material to maintain the optimum level of warmth. Apparently, the warmer the temperature, the higher the number of females that eventually hatch out, full fledged and ready to fly away.

This was a fitting bit of knowledge to acquire after wrapping up revisions to the 1992 edition of the *Rodale Book of Composting*. First published in 1967 as *The Complete Book of Composting*, the book was originally authored by J. I. Rodale. It was an honor to have the opportunity to help create a more compact and useful version of this classic in 1992, and when I was asked to revise and update the book again for the edition you have in your hands, I could hardly decline.

The pace of change in the world has seemed to accelerate since 1992, when the internet was yet to dominate the world of publishing and information sharing. While compost is a timeless substance, scientific understanding and practical applications of compost and the composting process have also expanded considerably in that time. Rapidly growing public awareness of the importance of recycling organic materials to build healthy soil and healthy humans has translated into proliferating public policies that support organics recycling. Let's hope that the speed of change for the better—more organic production and household composting—outpaces change for the worse—increased climate chaos and pollution.

Some of the changes that have helped compost assume a greater level of importance in the United States include:

- Organic food and fiber has become a $50 billion industry in the United States, with a wide range of organic products available to consumers everywhere. As a result, the public is increasingly aware of environmental and health-related problems of the existing food system.
- Organic methods, including making and using compost, are now considered the best practices in farming and gardening by many farmers, researchers, and educators. As land under organic management increases, so too does stable soil organic content–a key strategy for sequestering atmospheric carbon and countering climate change.
- In 2017 curbside organics collection programs were accessible to more than 5 million residents in hundreds of communities–nearly doubling the number in 2014.
- Urban farming and community gardening have taken root in diverse communities, from Boston to Seattle, as well as heartland cities like Milwaukee, Detroit, and Cleveland. Food justice activists recognize that compost and organic waste recycling are key to making fresh, healthy produce available to all.

In revising this classic book, we have sought to keep as much as possible of the interesting and useful information that never goes out of date. At the same time we have trimmed some of the information no longer relevant to today's environmental landscapes and updated information about soil biology, innovative composting methods, and state and local policies to promote wider use of composting for organic recycling and soil improvement. Some new material you will find in this edition includes:

- Emphasis on the historical development of composting knowledge through indigenous cultures in different environments
- More attention to the importance of fungi and how to promote increased fungal growth in compost
- The emergence of community composting programs throughout the country
- Emphasis on avoiding soil disturbance when applying and incorporating compost

- Diverse methods and technologies for farm-scale and municipal composting
- Updated regulatory considerations with the advent of USDA's National Organic Program
- A new appendix with expanded resources for information specific to your community, with websites to help you find any compost-related needs. Also included are a few classic books related to composting and organic soil management.

With a plethora of great information about how to build compost structures and practical composting techniques available on the internet, we have eliminated the more elaborate plans for building compost structures at home. The internet is also the best place to find sources for compost tools and supplies, and a wide range of compost-related gadgets and equipment can easily be found at home and garden supply centers throughout the country.

The potential to protect our soil and water and restore nutrition to our food through learning to compost and working with our neighbors to recycle food and yard wastes can inspire hope in a time when threats to the health of our planet and the public loom large. With this in mind, please apply this knowledge to the extent you are able, and enjoy witnessing the magical transformation of garbage into gold.

—Grace Gershuny
November 2017

COMPOSTING THROUGHOUT HISTORY

Composting is, in broadest terms, the biological reduction of organic wastes to humus. Whenever a plant or animal dies, its remains are attacked by soil microorganisms and larger soil fauna and are eventually reduced to an earth-like substance that forms a beneficial growing environment for plant roots.

This process, repeated continuously in endless profusion and in every part of the world where plants grow, is part of the ever-recurring natural process that supports all terrestrial life. The entire composting process is difficult to contemplate in its full dimensions. Let's just say that compost and composting are, like water and air, essentials of life.

A different, more common, definition of compost requires human participation in the process. The word *compost* comes from the Old French, meaning a mixture of various organic materials. The word *humus* comes from the same root as *human* and *humility*. Ordinarily, when we speak of compost and composting, we are referring to the process by which we transform organic wastes into a soil-building substance for farm, orchard, or garden.

Even when considering this common definition, however, the origins of human composting activities quickly become buried in the sands of prehistory. The best we can surmise is that sometime after people began to cultivate food to augment hunting and food-gathering activities, they discovered the benefits of compost, probably in the form of animal manure. Noting, perhaps, that food crops grew more vigorously in areas where manure had been deposited, they made the connection between the two phenomena and began a more selective application of the composting process.

INDIGENOUS COMPOST KNOWLEDGE

Ancient and indigenous cultures worldwide have handed down their knowledge to guide modern composters.

Compost was known to the Romans; the Greeks had a word for it, and so did the ancient Middle Eastern civilizations. The Bible is interspersed with references to the cultivation of soil. Dung was used as fuel and as fertilizer. Manure was sometimes spread directly onto fields. It was also composted, along with street sweepings and organic refuse, on the dunghill outside city walls.

According to the Talmud, raw manure was not to be handled by the truly religious because it was unclean. A Talmud commentator set down the rule for the faithful: "Do not use your manure until some time after the outcasts have used theirs," thus advocating the use of rotted or composted manure instead of fresh animal matter.

Beyond Europe, rotted organic materials were widely used by indigenous cultures on every continent, including the Americas. The practice of burying fish in corn planting hills was taught to early European settlers in New England, along with the collection of seaweed from coastal areas. The ancient Mayans and other Mesoamerican peoples used sophisticated systems that integrated fish culture and plants to fertilize crops with the rich sediment from their fishponds.

Sub-Saharan African civilizations began to domesticate cattle and presumably used their manure to help improve crops such as millet and sorghum as these crops entered cultivation. Ancient African village sites later became fertile ground when farmers found rich black earth in decomposed middens, which had mixed with ash from cook fires. Similarly, ancient Amazonian civilizations are believed to have grown on soil made fertile by incorporating charcoal to create the rich "terra preta," a recent discovery that has spurred interest in using biochar (a form of charcoal created by heating carbonaceous material under conditions of low oxygen) in composts.

Back in the early 20th century, American agricultural scientist Franklin Hiram King traveled to Asia to document the farming practices that had allowed some of these lands to be maintained under continuous cultivation for thousands of years. His *Farmers of Forty Centuries* remains a classic treatise on sustainable practices of the peasants of China, Southeast Asia, and India that include use of human manure and meticulous collection and return of organic matter to the soil on terraced hillsides.

COMPOSTING IN EUROPE AND ITS COLONIES

Much of the agricultural wisdom of the ancients survived the European Dark Ages to reappear—along with other fundamental scientific knowledge—in the writings of learned Arabs. Ibn al-'Awwam, variously assigned to the 11th and 12th centuries, goes into extensive detail on the processing and use of compost and other manures in his *Kitab al-Falahah*, or Book of Agriculture.

The medieval Catholic Church was another repository of knowledge and lore, thanks to the efforts of a few devoted monks. Within monastery enclosures, sound agricultural practices were preserved, applied, and, in some instances, taught to the neighboring farmers by the abbot, acting as a sort of medieval local extension agent.

Renaissance literature makes numerous references to compost. Shakespeare's Hamlet advises: "And do not spread the compost on the weeds, / To make them ranker."

Public accounts of the use of stable manure in composting date to the 18th century. Early colonial farmers abandoned the fish-to-each-hill-of-corn system of fertilizing when they discovered that by properly composting two loads of muck and one load of barnyard manure, they obtained a product equivalent to three loads of manure in fertilizing value.

Many New England farmers found it economical to use the whitefish or menhaden abundant in Long Island Sound, as well as manure, in their compost heaps. Stephen Hoyt and Sons of New Canaan, Connecticut, made compost on a large scale, using 220,000 fish in one season. A layer of muck 1 foot in thickness would be spread on the ground, then a layer of fish on top of that, a layer of muck, a layer of fish, and so on, topped off with a layer of muck, until the heap reached a height of 5 or 6 feet. This was periodically turned until the fish (except the bones) was completely disintegrated.

Our first president was a skilled farmer and a strong advocate of proper composting methods. According to Paul L. Haworth, author of the 1915 biography *George Washington: Farmer,* Washington "saved manure as if it were already so much gold, and hoped with its use and with judicious rotation of crops to accomplish" good tilth.

Thomas Jefferson was also an innovative farmer. Noting the difficulty and expense entailed in carrying manure to distant fields, he came upon the idea of stationing cattle for extended periods of time in the middle of the field that needed fertilization. Both Washington and Jefferson were slaveholders who undoubtedly relied on the skill and expertise of their enslaved workers. It is well established that African slaves were responsible for the introduction of rice as well as cattle raising in the "new world."

The famed African American botanist, chemist, and agriculturist George Washington Carver advised the farmer to compost materials and return them to the land. In a 1936 agricultural experiment station bulletin titled *How to Build Up and Maintain the Virgin Fertility of Our Soil,* Dr. Carver wrote, "Make your own fertilizer on the farm. Buy as little as possible. A year-round compost pile is absolutely essential and can be had with little labor and practically no cash outlay."

Dr. Carver also stressed the importance of covering the heap to prevent the leaching away of nutrients by rain. He explained:

> It is easy to see that our farm animals are great fertilizer factories, turning out the cheapest and best known product for the permanent building up of the soil. In addition to this farmyard manure, there are also many thousands of tons of the finest fertilizer going to waste all over the South, in the form of decaying leaves of the forest and the rich sediment of the swamp, known as "muck." Every idle moment should be put in gathering up these fertilizers.

Relatively small quantities of plant material were composted in this period because there was plenty of barnyard manure. However, in some sections of the South, cottonseed was composted with muck. The heap was started with alternate 6-inch layers of muck and 3-inch layers of cottonseed, finished off with a layer of muck. This was turned and repiled once a month, with regular watering, until the cottonseed was completely decomposed.

As America grew older, many of the sons and daughters of the early New England settlers trekked westward, searching for more abundant, lower-priced land. Some of them found soil so rich in organic matter from buffalo droppings, plants, grasses, and dead animals, all nicely composted, that little thought was given to composting. Only a few farsighted settlers in this newly discovered land of plenty continued composting practices proven effective by farming poorer soil.

ORGANIC ORIGINS

Composting has been a basis of the organic method of gardening and farming since the days of Sir Albert Howard, father of the organic method. Howard, a British government agronomist, spent the years from 1905 to 1934 in the district of Indore in India, where he slowly evolved the organic concept. By carefully observing the practices of the farmers where he was stationed and conducting his own experiments, Howard found that the best compost consisted of three times as much plant matter as manure. By this means, he devised the Indore method of compost making, in which materials are layered sandwich fashion, then are turned (or mixed by earthworms) during decomposition.

Austrian philosopher Rudolf Steiner outlined the principles of biodynamic agriculture in 1924, emphasizing composting as a central practice. Biodynamic farmers and gardeners approach composting with a kind of reverence; making compost entails use of specific preparations, which are thought to inoculate it with beneficial organisms and stimulate their activity. Adherents of biodynamics have been highly influential in promoting the idea of gardening in harmony with nature.

In 1942, J. I. Rodale, pioneer of the organic method in America, began monthly publication of *Organic Farming and Gardening*. In his publications, Rodale assimilated the ideas of Howard as well as Steiner, through his contact with Steiner's student Dr. Ehrenfried Pfeiffer, and added knowledge gained by further experimentation. From the beginning, Rodale's advocacy of the organic method extolled the use of compost and stressed its importance as a garden necessity. Subsequent developments in composting included adding ground rock powders to the heap, sheet composting, shredding materials for quicker decomposition, digester composting, and numerous other innovations discussed later in this book.

J. I. Rodale introduced American gardeners to the value of composting as a means of building soil quality.

The history of compost, then, is both ancient and modern. Compost has been understood by indigenous cultures on every continent as a transitional force in the life cycle. For millennia, people depended on compost to sustain croplands and to feed themselves. It was not until the 19th century, in fact, that we began to substitute chemical fertilizers for compost in the new "scientific" method of farming.

France's Jean-Baptiste Boussingault laid the foundations of agricultural chemistry in 1834. Then, in 1840, the great German scientist Justus von Liebig published his classic monograph on agricultural chemistry. Up until that time, the humus theory had prevailed. It was believed that plants actually ate humus in order to grow. Liebig disproved this theory, demonstrating that plants obtained nourishment from certain chemicals in solution. Since humus was insoluble in water, Liebig dismissed its significance in plant growth.

For the next century, agricultural practice became increasingly chemical in nature. It is ironic that in 1940, exactly 100 years after Liebig's classic work, Sir Albert Howard published his own magnum opus, *An Agricultural Testament*, which set in motion the movement to organic farming and gardening that today is widely accepted throughout the world. Even farmers and gardeners who depend heavily and routinely on chemical fertilizers now know of the value of compost and organic matter.

Today, the organic method of farming and gardening is more popular than it has ever been. Gardeners have led the way in reestablishing organic methods, and increasing numbers of farmers are making the transition to eliminate harmful pesticides and fertilizers. After Rachel Carson galvanized the environmental movement in the 1960s, waves of new farmers began learning about the dangers of agrichemicals, and consumers have become increasingly aware of the nutritional and environmental damage caused by the industrial system of agriculture. Thanks to the introduction of the USDA's National Organic Program, implemented in 2002, certified organic products of every description are available throughout the world. Organic farming, once considered the province of fanatics, has become established as a legitimate agricultural alternative.

With the advent of a federally sanctioned organic marketing program has come increased funding for research and education concerning best organic practices. The benefits of organic management systems and innovations that improve production and efficiency are being demonstrated at numerous land grant agricultural institutions as well as independent nonprofit organizations. The Rodale Institute, founded by J. I.'s son, Robert Rodale, has led the way in establishing long-term research plots comparing organic and conventional methods. In addition to improved soil health and water quality, organic methods are promoted for their support of healthy biodiversity and endangered pollinators. Not least among its many benefits is the mounting recognition that organic land management can mitigate the planetwide crisis of climate change. The sequestration of carbon in the form of soil organic matter, combined with eliminating the use of highly soluble synthetic fertilizers—especially nitrogen—can actually begin to draw down the dangerous levels of carbon dioxide and other greenhouse gases in our atmosphere, in addition to benefiting the health of everyone who eats.

Composting has also gained considerable attention as a solution to the solid-waste crisis now facing municipalities nationwide. Whereas just a few years ago proponents of municipal composting were generally regarded as impractical, now escalating landfill costs and tighter restrictions on disposal of potentially hazardous sewage sludge have dramatically increased the economic attractiveness of large-scale municipal and industrial composting systems. Urban gardeners now have a wide array of bins and barrels available commercially that allow them to make compost quickly and easily. Even non-gardening urbanites have begun saving kitchen scraps and yard wastes for their composting neighbors, in order to cut their trash disposal costs. Several municipalities have instituted mandatory food-scrap recycling programs, complete with curbside pickup available to residents.

It seems clear that composting, which has sustained us since the beginning of history, is now entering an era in which the intelligent use of scientific methods will enhance the quality of life instead of destroying it. In this scenario, compost and composting will find an increasingly welcome place.

2

THE BENEFITS OF COMPOST

Plants, animals, insects, and people are all inextricably linked in a complex web of interrelationships with air, water, soil, minerals, and other natural resources playing vital roles. Compost, too, plays an important role. There is a cycle, a continuity, to life.

We are only at the very beginning of an understanding of all the parts of this cycle of life. But we are learning that upsetting the life patterns of only one kind of plant or animal, even in a seemingly minor way, can have effects on many other living things. All of the environmental problems we face are rooted in a failure to appreciate the life cycle and to keep it intact. We can use our understanding of the interrelationships of living things in active ways, too, to increase the productivity of our fields, forests, orchards, and gardens. Composting is one way to work within the life cycle in the furthering of our welfare.

Compost is more than a fertilizer, more than a soil conditioner. It is a symbol of continuing life. Nature has been making compost since the appearance of primitive life on this planet, eons before humans first walked the earth. Leaves falling to the forest floor are soon composted, returning their nutrients to the trees that bore them. The dead grass of the meadow, seared by winter's frost, is made compost in the dampness of the earth beneath. The birds, the insects, and the animals of field and forest contribute their wastes and eventually their bodies, helping to grow food so that more of their kind may prosper. The greenness of the earth itself is a strong testament to nature's continuing composting program.

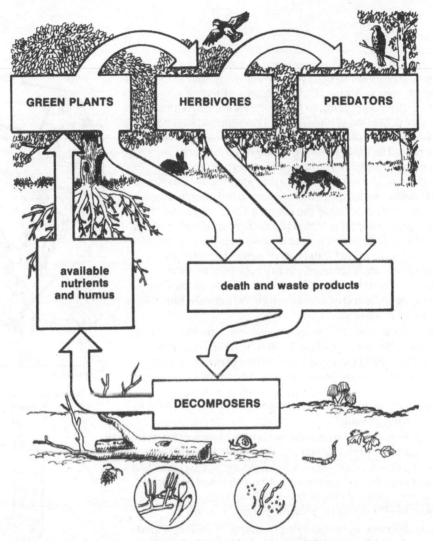

GREEN PLANTS

HERBIVORES

PREDATORS

available nutrients and humus

death and waste products

DECOMPOSERS

In the forest, nutrients are recycled through the natural decomposition of plant and animal waste.

The compost heap in your garden is an intentional replication of the natural process of birth and death that occurs almost everywhere in nature. It did not take long for people to learn to imitate nature by building compost piles, as we saw in Chapter 1. It is ironic that composting, the oldest and most universally practiced form of soil treatment in the world, should today be claiming so many converts.

The realization of the proper place of compost in a complex society strikes many of us in different ways, and at different times. It struck Wayne H. Davis, a professor at the University of Kentucky, in June 1971. He canceled his garbage collection service after having carried two bags of garbage to the curb almost every week of his adult life up to that time. The idea of having to pay more for garbage collection than for his daily newspaper was part of his motivation, but the most important factor was "a desire to find an alternative to what I consider a self-destructive lifestyle that grew out of the country's 'use it once and throw it away' philosophy which replaced the hated rationings of World War II days and led economists into the practice of measuring progress by the rate at which we turn our natural resources into junk. Man's system of moving nutrients from the farm to the ocean by way of sewers and of moving industrial materials from the mines to landfills, is not a viable life-style."

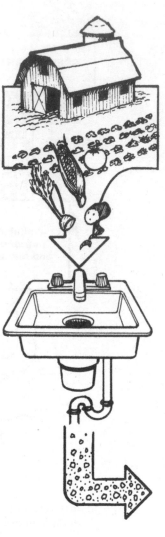

Composting is an ideal form of recycling, returning organic wastes to the use of the land from which they originally came. It is one of the most basic means of conservation, ensuring that future generations will have the same benefit of the earth as we do now. Composting can be seen, in one of its aspects, as an essential part of responsible and efficient home management.

An anthropological study carried out by classes of Dr. William L. Rathje at the University of Arizona reached some startling conclusions about household wastes. Originally a project designed to determine how much could be learned about the habits of people by examining their wastes, the project taught the students some pointed lessons.

It was discovered, by studying a sample of 380 representative household units, that Tucson's population of 450,000 was throwing away more than 9,500 tons of edible food each year. The average middle-income household in the study disposed of 10 percent of the food brought into the home. Students involved in the Tucson study became aware of the tremendous ecological impact of this waste and of its loss to the earth from which it originally came. In addition to loss of nutrients, energy is wasted once as the crops are grown, processed, and transported, and then again as they are transported as "waste" to the incinerator or landfill.

Like the man who canceled his garbage service, many others have achieved a sense of independence and freedom and have realized the satisfactions of sane

Because the compost heap is symbolic of nature's best efforts to build soil, and because compost is such an efficient and practical soil builder, it has become the heart of the organic method of farming and gardening. Composting is among the most important tasks of the organic gardener or farmer because compost builds soil health, and success in gardening and farming depends on the health of the soil.

Compost improves soil texture and structure, qualities that enable soil to retain nutrients, moisture, and air for the support of healthy crops. By increasing the soil's moisture-holding capacity, compost helps control erosion that otherwise would wash topsoil into waterways. Compost is the best recycler of biological wastes, turning millions of tons of our refuse into a food-growing asset. Compost provides and releases plant nutrients, protects against drought, controls pH, supports essential bacteria, feeds helpful earthworms, stops nutrient loss through leaching, acts as a buffer against toxins in the soil, controls weeds, and conserves nonrenewable energy resources. Beyond this, we are learning that using compost in place of synthetic fertilizers, especially nitrogen, not only confers greater resilience in the face of increasingly severe weather events but also works to reverse the dangerous buildup of carbon dioxide in our atmosphere by storing carbon in the form of stable soil humus.

Every gardener knows that compost is valuable, but until we understand more fully all the benefits of compost, we won't understand why it is so important to the success of our organic gardening and farming efforts. In this chapter, we will examine those benefits more closely.

management from dealing responsibly with their own wastes, through composting and through other forms of recycling. Now, thanks to increased economic incentives to compost, generated by the solid waste crisis, it has at last become profitable to act responsibly.

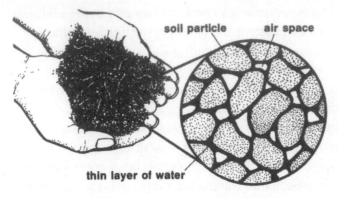

soil particle   air space

thin layer of water

The addition of organic matter to the soil promotes the development of good granular structure that, in turn, helps maintain the balance of air and water.

RESTORING OUR ENVIRONMENT

Recycling garden and food wastes to return to the soil is essential to protecting our environment. It is a truism that there is no such thing as waste in nature. Organic waste can be disposed of by chemical means (burning) or by largely physical means (landfill), but only when it is disposed of by biological means (composting) are plant nutrients conserved to the advantage of the entire ecosystem. Returning wastes to nourish the soil helps restore the balance of our planetary ecosystem.

By drastically reducing the need for synthetic fertilizers, compost reduces damage to our soil and water resources from overuse of these highly soluble materials, and at the same time actually helps reduce the load of greenhouse gases now approaching critical limits in our atmosphere. The manufacture of nitrogen fertilizer in particular is highly energy intensive, accounting for an estimated 2 to 3 percent of all natural gas consumed in the world today. Similarly, highly soluble synthetic phosphate fertilizers are causing increasing problems of algae blooms in lakes and rivers, while nitrate from fertilizer pollutes drinking water downstream. Meanwhile, worldwide phosphorus reserves are dwindling as we must travel farther and work harder to extract them. When food scraps and other organic wastes are composted instead of being sent to landfills, where they emit methane gas (another powerful greenhouse forcer), both the environment and our health win.

Composting is a giant step toward recycling wastes, conserving precious energy reserves, stabilizing our climate, and regaining control of our food supplies. Backyard composting is the first step and the easiest. Farm-scale composting is more difficult to effect but potentially far more beneficial to society as a whole. Municipal composting–the transformation of a city's wastes into compost for farm and garden–is the most far-reaching and potentially beneficial of all.

BUILDING SOIL STRUCTURE

Compost builds good soil structure.

In good garden soils, the individual particles of sand, clay, and silt will naturally group together into larger units called aggregates. This process is essential to a good garden soil, since it promotes aeration and water drainage. The shapes of these aggregates determine the soil structure; the ideal garden soil has a granular, or a crumb, structure. Sandy soils will have poor structure, since sand is too coarse to form aggregates, while a heavy clay soil compacts when wet, inhibiting good plant growth. Compost can correct a soil that is either too sandy or too clayey by adding organic matter and soil-building microbes that encourage aggregate formation. Soils that have been chemically treated, with little or no addition of organic matter, will gradually lose structure, necessitating increased fertilization, cultivation, and irrigation.

Good structure allows a soil to breathe and facilitates circulation. A heavy clay soil tends to become waterlogged quickly, preventing water and air penetration. Adding compost works to loosen this packed soil by stimulating soil biological activity, which helps to open up pore spaces that, like little tunnels, carry air and water down into the soil. A granular structure forms, and a thin film of moisture is held on each granule where plant roots can utilize it as needed.

Sandy soils, which tend to let water drain away too rapidly, are also rebuilt by the addition of compost. The fine particles are held together by fungal secretions such as glomalin, which enables the larger particles to hold greater quantities of water in films on their surfaces.

The higher the humus content, the more moisture a soil can absorb and retain. Soil with ample organic matter and a good cover of living plants or mulch lets raindrops seep gently into it, instead of splattering and churning up soil particles. In the case of packed, crusted soil, a muddy drop of water is formed that will run over the soil surface as the first stage of erosion. A heavy rainstorm may result in considerable runoff that carries away soil.

AGGREGATE FORMATION

The mystery of aggregate formation was solved in great part by two scientists from the National Institute of Agricultural Sciences, Tokyo, many decades ago. In tests made on the decomposition of organic matter and aggregate formation, it was learned that various soil fungi grow on the organic matter. Soil bacteria then come along to turn the fungal products into "cementing materials." These cementing materials "glue" together tiny particles of soil into coarse grains or crumbs.

At the Rothamsted Experimental Station in England, soil microbiologist Dr. R. J. Swaby did extensive research in the 1940s on the mechanism of aggregation. At the beginning, Dr. Swaby reasoned that improved structure must be due to one or all of several things—the roots themselves, microorganisms associated with the roots, or gums and resins produced by these organisms. So his experiments began.

First, he grew grasses in a sterilized soil and measured the structural changes. There were scarcely any. The grass roots were incapable of doing the job without the microorganisms that live and feed on them. These microorganisms were apparently the real soil binders; the grass roots were acting merely as food.

Was it the microorganisms themselves or was it their gummy by-products that bound the soil into desirable water-stable aggregates? Microorganisms known to be gum and resin producers were isolated from soil and grown in laboratory cultures. Their gummy products were added to unstructured soil. There was little improvement in granulation. Apparently the gummy substances were not important.

One by one, the important groups of soil organisms were added to poorly structured, sterilized soil at this stage and allowed to grow and increase. The effect on structure was carefully measured. There was a remarkable improvement when some were added. The soil became granulated and permeable to water.

Easily the most effective organisms were the fungi, or molds. Plants grown in poorly structured soil increased dramatically in size when these were added to the pots. Soil aeration was improved, and water permeability increased. Microscopic bacteria had no such beneficial effects. The threadlike mycelium of the fungi apparently wound itself around soil particles and held them together.

Walking on Harpenden Common at Rothamsted one late-winter morning, Dr. Swaby noticed that some earthworm casts on permanent grassland were more resistant to the disintegration action of thawing snow than were similar casts on nearby wheatland. So the role of earthworms was investigated. Worm casts from various types of soils were collected and tested in the laboratory.

Results showed that earthworms improved the permanence of aggregation of all soils they devoured. Their casts on grassland soil were particularly stable. Evidently, binding substances were derived as grass roots present in the soil passed through the worm.

The extra organic matter in the grassland soil, with its greater number of roots, encouraged a vigorous microbial population in the worms' intestines. These glued the soil into very stable aggregates. Earthworms accounted for another small portion of the field aggregation, but there was still some to be explained. Also, there was still the mystery of the very permanent aggregates found in the field. These were more stable even than worm casts.

Now thinking in terms of humus, Dr. Swaby began to treat soil crumbs with certain extracts. One extract, known as humic acid, gave remarkable results. It not only improved aggregation but increased the permanence of the crumbs already formed.

Humic acid is a complicated product formed during the breakdown of organic matter in the soil. It has so far resisted attempts to unravel its involved chemical formula. In the presence of some minerals, such as calcium and iron, a salt such as calcium humate was formed. This substance often proved more potent than humic acid as a means of increasing the permanence of aggregation, and it explained the extreme stability of the crumb structure of some heavy red and black soils.

With x-ray analysis, chains of humic acid molecules could be detected inside actual clay particles, where they were held electrostatically. The presence of positively charged metals in solution increased the strength of the electrostatic bond and made the aggregate more permanent.

The picture was clearer now. Fungi that are symbiotic with plant roots bound soil particles into aggregates. Earthworms also helped to make soil aggregates. These aggregates were made stable by mobile humic acid compounds formed during the active breakdown of organic matter. Organic matter improved the quantity and quality of aggregation.

But even the strong, humus-bound crumbs are broken down by bacteria. When bacteria help break down organic matter to produce the humus extracts that aid aggregation, other bacteria destroy both these and aggregates bound together by fungal mycelia. Recent studies have focused on one particular type of organism, arbuscular mycorrhizae (sometimes abbreviated as AMF), and their unique protein secretion, called glomalin, as an important component of stable soil aggregates. Although bacteria do not produce these aggregate-forming secretions, they do provide food for the mycorrhizae.

What does this mean agriculturally?

It means that provision must be made in crop rotations to feed organic matter constantly back into the soil to replace that which is broken down by bacteria. If this is not done, the soil structure will suffer.

Drought Protection

Soil improved with compost holds more moisture. The permeability of soils amply supplied with organic matter is a potent weapon against drought damage. Water is soaked up like a sponge and stored on the soil granules (100 pounds of humus hold 195 pounds of water). When the tiny hairs on plant roots can absorb all the water the plant needs from the films on these granules, they do not suffer from long rainless periods.

Granular structure is built not merely by mechanical means but with the help of soil bacteria and fungi. Here, the vital ecology of soil and compost comes sharply into focus.

Stopping Erosion

Erosion is both a cause and a result of a gradual loss of soil fertility. The most important way to prevent erosion is to keep soil under plant cover, so that soil that has been tilled or cultivated is not subject to wind or water damage. Compost helps to stimulate vigorous plant growth and build the good soil structure that encourages optimum fertility and resists erosion. Shortsighted agricultural practices have already led to the erosion and subsequent loss of frightening amounts of America's topsoil. The US Department of Agriculture monitors and reports on soil erosion resulting from agriculture, and despite some improvements implemented through various soil conservation efforts, billions of tons of soil erode away each year in this country. Agricultural activities have been linked to 69 percent of all erosion; for every pound of food consumed in the United States, water erodes an estimated 22 pounds of agricultural soil. Really fertile soil is resistant to erosion, especially wind erosion, as the humus content helps to bind it together in a healthy crumb structure. Keeping soil covered, together with good structure, are key to preventing soil erosion.

The loss of structure, then, is related closely to soil erosion, and the solution to good structure is the incorporation of organic materials into the soil, stimulating more vigorous plant growth and promoting higher populations of beneficial soil organisms. Keeping soil covered and building organic matter by adding compost are key strategies in the fight against erosion.

Improving Aeration

Aeration is also extremely important to soil health. Air plays a vital role in the maintenance of soil productivity. Plant roots and the majority of beneficial soil organisms need to breathe to proliferate. Organisms that can handle poor aeration—known as anaerobic conditions—do not perform the vital functions needed to properly decompose organic matter and release its nutrients to feed the plants. Without air, soils tend to become alkaline, organic matter content decreases, active humus becomes deactivated, total and active humus content decreases, nitrogen content is reduced, and the carbon/nitrogen (C/N) ratio is lowered.

The presence of sufficient air in the soil is necessary for the transformation of minerals to forms usable by plants. Scientists have discovered that forced aeration increases a plant's intake of potassium, one of the macronutrients, or elements most responsible for plant health.

Many of the processes in the soil are oxidative—such as when sulfur is transformed to sulfur dioxide, carbon to carbon dioxide, ammonia to nitrate. Oxygen is essential in these processes, and air is an urgent need of the many beneficial soil organisms that aid in these transformations. In addition, aeration stimulates the mycorrhizal fungi, which help create stable aggregates as well as form a symbiotic relationship with plant roots that acts to feed the plant valuable nutrients.

Compost helps build soil structure that will allow for optimum aeration at

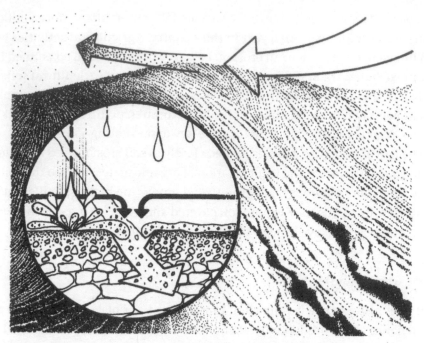

Topsoil erosion is a serious problem in many areas of the United States. Bare mineral soil is easily eroded by wind and water. Knocked loose by raindrops, particles of soil wash away over the soil's surface. Surface runoff comes together into little rivulets or rills that then join to form gullies. The greater the water flow, the more soil is washed away.

all times. Just as organic matter enables soils to hold more water through the enhanced formation of soil aggregates, it also allows more spaces for air between soil granules. In your garden, poor structure and lack of aeration may show up as crusting of the soil surface. Since aggregates are not forming, soil particles become packed together, limiting the entry of water and air into the soil. Newly planted seeds suffer greatly under such conditions: Lack of air and water reduces germination, while seeds that do sprout have difficulty breaking through the soil's hard surface crust.

Nutrients When Plants Need Them

Compost is an excellent vehicle for carrying nutrients to your soil and plants. In a well-planned and -executed composting program, in fact, food crops

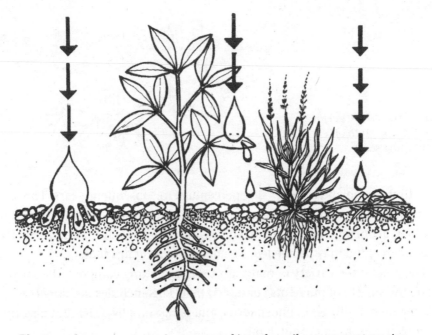

Plants and organic matter incorporated into the soil can prevent erosion by breaking the impact of raindrops, causing more water to be absorbed by the soil and slowing the flow of water over the surface.

and ornamentals will need no other form of fertilization besides good compost.

Further, the naturally occurring nutrients in compost are released slowly at a rate at which the plants can best use them for optimum growth. Compost, then, is not only a source of nutrients, but a storehouse for them.

Compost doles out nutrients slowly when plants are small and at greater rates as soil temperatures warm up and the crops' major growth period begins. This is because soil microorganisms that release the nutrients from compost grow and die faster as temperatures increase. Chemical fertilizer companies have tried to reproduce this effect by marketing their products in timed-release form. Rather than saturating a field with quickly available nitrogen–a major factor in nitrogen pollution of ground and surface waters–such fertilizers slowly release their nitrogen over a period of time. Unfortunately, they are expensive–unlike compost.

For example, when composted, manure releases 50 percent of its nutrients

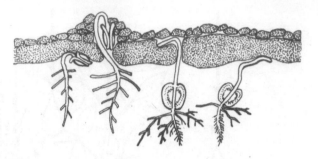

A hard-crusted soil surface hinders the growth of germinating seeds.

in the first season and a decreasing percentage in subsequent years. This means that with constant additions of compost, the reserves of plant nutrients in the soil are being built up to the point where, for several seasons, little fertilizer of any kind may be needed. No chemical can claim that.

The greater the variety of materials used in making compost, the greater will be the variety of nutrients contained in it. This includes not only the major elements–nitrogen, phosphorus, and potassium (N-P-K)–but also the minor elements, or micronutrients.

Although micronutrients are needed by plants in very small amounts in comparison with major elements, they are nevertheless just as essential to plant growth and reproduction. Micronutrients commonly found to be deficient in many soils include iron, cobalt, manganese, boron, zinc, copper, molybdenum, and iodine. Similarly, too much of these elements will affect plant growth. As little as 25 parts per million of nickel will reduce the growth of an orange seedling, for example. Manure and compost usually contain a balanced amount of minor elements, and farmers who still use large amounts of these materials are less likely to encounter deficiencies of minor elements.

Colloids and Minerals

Humus holds nutrients in the soil and makes them readily available to plants. The medium by which organic matter transfers nutrients to plant roots is called base exchange. Colloidal (very tiny) humus particles are negatively charged and attract positive elements, such as potassium, sodium, calcium, magnesium, iron, and copper. Colloidal clay particles have this same ability, but not to as great an extent as humus. When a tiny rootlet moves into contact with some humus, it exchanges hydrogen ions for equivalent quantities of the mineral ions. These are then taken up into the plant.

The mineral-holding capacity of colloidal particles is very important to the maintenance of soil fertility. Lack of soil colloids means that minerals are easily leached out by rain. As Dr. Ehrenfried Pfeiffer, a pioneer of the biodynamic method, pointed out in 1938 in *Bio-dynamic Farming and Gardening*:

One can wash out a soil by frequent percolation until the filtrate no longer contains any minerals in solution. In many cases, the analysis of the soil before and after the washings does not correspond with the amount of minerals washed out. The holding capacity is quite different in soils with a high organic matter content from that of soils with low organic matter. In fact, a soil with high organic matter loses very little through washing out. In the same procedure, a soil plus soluble mineral fertilizer loses not only the added minerals, but quite a bit of its own hidden reserves, too.

One can pour seven times their weight in water through soils with high organic matter in 12 washings, and not lose any appreciable amount of minerals.

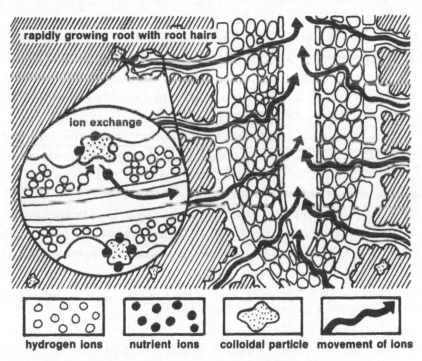

As roots grow, their root hairs encounter soil colloids holding mineral ions. The mineral ions are replaced on the colloid by hydrogen ions that are exuded from the root. The freed mineral ions are then absorbed by the root.

Dr. Pfeiffer explained that this is why crops on low-humus soils exhibit fast growth after a rain—they are absorbing the minerals in solution—but "when drought sets in these crops come to a standstill, and start to head out much too early. Organic soils result in a slower growth during the same period, but the plants continue to grow on into the dry season, head out later, and thus accumulate more weight." They are drawing on the minerals held on the colloids that are plentiful in a humus-rich soil.

NEUTRALIZING TOXINS

Another service of compost occurs in the neutralization of soil toxins. For example, an overabundance of aluminum in the soil solution is highly toxic to plants, since it prevents them from taking up phosphorus. Actively decomposing organic matter results in more effective use of applied phosphorus in soils by the production of organic acids, some of which form stable complexes with iron and aluminum. The aluminum is thus "locked up" in a stable complex, unable to harm plants.

Dr. Selman A. Waksman in his book *Humus: Origin, Chemical Composition, and Importance in Nature* says, "The toxicity of plant poisons becomes less severe in a soil high in humus than in a soil deficient in humus; high salt concentrations are less injurious; and aluminum solubility and its specific injurious action are markedly decreased."

"Organic matter has a high capacity to fix heavy metals and many papers have been written on the subject," observed Dr. M. B. Kirkham, who conducted a study on organic matter and heavy metals at the University of Massachusetts. "Indigenous soil organic matter and that added in sewage sludge, farmyard manures, composts, crop residues, and peat, bind heavy elements in soil. Most heavy metals associated with soil organic matter are in insoluble and stable combinations and are relatively unavailable for plant uptake. The ability of soil organic matter to hold heavy elements necessary for growth for a long time and release them as needed to crops is one of the most important benefits derived from its presence in soils."

Compost can also function as a "probiotic" for soil that has been damaged by overuse of toxic substances such as herbicides. According to retired Perdue University plant pathologist Dr. Don Huber, the mode of action of all herbicides is similar to that of antibiotics. Soil organisms take a beating from repeated doses of any herbicide, so inoculating soil that has been treated with herbicides is a good first step in restoring its microbial workforce. Beyond this, composts can be specifically managed to support disease-suppressing organisms that can keep plant pathogens like blight and damping-off fungus in check.

A BETTER BUFFER

By adding humus to the soil, compost helps plants overcome soil pH levels that are either too low (acidic) or too high (alkaline). Humus acts as a buffer in the soil. Garden and crop plants are less dependent upon a specific soil pH when there is an abundant supply of humus. For instance, in soils where the humus content is low, potatoes require acidic conditions. If such soils are more alkaline, potatoes are highly susceptible to potato scab. In soils better supplied with humus, they suffer no potato scab even when the soil is slightly alkaline.

Soils in certain regions of the United States exhibit characteristic pH levels. Throughout the Southwest, soils are typically alkaline. High pH levels reduce the number of soil microorganisms and make growing vegetables—most of which prefer slightly acidic conditions—difficult or impossible. In parts of New England, northern Michigan and Wisconsin, northwestern Minnesota, New York, New Jersey, and Alaska, sandy soil covers heavy colloidal clay and is in turn covered by a thin layer of acidic humus, creating equally inhospitable growing conditions.

In both cases, the addition of humus to the soil reduces plants' reliance on specific soil pH levels. Often, plants that are known to "prefer" acidic or alkaline soils are actually in need of nutrients that become unavailable when the pH falls out of a desired range. Compost makes those nutrients more available and helps keep extreme pH from rendering them insoluble.

WELCOME WORMS

Earthworms, in passing soil and organic matter through their bodies, gradually make acidic soil less acidic and alkaline soil less alkaline, slowly drawing any out-of-balance soil into the neutral range. Compost feeds earthworms and allows them to multiply, thus enhancing their ability to correct soil pH. A compost mulch keeps soil temperatures in the range earthworms need to survive, and it encourages such active soil builders as red worms and brandling worms that require copious amounts of organic matter in the surface soil. Earthworms and compost work together in many ways to improve soil for growing plants, including improved aeration as they tunnel through the soil, and secretions similar to glomalin that help form stable soil aggregates. This relationship is discussed more fully in Chapter 9.

GROWTH STIMULATORS

Compost produces compounds that act as growth stimulators. Experiments on wheat, barley, potatoes, grapes, tomatoes, beets, and other crops show that, even in very low concentrations, humic acids act to stimulate plant growth. At concentrations as low as 0.01 to 0.1 percent, increased growth has been observed. Root systems in particular respond rapidly to the stimulating action of humic acids.

Tests to determine just how humic acids work revealed that they are in an ionically dispersed state. In this form, they are readily assimilated by the plants as a nutrient, over and above any normal mineral nutrition that plants get. Humic acids improve oxygen assimilation as well. This is particularly noticeable in the early stages of plant growth.

It was also noted during tests with humic acids that plants are able to assimilate other physiologically active substances, including bitumens, vitamins, and vitamin analogs. All of these substances, including the humic acids, are either supplied in fresh organic matter or derived from it during the decaying process.

CHEMICALS VERSUS COMPOST

It should be obvious, if you have read this far about the benefits of compost, that chemical fertilizers are no substitute for compost. Chemicals supply major nutrients—period—in quick-release forms. Plants obtain fast growth, but long-term benefits are few. And living soil and living plants need far more than a few isolated chemical elements. Plants take their nourishment through infinitely complex biological processes that we still do not understand fully. To use chemical fertilizers to the neglect of compost is to disregard the soil's need for life.

Further, the chemical system of gardening and agriculture depends extensively on the use of greenhouse gas–producing fossil fuels. It is estimated that 2 to 3 percent of the world's natural gas is used for the manufacture of nitrogen fertilizer alone. As nonrenewable energy supplies dwindle and as the availability of fertilizer resources becomes increasingly tied to geopolitical issues, farmers and gardeners will find energy-intensive chemical fertilizers ever more unaffordable.

Thirty-five percent of synthetic nitrogen and from 15 to 20 percent of the phosphorus and potassium applied to land is lost because farmers and gardeners apply these chemicals in amounts greater than can be immediately assimilated by plants or soil. Since the synthetic material, unlike the major constituents of compost, is immediately soluble, it is easily leached out during a rain.

Runoff of fertilizers from farm fields has led to "dead zones" that appear seasonally near the mouths of most major rivers, including the Gulf of Mexico and Chesapeake Bay. According to a 2008 story in *Scientific American*, such "lifeless waters" may cover close to 8,000 square miles in the summer months, and 2017 was predicted to set a new record for the size of the Gulf of Mexico dead zone–10,000 square miles! Nitrogen and phosphorus that are washed into streams and rivers find their way into lakes, where they stimulate growth of algae that lead to blooms that choke off oxygen and aquatic life, while cities in the Corn Belt struggle to remove toxic nitrate from drinking-water supplies.

Nitrates and other substances in synthetic fertilizers have also been linked to nitrate poisoning, cancer, deterioration of soils' healthy structures, creation of hardpans, and destruction of earthworms and other beneficial microorganisms. These chemicals can alter the vitamin and protein content of certain crops and make some crops more vulnerable to disease. Some experts have even said that vegetables grown with chemical fertilizers lose the power to reproduce in kind after a period of years. For example, Sir Albert Howard (one of the original promoters of composting) felt that cultivars would have to be introduced frequently from areas of the world where chemicals were not traditionally used if vegetable species were to maintain their strength when planted for several generations and nourished with chemicals.

The foundation of the agrochemical industry rests on the assumption that what a plant removes from the soil can be analyzed and replaced in chemical form. Though this would seem to be a logical assumption, it fails to take into account the complex biological processes and mechanisms through which the chemical transactions are performed, processes and mechanisms aided by finely tuned and highly specialized living organisms whose operations cannot be duplicated or even completely understood. In general, the use of synthetic fertilizers trades short-term rapid growth for long-term gain in structure and soundness.

LIFE INSIDE A COMPOST HEAP

The two most important aspects of a compost pile are the chemical makeup of its components and the population of organisms in it. Compost piles are intricate and complex communities of animal, vegetable, and mineral matter, all of which are interrelated, and all of which play a part in the breakdown of organic matter into humus. Composting is the result of the activities of a succession of organisms, each group paving the way for the next group by breaking down or converting a complex biodegradable material into a simpler or more usable material that can be utilized by its successor in the chain of breakdown. Generally speaking, the more "simple" the molecular structure of the material, the more resistant it becomes to bacterial attack and, hence, the more biologically stable it becomes. Whether the decomposition process takes place on the forest floor or in a gardener's compost heap, the biochemical systems at work are the same, and humus is always the result.

HUMUS

Humus, the relatively stable end product of composting, is rich in nutrients and organic matter and highly beneficial to both the soil and crops grown in the soil.

As we saw in Chapter 2, the advantages of humus are twofold. First, when it is mixed with the soil, the resulting combination becomes a heterogeneous, loosely structured soil mixture allowing air and water to penetrate to soil organisms and growing plants. Because of its loose spongelike texture, humus-rich soil soaks up water in its pores so that less runoff occurs. Second, humus contains a number of chemical elements that enrich the soil with which it is mixed, providing nutrients for growing plants.

The major elements found in humus are nitrogen, phosphorus, potassium, sulfur, iron, and calcium, varying in amounts according to the original composition of the raw organic matter thrown on the heap. Minor elements are also present, again in varying amounts depending on the type of compost. The N-P-K percentages of finished compost are relatively low, but their benefit lies in the release of nitrogen and phosphorus in the soil at a slow enough rate that plants can use them and that they aren't lost through leaching.

Soil mixed with humus becomes a rich, dark color that absorbs far more heat than nonorganic soils, making it a more favorable environment in which to grow crops and ornamental plants.

HOW COMPOST IS PRODUCED

The road from raw organic material to finished compost is a complex one, because both chemical and microbial processes are responsible for the gradual change from one to the other.

Decomposition of compost is accomplished by enzymatic digestion of plant and animal material by soil microorganisms. Simultaneously, the chemical processes of oxidation, reduction, and hydrolysis are going on in the pile, and their products at various stages are used by microorganisms for further breakdown.

Bacteria use these products for two purposes: (1) to provide energy to carry on their life processes and (2) to obtain the nutrients they need to grow and reproduce. The energy is obtained by oxidation of the products, especially the carbon fraction. The heat in a compost pile is the result of this biological "burning," or oxidation. Some materials can be broken down and oxidized more rapidly than others. This explains why a pile heats up fairly rapidly at the start. It is because the readily decomposed material is being attacked and bacterial activity is at its peak. If all goes well, this material is soon used up, so bacterial activity slows down—and the pile begins to cool. Of course, if the mass of the material is big enough, it acts as an insulator to prevent heat loss, and the high temperature may thus persist for some time after the active period is over, especially if the pile is not turned. Persistent high temperatures are the result of uneven breakdown.

The raw materials that you add to your compost can be anything of biological origin. Wood, paper, kitchen trimmings, crop leavings, weeds, and manure can all be included in the heap. As compost is broken down from these raw materials to simpler forms of proteins and carbohydrates, it becomes more available to a wider array of bacterial species that will carry it to a further stage of decomposition.

Carbohydrates (starches and sugars) break down in a fairly rapid process to simple sugars, organic acids, and carbon dioxide that are released in the soil. When proteins decompose, they readily break down into peptides and amino acids, and then to available ammonium compounds and atmospheric nitrogen. Finally, species of nitrifying bacteria change the ammonium compounds to nitrates, in which form they are available to plants.

At this stage of decomposition, the heap is near to becoming finished compost, with the exception of a few substances that still resist breakdown. Through complex, biochemical processes, these substances and the rest of the decomposed material form humus. There is some evidence that humus is largely the remains of microbial bodies.

The microorganisms of the compost heap, like any other living things, need both carbon from the carbohydrates, and forms of nitrogen from the proteins in the compost substrate. To thrive and reproduce, all microbes must have access to a supply of the elements of which their cells are made. They also need an energy source and a source of the chemicals they use to make their enzymes. The principal nutrients for bacteria, actinomycetes, and fungi are carbon (C), nitrogen (N), phosphorus (P), and potassium (K). Sulfur and magnesium are important minor nutrients, while micronutrients such as boron, manganese, copper, zinc, iron, selenium, and molybdenum, among others, are essential components of the enzyme systems that all organisms need to grow and reproduce.

In addition to proteins and carbohydrates, all organisms need to consume fats or lipids, which are key constituents of cell membranes. Microbes rely on lipids to be able to secrete the gums that are so crucial to soil aggregation and the formation of stable humus.

Essential nutrients occur in multiple forms, depending on the stage of decomposition in which they are found. For example, at any given moment,

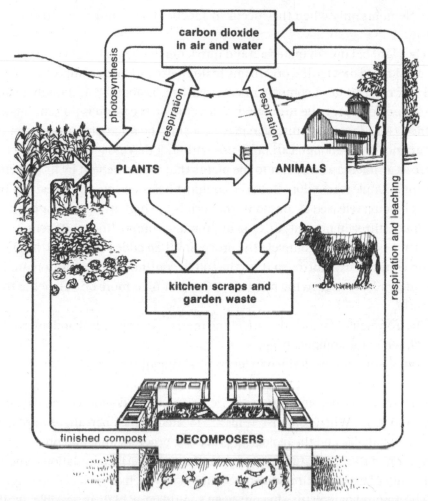

The carbon cycle. Green plants use carbon dioxide gas, water, and sunlight to make sugars and other carbon-containing compounds that animals use as food. Carbon compounds in plant and animal wastes provide food for decomposers in the compost pile. Materials that have passed through the decomposers' bodies and the microbial bodies themselves contain nutrients used by plants to continue the carbon cycle.

nitrogen may be found in the heap in the form of nitrates and nitrites, in ammonium compounds, in the complex molecules of undigested or partly digested cellulose, and in the complex protein of microorganism protoplasm. There are many stages of breakdown and many combinations of nutrient elements. What's more, microorganisms can make use of nitrogen and other elements only when they occur in specific forms and ratios to one another.

The right balance of materials and nutrients in raw materials helps provide a balanced diet for the organisms to do their work of decomposition. The ideal C/N ratio for most compost microorganisms is about 25:1, though it varies from one compost pile to another. When too little carbon is present, making the C/N ratio too low, nitrogen may be lost to the microorganisms because they are not given enough carbon to use with it. It may float into the atmosphere as ammonia and be lost to the plants that would benefit by its presence in humus. Unpleasant odors from the compost heap are most often caused by nitrogen being released as ammonia. Materials too high in carbon for the amount of nitrogen present (C/N too high) make composting inefficient, so more time is needed to complete the process. When added to the soil, high-carbon compost uses nitrogen from the soil to continue decomposition, making it unavailable to growing plants. See Chapter 6 for more on balancing the C/N ratio.

Environmental factors also affect the interwoven chemical and microbial breakdown of the compost heap.

Composting can be defined in terms of availability of oxygen. Aerobic decomposition means that the active microbes in the heap require oxygen, while in anaerobic decomposition, the active microbes do not require oxygen to live and grow. When compost heaps are located in the open air, as most are, oxygen is available and the biological processes progress under aerobic conditions. Temperature, moisture content, the size of bacterial populations, and the availability of nutrients limit and determine how much oxygen a heap uses.

The amount of moisture in your heap should be as high as possible, while still allowing air to filter into the pore spaces for the benefit of aerobic bacteria. Individual materials hold various percentages of moisture in compost and determine the amount of water that can be added. For example, woody and fibrous materials, such as bark, sawdust, wood chips, hay, and straw, can hold moisture equal to 75 to 85 percent of their dry weight. "Green manures," such as lawn clippings and vegetable trimmings, can absorb moisture equaling 50 to 60 percent of their weight. According to longtime composting advocate and researcher Dr. Clarence Golueke in *Composting: A Study of the Process and Its Principles*, "The minimum content at which bacterial activity takes place is from 12 to 15 percent. Obviously, the closer the moisture content of a

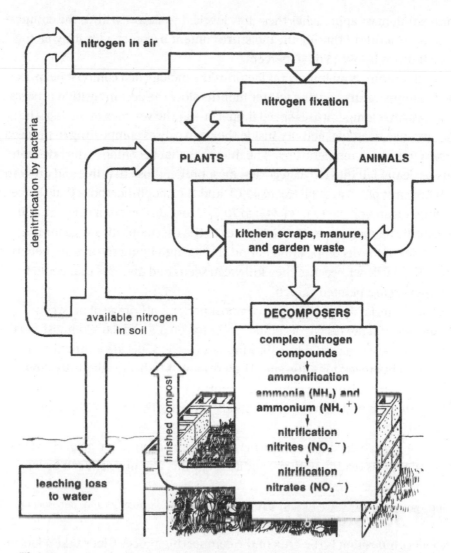

The nitrogen cycle. Shortage of available nitrogen is often a limiting factor in plant growth, since plants can't make use of abundant atmospheric nitrogen gas. (So-called nitrogen-fixing plants rely on symbiotic bacteria.) Composting plant and animal wastes exposes the nitrogen they contain to nitrogen-fixing microorganisms and decomposers that break it down into forms available to plants.

composting mass approaches these low levels, the slower will be the compost process. As a rule of thumb, the moisture content becomes a limiting factor when it drops below 45 or 50 percent."

Temperature is an important factor in the biology of a compost heap. Low outside temperatures during winter months slow the decomposition process, while warmer temperatures speed it up. During the warmer months of the year, intense microbial activity inside the heap causes composting to proceed at extremely high temperatures. The microbes that decompose the raw materials basically fall into two categories: mesophilic, those that live and grow in temperatures of 50° to 113°F (10° to 45°C), and thermophilic, those that thrive in temperatures of 113° to 158°F (45° to 70°C). Most garden compost begins at mesophilic temperatures, then increases to the thermophilic range for the remainder of the decomposition period. These high temperatures are beneficial to the gardener because they kill weed seeds and diseases that could be detrimental to a planted garden.

The bacterial decomposers in compost prefer a pH range of between 6.0 and 7.5, and the fungal decomposers between 5.5 and 8.0. Compost must be within these ranges if it is to decompose. Levels of pH are a function of the number of hydrogen ions present. (High pH levels indicate alkalinity; low levels, acidity.) In finished compost, a neutral (7.0) or slightly acidic (slightly below 7.0) pH is best, though slight alkalinity (slightly above 7.0) can be tolerated.

Lime is often used to raise the pH if the heap becomes too acid. However, ammonia forms readily with the addition of lime, and nitrogen can be lost.

COMPOST ORGANISMS

Since decomposition is the crux of the composting process, let's take a look at the various organisms involved in this vital function of the working compost heap. Most are microscopic, some are large enough to be observed with the unaided eye, but nearly all are beneficial, each having a role in breaking down raw organic matter into finished compost. They are known as decomposers.

Biologists now recognize six kingdoms of life-forms, replacing the original two (plants and animals) initially identified by Linnaeus. These include plants, animals, protists, fungi, archaebacteria, and eubacteria. Plants and animals are the familiar macroscopic creatures, while the microscopic

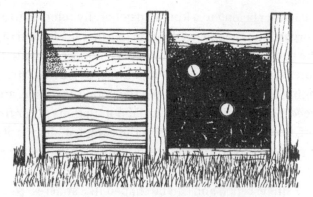

You can gauge the progress of your compost by regularly checking the temperature inside the heap. Mesophilic decomposers work best at temperatures of 50° to 113°F (10° to 45°C); as decomposition progresses, temperatures increase to 113° to 158°F (45° to 70°C) and thermophilic microorganisms continue the breakdown process.

universe has been more finely broken down according to characteristics such as complexity and cellular structure. Some of these kingdoms, like the protists, may include a wide range of organisms, from unicellular protozoans to multicellular photosynthesizers like algae.

Microscopic Decomposers

By far the most important microscopic decomposers are bacteria, which do the lion's share of decomposition in the compost heap. But there are other microscopic creatures, such as actinomycetes, protozoa, and fungi, that also play important roles. Together, these microscopic decomposers change the chemistry of the organic wastes, they carry the name of chemical decomposers.

The larger fauna in the heap include mites, millipedes, centipedes, sow bugs, snails, slugs, spiders, springtails, beetles, ants, flies, nematodes, flatworms, rotifers, and, most important, earthworms. Collectively, these are called the physical decomposers, since they bite, grind, suck, tear, and chew the materials into smaller pieces, making them more suitable for the chemical work of the microscopic decomposers.

Bacteria. Bacteria belong to a kingdom generally referred to as Eubacteria, single-celled organisms that do not contain distinct nuclei and rarely contain organelles. The bacteria likely to be found in a compost heap are those that specialize in breaking down organic compounds, those that thrive in temperatures ranging up to 170°F (77°C) in the thermophilic range, and those that are aerobic, needing air to survive. Bacterial populations differ from pile to pile, depending upon the raw materials of the compost, degree of heat, amount of air present, moisture level, geographic location of the pile, and other considerations.

Bacteria are single celled and can be shaped like spheres, rods, or spiral twists. They are so small that it would take 25,000 bacteria laid end to end to take up 1 inch on a ruler, and an amount of garden soil the size of a pea may contain up to a billion bacteria. Most bacteria are colorless and cannot make carbohydrates from sunshine, water, and carbon dioxide the way green plants can. Some bacteria produce colonies; others are free-living. All reproduce by means of binary fission.

Bacteria are the most nutritionally diverse of all organisms, which is to say, as a group, they can eat nearly anything. Most compost bacteria, similar to fungi and animals, can use living or dead organic materials. Some are so adaptable they can use more than 100 different organic compounds as their source of carbon because of their ability to produce a variety of enzymes. Usually, they can produce the appropriate enzyme to digest whatever material they find themselves on. In addition, respiratory enzymes in the cell membrane make aerobic respiration possible.

Since bacteria are smaller, less mobile, and less complexly organized than most organisms, they are less able to escape an environment that becomes unfavorable. A decrease in the temperature of the pile or a sharp change in its acidity can render bacteria inactive or kill them.

When the environment of a heap begins to change, bacteria that formerly dominated may be decimated by another species. At the beginning of the composting process, mesophilic (medium-temperature) bacteria and fungi predominate. They gradually give way to thermophilic (high-temperature) bacteria as the pile becomes hotter; the more thermophilic bacteria that are present, breaking down compounds and releasing heat as a by-product, the hotter the pile becomes. As stability approaches, actinomycetes and fungi that have so far been confined to the cooler edges of the pile begin to dominate the compost and hasten it toward further stability.

Actinomycetes. The characteristically earthy smell of newly plowed soil in the spring is caused by actinomycetes, higher-form bacteria similar to fungi and molds. Actinomycetes are especially important in the formation of humus. While most bacteria are found in the top foot or so of topsoil, actinomycetes may work many feet below the surface. Deep under the roots, they convert dead plant matter to a peatlike substance.

While they are decomposing animal and vegetable matter, actinomycetes liberate carbon, nitrogen, and ammonia, making nutrients available for higher plants. They are found on every natural substrate, and the majority are aerobic and mesophilic. Actinomycetes comprise 5 percent or more of the soil's bacterial population.

The reason that other bacteria tend to die rapidly as actinomycete populations grow in the compost pile is that actinomycetes have the ability to produce antibiotics, chemical substances that inhibit bacterial growth.

Protozoa. Protozoa belong to the kingdom Protista, which is characterized by single or multicelled organisms that do not form differentiated tissues and whose cells contain distinct nuclei and organelles. Even though they are microscopic in size, they are larger and more complex in their activities than most bacteria. A gram of soil can contain as many as a million protozoa, but compost has far fewer, especially during the thermophilic stage. Protozoa obtain their food from organic matter in the same way bacteria do, and may also feed on bacteria.

Fungi. Like plants, fungi have rigid cell walls and do not move independently, but unlike plants, they have neither chlorophyll nor cellulose. They must therefore consume external organic matter for energy. Fungi may be single celled or many celled; the kingdom Fungi is quite diverse and includes everything from edible mushrooms to molds and yeasts. Most fungi are classified as saprophytes because they live on dead or dying material and obtain energy by breaking down organic matter in dead plants and animals, but they will also happily consume smaller organisms such as bacteria and protozoans and are even known to attack nematodes. Like the actinomycetes, fungi take over during the final stages of the pile when the compost has been changed to a more easily digested form. The best temperature for active fungi in the compost heap is around 70° to 75°F (21° to 24°C), although some thermophilic forms prefer much greater heat and survive to 120°F (49°C).

Physical Decomposers

The bacteria, actinomycetes, protozoa, and fungi that we have looked at so far have to do mainly with chemical decomposition in the compost heap. The larger organisms, though, that chew and grind their way through the compost heap, are higher up in the food chain and are known as physical decomposers.

All of the organisms, from the microscopic bacteria to the largest of the physical decomposers, are part of a complex food chain in your compost pile. They can be categorized as first-, second-, and third-level consumers, depending upon what they eat and by what they are eaten. First-level consumers attract and become the food of second-level consumers, which in turn are consumed by third-level consumers. The organisms comprising each level of the food chain serve to keep the populations of the next lower level in check, so a balance can be maintained throughout the compost. Soil ecologist Dr. Daniel L. Dindal gives an example in *Ecology of Compost*:

> Mites and springtails eat fungi. Tiny feather-winged beetles feed on fungal spores. Nematodes ingest bacteria. Protozoa and rotifers present in water films feed on bacteria and plant particles. Predaceous mites and pseudoscorpions prey upon nematodes, fly larvae, other mites, and collembolans. Free-living flatworms ingest gastropods, earthworms, nematodes, and rotifers. Third-level consumers such as centipedes, rove beetles, ground beetles, and ants prey on second-level consumers.

The following is a rundown of some of the larger physical decomposers that you may find in nearly any compost heap. Most of these creatures function best at medium or mesophilic temperatures, so they will not be in the pile at all times.

Mites. Mites are related to ticks, spiders, and horseshoe crabs because they have in common eight leglike, jointed appendages. They can be free living or parasitic, sometimes both at once. Some mites are small enough to be invisible to the naked eye, while some tropical species are up to $1/2$ inch in length.

Mites reproduce rapidly, moving through larval, nymph, adult, and dormant stages. They attack plant matter, but some are also second-level consumers, ingesting nematodes, fly larvae, other mites, and springtails.

Millipedes. The wormlike body of the millipede has many segments, each except the front few bearing two pairs of walking legs.

The life cycles of millipedes are not well understood, except that eggs are laid in the soil in springtime, hatching into small worms. Young millipedes molt several times before gaining their full complement of legs. When they reach maturity, adult millipedes can grow to a length of 1 to 2 inches. They help break down plant material by feeding directly on it.

Centipedes. Centipedes are flattened, segmented worms with 15 or more pairs of legs–1 pair per segment. They hatch from eggs laid during the warm months and gradually grow to their adult size. Centipedes are third-level consumers, feeding only on living animals, especially insects and spiders.

Sow bugs. The sow bug is a fat-bodied, flat creature with distinct segments. Sow bugs reproduce by means of eggs that hatch into smaller versions of the adults. Since females are able to deposit a number of eggs at one time, sow bugs may become abundant in a compost heap. They are first-level consumers, eating decaying vegetation.

Snails and slugs. Both snails and slugs are mollusks and have muscular disks on their undersides that are adapted for a creeping movement. Snails have a spirally curved shell, a broad retractable foot, and a distinct head. Slugs, on the other hand, are so undifferentiated in appearance that one species is frequently mistaken for half of a potato. Both snails and slugs lay eggs in capsules or gelatinous masses and progress through larval stages to adulthood.

Their food is generally living plant material, but they will attack fresh garbage and plant debris and will appear in the compost pile. It is well, therefore, to look for them when you spread your compost, for if they move into your garden, they can do damage to crops.

Spiders. Spiders, which are related to mites, are one of the least appreciated animals in the garden. These eight-legged creatures are third-level consumers that feed on insects and small invertebrates, and they help control garden pests.

Springtails. Springtails are very small insects, rarely exceeding ¼ inch in length. They vary in color from white to blue-gray or metallic and are mostly

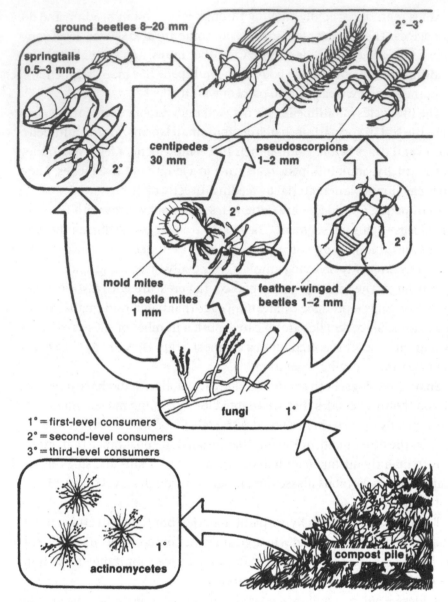

ground beetles 8–20 mm

springtails 0.5–3 mm

2°–3°

2°

centipedes 30 mm

pseudoscorpions 1–2 mm

mold mites

beetle mites 1 mm

2°

feather-winged beetles 1–2 mm

2°

1° = first-level consumers
2° = second-level consumers
3° = third-level consumers

fungi 1°

actinomycetes 1°

compost pile

Energy flows in the direction of the arrows.
(*Daniel L. Dindal*, Ecology of Compost: A Public Involvement Project)

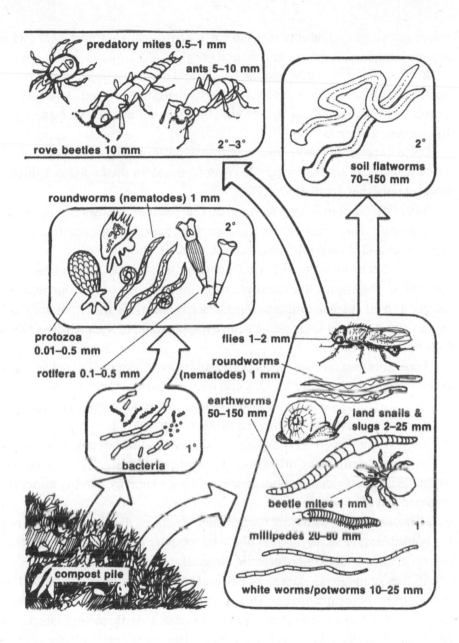

predatory mites 0.5–1 mm

ants 5–10 mm

rove beetles 10 mm

2°–3°

soil flatworms
70–150 mm

2°

roundworms (nematodes) 1 mm

2°

protozoa
0.01–0.5 mm

rotifera 0.1–0.5 mm

flies 1–2 mm

roundworms
(nematodes) 1 mm

earthworms
50–150 mm

land snails &
slugs 2–25 mm

beetle mites 1 mm

millipedes 20–80 mm

1°

white worms/potworms 10–25 mm

bacteria

1°

compost pile

distinguished by their ability to jump when disturbed. They feed by chewing decomposing plants, pollen, grains, and fungi.

Beetles. The rove beetle, ground beetle, and feather-winged beetle are the most common beetles in compost. Feather-winged beetles feed on fungal spores, while the larger rove and ground beetles prey on other insects as third-level consumers.

Beetles are easily visible insects with two pairs of wings, the more forward-placed of these serving as a cover or shield for the folded and thinner back-set ones that are used for flying.

A beetle's immature stage is as a grub that feeds and grows during the warm months. Once grubs are full grown, they pass through a resting or pupal stage and change into hard-bodied, winged adults.

Most adult beetles, like the larval grubs of their species, feed on decaying vegetables, while some, like the rove and ground beetles, prey on snails, insects, and other small animals. The black rove beetle is an acknowledged predator of snails and slugs. Some people import them to their gardens when slugs become a problem.

Ants. Ants feed on a variety of material, including aphid honeydew, fungi, seeds, sweets, scraps, other insects, and sometimes other ants. Compost provides some of these foods, and it also provides shelter for nests and hills. Ants will remain, however, only while the pile is relatively cool.

Ants prey on first-level consumers and may benefit the composting process by bringing fungi and other organisms into their nests. The work of ants can make compost richer in phosphorus and potassium by moving minerals from one place to another.

Flies. Many flies, including black fungus gnats, soldier flies, minute flies, and houseflies, spend their larval phase in compost as maggots. Adults can feed upon almost any kind of organic material.

All flies undergo egg, larval, pupal, and adult stages. The eggs are laid in various forms of organic matter. Houseflies are such effective distributors of bacteria that when an individual fly crawls across a sterile plate of lab gelatin, colonies of bacteria later appear in its tracks. During the early phases of the composting process, flies provide ideal airborne transportation for bacteria on their way to the pile.

If you keep a layer of dry leaves or grass clippings on top of your pile and cover your garbage promptly while building compost, your pile will not provide a breeding place for horseflies, mosquitoes, or houseflies that may become a nuisance to humans. Fly larvae do not survive thermophilic temperatures. Mites and other organisms in the pile also keep fly larvae reduced in number. Though many flies die with the coming of frost, their rate of reproduction is so rapid that a few survivors can repopulate an area before the warm season has progressed very far.

Nematodes, flatworms, and rotifers. Nematodes, or eelworms, plus free-living flatworms and rotifers, all can be found in compost.

Nematodes are microscopic creatures that can be classified into three categories: (1) those that live on decaying organic matter; (2) those that are predators on other nematodes, bacteria, algae, protozoa, and so on; and (3) those that can be serious pests in gardens, where they attack the roots of plants. As is true with most other soil organisms, very few nematode species are pathogenic, and these are kept in check by a diverse population of fungi as well as faunal predators. A diverse mix of nematode species is considered an indicator of overall soil health.

Flatworms, as their name implies, are flattened organisms that are usually quite small in their free-living form. Most flatworms are carnivorous. They live in films of water within the compost structure.

Rotifers are small, multicellular animals that live freely or in tubes attached to a substrate. Their bodies are round and divisible into three parts: head, trunk, and tail. They are generally found in films of water, and many forms are aquatic. The rotifers in compost are found in water that adheres to plant substances, where they feed on microorganisms.

Earthworms. If bacteria are the champion microscopic decomposers, then the heavyweight champion is doubtless the earthworm. Pages of praise have been written to the earthworm, ever since it became known that this creature spends most of its time tilling and enriching the soil. The great English naturalist Charles Darwin was the first to suggest that all the fertile areas of this planet have at least once passed through the bodies of earthworms.

The earthworm consists mainly of an alimentary canal that ingests, decomposes, and deposits casts continually during the earthworm's active periods. As soil or organic matter is passed through an earthworm's digestive system, it is broken up and neutralized by secretions of calcium carbonate from calciferous glands near the worm's gizzard. Once in the gizzard, material is finely ground prior to digestion. Digestive intestinal juices rich in hormones, enzymes, and other fermenting substances continue the breakdown process. The matter passes out of the worm's body in the form of casts, which

🌿 CREATING A SMALL-SCALE ECOSYSTEM

"Sometimes people need a small object in order to understand a big idea," says artist Barbara Bodle Kirschenstein, who calls one of her works the "Compost Pet Tank." Described in *Green Scene*, the magazine of the Pennsylvania Horticultural Society, Kirschenstein's compost pet tank is a vivarium (an enclosure for keeping or raising and observing animals indoors) that seeks to approximate larger ecosystems—such as the one in which we live—by copying the smaller ecosystem of the compost pile.

While the amount of compost produced by a compost pet tank is only enough for a few houseplants, this small-scale ecosystem does provide an entertaining and educational way to show children how a compost pile works. For insect-tolerant apartment dwellers, the compost pet tank offers a link to nature that might otherwise be missing.

Pet Tank Basics

Start with a large aquarium; 24 by 18 by 10 inches is a good size. A covering for the aquarium is necessary to ensure that your small ecosystem doesn't invade your larger one; fine wire mesh works best. Select a spot where your tank can get light. The tank should also be in a spot where household temperatures can be maintained (50° to 90°F/10° to 32°C). The warmer the temperature, the quicker the composting process.

Four Components

Kirschenstein's tanks consist of four areas:

- A watering system is placed between rocks and plants.
- A composting area, built up with coarse organic matter such as sticks and branches and covered with finished compost or garden soil, should

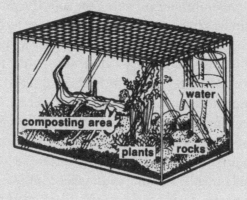

be located next to growing plants and should take up about half the tank.

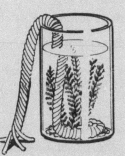

- Growing plants in soil should account for about a quarter of the space.
- The remaining quarter can be filled with rocks, shells, or driftwood.

Water

Water is an important part of any ecosystem. Here are three ways to provide water to your tank:

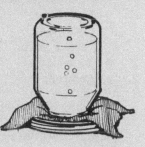

- Place water in jar lids or shells positioned around the tank.
- Suspend a wick from a jar of water, letting the end dangle over the top of the container into the tank. For added interest, try growing a water plant in the jar.
- Place a piece of cloth on a large plastic lid. Turn a water-filled jar upside down on top of the cloth. The fabric will soak up the water, allowing it to seep into the tank.

Suggested Inhabitants

Insects/Arthropods

- Milkweed bugs
- Mealybugs/darkling beetles (start with about 100)
- Millipedes
- Crickets (start with about 500)

Predators

(Allow insects to multiply for about 2 months before introducing predators.)

- Tree frogs
- Toads
- Lizards and salamanders

Recommended Plants and Kitchen Scraps

(No wet things, which attract fruit flies)

- Succulents
- Carrot-top plants
- Weeds
- Herbs
- Hens-and-chicks
- Cedar chips (to help control odors)
- Potatoes (to provide insect homes and moisture)
- Small bones
- Citrus peels
- Lettuce leaves
- Tomatoes
- Corncobs

Arrange your tank as artistically as you want. Watch this new ecosystem: Is there a balance of wet and dry materials? Is there a balance between predators and prey? If the ecosystem fails—if plants or animals die, or if the composting area smells—try again, altering different aspects until you find a system that suits your needs and those of the tank's inhabitants.

are the richest and finest quality of all humus material, essentially a condensed packet of the essential nutrients extracted from the worm's diet. Fresh casts are markedly higher in bacteria, organic material, and available nitrogen, calcium, magnesium, phosphorus, and potassium than soil itself. Earthworms thrive on compost and contribute to its quality through both physical and chemical processes.

Both male and female reproductive systems are in one earthworm, but fertilization can occur only between two separate individuals during copulation. The fertilized eggs are deposited and contained in a cocoon, out of which the young worms emerge after 8 to 10 days.

Since earthworms are willing and able to take on such a large part in compost making, wise gardeners adjust their composting methods to take full advantage of the earthworm's talents. The earthworm's contributions to compost making will be discussed more fully in Chapter 9.

4

COMPOST AND PLANT HEALTH

Plants grown in compost-rich soil will be healthier and more resistant to both insects and plant diseases.

All higher plants have the same basic requirements for growth, although their requirements vary widely in amount and degree. The essentials are light, heat, water, air, and certain nutrient elements in reasonable amounts and in suitable balance. Plants obtain needed moisture and nutrients, with the exception of carbon dioxide, from the soil. The soil also helps control the temperature in the root zone and, to a lesser extent, in the aerial portions of plants.

For a plant to thrive, its soil must not contain toxic substances in a form and concentration that is likely to be taken up by the roots. The soil microbiome must be healthy enough to suppress any disease organisms present.

TEMPERATURE AND PLANTS

Of the various factors that influence seed germination and plant growth, temperature is one of the most crucial. It seems to take forever for the first planting of peas in early spring to be seen above the soil's surface. But in July, beans and new sowings of lettuce seem to germinate overnight. Temperature is also one of the most difficult factors to adjust to benefit your plants. Compost helps moderate soil temperatures, but other methods such as row covers, mulches, and shade are more useful for improving the temperature environment of your plants.

The heat necessary for plant growth comes from the sun. Plants are the original solar collectors and are still unsurpassed as human ingenuity attempts to mimic their design. But the earth quickly reradiates much of the heat it receives from the sun, even though the buildup of carbon dioxide and other greenhouse gases in our atmosphere has already started to diminish this vital function. Heat is lost more quickly when the sun shines on bare, light-colored fields or on the ever-increasing expanses of concrete on this planet's surface. Dark colors absorb heat, however, and the black color of humus helps it retain heat from the sunlight. When you put compost into your garden, you are helping the earth absorb and store heat for your plants, moderating soil temperatures. Just be vigilant about covering that exposed soil as quickly as possible to avoid overheating and soil degradation.

During the growing season, soil temperatures to a depth of several inches vary greatly over a 24-hour period. Low-growing roots must function at temperatures cooler than those for surface roots. The temperature differences influence the uptake of water and nutrients by plants. Experiments have shown that there is a marked increase in nutrient accumulation in plants as temperatures rise–up to a point.

The absorption of water by plant roots is retarded by both low and high temperatures. Plants adapted for growth at low temperatures will continue to absorb water in soils under 40°F (4°C), but warm-temperature plants will not. Heat also leads to faster transpiration of water through plant leaves, making the roots work harder to quench the plant's thirst–just as you need to drink more water when working in the garden on a hot day. Adding compost to soil tends to keep it from heating up or cooling down rapidly, so water absorption continues at a relatively constant rate.

Root growth is greatly influenced by soil temperature. In general, growth of roots increases as temperatures rise to a certain point, then decreases rapidly if temperatures exceed that level. For example, root growth is most rapid in most plants before midsummer.

Most beneficial soil microorganisms multiply rapidly at temperatures between 50° and 104°F (10° and 40°C). Organic matter in soil decomposes more quickly, due to the work of microorganisms, as temperatures rise toward 80.6°F (27°C); beyond this level, soil organism balances may change, and organic matter reserves will be depleted. Tropical soils tend to contain little organic matter, due partly to year-round high temperatures.

Disease organisms are influenced by temperature. Some do better at high temperatures, especially when such temperatures weaken their plant hosts. By helping to maintain soil temperatures at optimum levels for vigorous plant growth, humus improves disease resistance.

RESPIRATION AND THE USE OF AIR

Respiration is a process common to all living cells. Most plants need oxygen from the air; a large part of the carbon dioxide used by plants in photosynthesis and other processes also comes from the air.

The amount of water vapor in air is an essential factor in plant growth as well.

Proportions of oxygen, nitrogen, and carbon dioxide do not vary widely in unpolluted air. Air normally contains 0.03 percent CO_2 and 20.96 percent O_2. However, the concentration of CO_2 in the atmosphere has been increasing exponentially since the advent of the industrial revolution, due in no small part to industrialized food-production systems. Most plants thrive on the normal atmospheric percentages. Some apologists for industrial agriculture even suggest that plant growth will benefit from higher CO_2 levels that threaten the stability of our climate.

Soil air–the air in soil and the spaces between soil aggregates–contains widely varying amounts of CO_2 and less O_2 than atmospheric air. Roots obtain their oxygen and CO_2 from this soil air, where concentrations rise as organic matter decomposes through microbial activity.

Compost promotes aeration and its many benefits to plants. Poorly aerated soils absorb water poorly, and water use by plants in humus-rich soil is more efficient than in unaerated clay. Plants also absorb more nutrients of all kinds in well-aerated soils, as long as oxygen and carbon dioxide are in balance. In experiments, forced aeration of soils increased plants' absorption of nutrients, particularly of potassium and phosphorus.

Compost is being used as a source of heat as well as CO_2 in greenhouses, one of the frontiers of compost discussed in the next chapter.

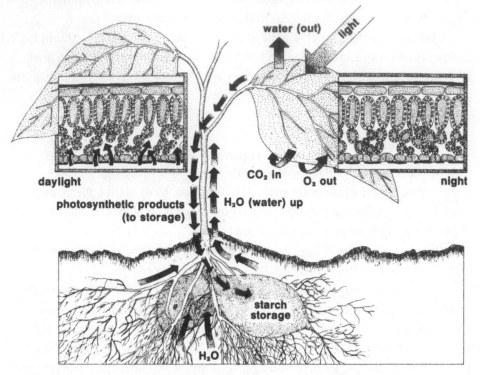

In the process of photosynthesis, carbon dioxide (CO_2) from the air and water (H_2O) from the soil combine in the presence of sunlight to form glucose ($C_6H_{12}O_6$) plus oxygen (O_2). Stomata open during daylight hours to admit CO_2 and release O_2, and they close at night. Excess water exits through the leaves via transpiration. Glucose is transformed into starch for storage in fleshy roots or tubers to nourish the plant and provide energy for growth. In respiration, plants reverse the chemical processes of photosynthesis to release energy for cellular functions. Oxygen (O_2) is absorbed from soil by the roots and is used to break down stored starches ($C_6H_{12}O_6$). Carbon dioxide (CO_2) and water (H_2O) are released.

WATER AND PLANT GROWTH

All living tissue contains water. Plants need and absorb more water than they do any other component of the soil. Much of the water they take in is given off again as they transpire, but some is kept in plant tissues and some is broken down to supply the hydrogen and part of the oxygen plants use or store in the form of carbohydrates. Drought is the most common cause of crop failure.

Green tissues of plants contain an average of 75 percent water. Growing tips may be as much as 93 percent water. Some plants contain more water than others. Tomato leaves are 84 percent water, and cabbage leaves 86 percent.

A plant must be turgid—full of water—for vital processes to take place within it. Too little water in leaf tissues causes stomata (the pores in green plant leaves that allow them to "breathe") to close, reducing CO_2 uptake and thus photosynthesis.

Roots are essential for obtaining water and nutrients. Generally, roots grow in response to water need. However, plants differ widely in the amount of root they grow in reaching water. Soils also influence the growth of roots. In test plants, tomato roots at 12 weeks reached a depth of 11 inches in loam, but in other soils they were much shallower. Humus increases the potential for deep root penetration and for firm anchorage of root hairs by improving both soil friability and moisture-holding capacity.

The availability of water affects nutrient uptake, too. For example, nitrogen can be taken up from low-moisture soils more readily than phosphorus but less so than potassium. This, of course, can affect the growth pattern of the plant. The amount of water in the soil also has an effect on soil bacteria. The helpful nitrogen-fixing bacterium azotobacter can resist drying, but many other beneficial soil bacteria cannot. This is one reason why nitrates are produced in smaller quantity in dry soils. On the other hand, too much water in soils leads to anaerobic conditions and cessation of most beneficial bacterial activity. Also, soils that are too moist can promote formation of toxic substances and suppress nitrate formation as nitrifying bacteria shut down; with soil pores occupied by water, too little oxygen is available for respiration in the roots. Roots do not develop as quickly as topgrowth in plants. Very succulent vegetables grown in wet soils are more susceptible to disease than are vegetables grown elsewhere. Adding humus to the soil improves both its drainage and water-holding qualities. Heavy, waterlogged soils become less soggy, and light, droughty soils retain more water. This is especially significant in areas where water conservation is a priority.

HUMUS AND PLANT NUTRITION

The role of humus in plant nutrition has been the subject of much controversy among soil scientists throughout history, and it continues to be a subject on which there are varying opinions.

Until quite recently in history, people believed that plants "ate" humus and used its carbon content in their growth. In the 19th century, the study of chemistry and the early use of hydroponic techniques–growing plants without soil–led to the opposite thesis, that as long as plants can be fed artificial chemical nutrients, they need no humus. Attempts to isolate and synthesize the organic compounds in humus, mostly humic acids, were for some time unsuccessful. Artificial humic acids did not have the same influence on plants that natural humus did. Only recently, with new hydroponic techniques and sophisticated ways of measuring plant uptake of nutrients, such as the use of radioactive carbons, has the plant intake of the nutrients in humus been measured accurately.

In 1936, in *Humus,* Dr. Selman A. Waksman wrote of the early investigators of humus nutrients:

> Even those investigators that denied the presence of any plant-stimulating substances in soil organic matter had to admit that although green plants grow, remain healthy, and reproduce without any organic matter or bacteria, still certain types of organic substances, especially in the presence of bacteria, may markedly affect the constitution of the plant.

Scientists began to look to humus for vitamin-like substances, sometimes called "auximones," or for "phytamins," which they believed to be in compost and organic manures. Others studied the plant hormones present in organic matter.

COMPLEX RELATIONSHIPS

According to research by W. Flaig of the Institut für Biochemie in Braunschweig, Germany, soil organic matter contains physiologically active fractions of humic substances of low molecular weight that have an effect on the metabolism of plants after their uptake. Some of these substances, which are created in nature by the degradation of lignin (the woody substance found in the walls of plant cells), were synthesized in laboratory experiments. By using carbon 14 in the process, the scientists were able to observe the effect of the lignin-based humic substances in plant roots, and to some extent in sprouts, when they measured the radioactivity of the carbon 14. The plants exposed to these substances were found to give off large quantities of CO_2.

Flaig describes experiments in which amino acids (simple proteins) are taken up by plants as intact molecules and utilized in protein metabolism. The mechanism of uptake of humus nutrients by plants is somewhat like the transport of ions in a chemical reaction. It is not, as was earlier believed, always associated with capillarity. In poor environmental conditions, such as low levels of moisture and air, humic substances act more rapidly to increase the dry weights of plants. Here we find still another reason for using compost.

V. Hernando Fernandez of Madrid, Spain, has experimented with humic acids in solution. He found the humic acids derived from manure had even more effect on plants than the substances from peat (or lignin). Manure humic acids fostered nitrogen absorption by plants, but those made from peat did not. An increase in the weight of plants, according to Fernandez, is brought about as the result of the two most important influences of humic substances: their action on respiration and their action on synthesis and photosynthesis.

One part of humic acid molecules consists of a redox, or oxidation-reduction, system, in which a molecule loses electrons to another molecule. This part helps to liberate oxygen and so increases the rate of respiration in plants. The other part of the humic acid molecules consists of nitrogen compounds, principally amino acids and proteins. This part exerts an enzymelike effect on photosynthesis.

For a plant to increase in weight, these two influences must be in balance. Fernandez determined that the effect of humic acids in solution differed markedly from the effect of chemical fertilizers. Increasing the quantities of humic acids used did not bring about corresponding effects in plants the way increasing the amounts of chemical fertilizers would have. This indicated to him that the balance of respiration-connected and photosynthesis-connected acids is all important when humic acids are provided to plants in solution.

Both the Spanish and German scientists' experiments prove that humus and humus-produced substances do indeed influence plant growth but that their influence is extremely complex. For example, a plant's ability to assimilate and make use of soil nutrients or to produce carbohydrates through photosynthesis may be influenced by humus even when the humus itself does not provide the nutrients. This provides evidence that the theories of plant growth that contend that all the necessary nutrients can be provided with chemicals and that these alone will ensure plant growth and health are indeed oversimplifications. Nature's soil-building processes are incredibly complex.

KNOWN BENEFITS

On top of these discoveries about the influence of humic substances, earlier research bears witness to the benefits of humic materials to plants. As well as serving as a soil conditioner, humus provides for plant nutrition in a number of ways. Dr. Waksman, in *Humus*, listed the following:

1. Organic compounds can be directly assimilated by plants and can replace nitrates in solution.
2. Leguminous plants, whose roots carry nodules that host nitrogen-fixing bacteria, obtain nitrogen in the form of organic compounds.
3. Certain sugars in humus can be assimilated by plants; lecithin, which is found in humus, can be used as a source of phosphate; cystine can be used as a source of sulfur.
4. Humus can improve the availability of inorganic phosphorus in soil.
5. Humus is a source of available iron to plants and microorganisms in forms that are optimum for the growth of plants.
6. Humus contains varying levels and types of lipids, which can contribute to improved permeability of the protoplasmic membranes of plants, allowing them to assimilate more nutrients and better resist toxins and pathogens.
7. Vitamins, enzymes, and other complex organic molecules resulting from microbial decomposition can be taken up directly by plants.
8. Humus is an important source of CO_2 for plant growth.

In addition to these specific ways in which humus helps plants, a secondary characteristic of humus is that it contains, and can make available, major and minor plant nutrients. Most of the nutrients needed by plants are also needed by soil organisms, which in turn are able to provide plants with otherwise unavailable nutrients when they die. Microbes are responsible for gradually releasing the nutrients from humus over the course of a growing season—providing a good diet for these unseen workers will ensure one for your growing plants. This is what is meant by the phrase "feed the soil, not the plant." Although chemical fertilizers are more readily available at once, their nutrients can be lost through leaching or chemical immobilization and may actually harm plants and soil microbes when applied in large doses.

While a balanced diet for plants can be provided by compost alone, it is important to know if any nutrient may be deficient. If you suspect some deficiency, have your soil tested to give you more information to go on. (For a more complete discussion of soil nutritional balances, including soil testing, consult *The Soul of Soil: A Guide to Ecological Soil Management,* by Grace Gershuny and Joseph Smillie.) We'll now take a closer look at the plant nutrients that are supplied by humus.

Macronutrients

Nutrients that are needed in significant quantities by plants are called macronutrients. These include nitrogen, phosphorus, and potassium, the familiar N-P-K of fertilizer labels, as well as calcium, magnesium, and sulfur. All of these are supplied to plants through the soil, while the plants get carbon, which is a primary constituent of all living tissue, from the air.

Carbohydrates. Although we don't often think about it in these terms, plants manufacture most of what they "eat" themselves, using the raw materials of air and water, plus energy from sunlight. In fact, nearly all (95 to 99.5 percent) of plant tissue is composed of carbon, hydrogen, and oxygen in the form of carbohydrates. The hydrogen and oxygen come from water, and the carbon comes primarily from the carbon dioxide in the atmosphere. Plant roots are continually sloughing off dead cells and actually secreting excess sugars as they grow, which in turn helps to feed the microbial community that surrounds them.

Carbon. One of the key elements recycled through microbial action, carbon is likewise essential to microbe growth. Organic matter is the sole source of carbon for soil organisms, which give off carbon dioxide as they respire. The amount of CO_2 generated by abundant soil organisms can be significant to plants and should not be discounted when considering the benefits to plant nutrition of increasing soil humus content.

Nitrogen. Nitrogen is a vital component of all protein, essential for the formation of new plant protoplasm. Without sufficient nitrogen, a plant is stunted and turns pale green or yellow, starting with the lower leaves. The stems of members of the grass family, such as corn, will be slender, and the whole plant will lack vigor. (Remember, however, that other conditions, such as excess or lack of moisture, cold weather, or plant disease, can cause the same symptoms.)

The demand for nitrogen is particularly strong when new plant tissue is developing and growth is most rapid. Nitrogen tends to be used more by stems and leaves than in seed production, so plants mature more slowly in soils that are overrich in nitrogen. Too much nitrogen in plant tissues has been found to make them more susceptible to attack by pests and diseases. Also, excess nitrogen, most often present when fertilizer applications are not timed to match plants' nitrogen needs, leaches easily from the soil and becomes a significant source of water pollution. Release of nitrogen from humus parallels plant demand, since microbial activity speeds up at the same time. If your plants have nitrogen-deficiency problems, the best way to provide immediate help is with manure tea (see page 141).

Phosphorus. Phosphorus is necessary for photosynthesis, for energy transfers within plants, and for good flower and fruit growth. Unlike nitrogen, phosphorus has more to do with plant maturation than with plant growth. Most phosphorus in soil is present in the form of organic matter; the remainder is largely bound up in insoluble calcium, iron, or aluminum compounds. Plants need it in the form of phosphoric acid, which is released primarily through the action of soil microbes as they break down organic matter.

Deficiencies of phosphorus are characterized by stunted early growth, poor root development, and most notably by reddish or purple coloration on the undersides of leaves. Fruit tree leaves become bronzed and lose their luster, and some, like lemon leaves, show spots. Because seed production is influenced by phosphorus, seed abnormalities may also indicate a lack of this element.

Excess soluble phosphates are, like nitrates, subject to loss through leaching. Although not as injurious to soil life as nitrates, synthetic phosphates are among the five major pollutants measured to determine water quality. Slow-release sources such as rock phosphate and bonemeal are the best options for increasing long-term phosphorus availability to plants. Compost organisms turn phosphorus added as a rock powder into an organic form that is readily available to plants as humus breaks down. Adding phosphate to your compost also prevents nitrogen loss through ammonia volatilization.

Potassium. Potassium is used by plants in many life processes, including the manufacture and movement of sugars, and cell division. It is necessary for root development and helps plants retain water. Potassium, or potash, in soil is often bound up with silicates. Potassium is not, however, a constituent of the organic compounds within plants.

Symptoms of deficiency appear in older leaves first and take the form of yellowing at the edges. Later, leaf edges turn brown and may crinkle or curl. In the case of corn, streaks appear between the leaf veins, and dry, brown edges and tips appear on leaves. The brown spreads to the entire leaf. On legumes, yellow spots, turning brown, spread inward from leaf edges. Tomato and potato plants also show yellowing of leaf tips and edges and some curling. Beets, carrots, sweet potatoes, radishes, and similar crops are long and small in diameter when they lack potassium.

Compost made with a formula of 6 inches of green matter to every 2 inches of manure provides adequate potassium for garden needs. When the moisture of the green plants is eliminated and the material is broken down, a sizable percentage of the remaining solid matter consists of potassium. If your soil is extremely low in potassium, add greensand or granite dust to the compost heap. Heavy mulching seems to help maintain soil potassium supplies, too. In an experiment performed some years ago at Purdue University, Clarence E. Baker found that mulching with manure, straw, and soybean hay eliminated symptoms of potassium deficiency in a peach orchard. Use wood ashes or any highly soluble potassium source sparingly. They can damage soil organisms with their high salt content, increase alkalinity to undesirable levels, and stimulate excess potassium uptake in plants, known as "luxury consumption."

Calcium. A lack of calcium appears to affect the stems and roots of growing plants. Plants deficient in calcium are retarded in growth and develop thick woody stems; seedlings will have stubby little roots with brownish discoloration. The lower leaves of cereal crops roll in at the edges, and brown spots appear on them. In corn, the leaves sometimes stick together as if glued. Some plants show green veins with yellow tissue between them. Blossom end rot in tomatoes or peppers is a sure indicator of calcium deficiency.

It is difficult to diagnose calcium deficiency because its assimilation is influenced by the balance between magnesium, manganese, and potassium in the soil. Available calcium can be quickly leached from soil by prolonged heavy rains or overzealous irrigation. Calcium-deficiency symptoms often occur on plants growing in acidic or sandy soils; applications of ground limestone supply calcium and raise the pH. Calcium deficiencies in neutral or alkaline soils can be corrected with gypsum, which also supplies sulfur.

Magnesium. Although plants need magnesium in smaller quantities than calcium, this element plays a vital role at the center of the chlorophyll molecule, responsible for photosynthesis. It also functions as a carrier for phosphorus, and the two deficiencies often go together. Insufficient magnesium is manifested as discoloration in the tissue between veins, which may cause leaves to look streaked. In some plants, leaves develop a reddish or purplish coloration, and the leaf margins turn brown or yellow while the veins remain green.

Magnesium availability to plants may be blocked by an excess of other elements, most notably potassium. Acidic soils commonly lack magnesium, which is why dolomitic limestone, containing both calcium and magnesium, is often recommended.

Sulfur. Sulfur is another essential component of protein; its deficiency results in symptoms resembling those caused by lack of nitrogen. It is essential for onions, good fruit set in peppers, and tree fruit such as cherries and plums. Soils with adequate organic matter rarely lack sulfur, especially in areas suffering from acid rain.

Sulfur is sometimes provided as part of a fertilizer used to supply some other nutrient; in fact, in some places sulfur deficiencies started appearing when farmers began using highly concentrated artificial fertilizers that lack the "impurity" of sulfur. Any organic fertilizer material will provide sulfur, but it can also be added in the form of gypsum (calcium sulfate) or langbeinite (sulfate of potash magnesia), depending on which other nutrients are needed. Pure "flowers of sulfur" is sometimes used to acidify soil.

Micronutrients

Agronomists in the 1920s and 1930s discovered that the absence in the soil of a very small quantity of a variety of minerals such as iron, manganese, copper, zinc, boron, selenium, molybdenum, iodine, silicon, cobalt, chromium, tin, vanadium, nickel, and lithium could severely stunt the growth of crops. For example, a plant's ability to hold water is affected by such micronutrients. These minerals, again in minute quantities, have also proved beneficial to the health of animals and humans. Dietary deficiencies of micronutrients in plants, animals, and people reflect soil deficiencies in the areas where they live.

An excellent way of getting micronutrients in the proper balance back into the soil is to compost with a great variety of organic materials. By applying micronutrients with organic compost rather than in chemical form, you can avoid the risk of toxicity. Many poor soils already have enough micronutrients, but they are locked into compounds that plants can't use. Earlier we talked about the action of the humic acids that are manufactured in the process of composting. They can pull nutrients out of minerals already in the soil and make them available to plants. Some micronutrients, such as cobalt and molybdenum, are important to soil organisms that fix nitrogen.

Humus also acts as a regulator of soil micronutrient balances through its quality of forming chelates. *Chelate* is a term derived from the Greek word meaning "claw," which describes how complex organic molecules hold on to single micronutrient ions. These chelates are like a safe deposit box for micronutrients, protected from leaching away in rainwater, yet available to plants in an easily assimilated form. The same mechanism is known to work for some toxic heavy metals such as lead, thus keeping them safely out of the food chain.

Iron. Almost all soils have sufficient iron for crops, but iron may not be available to plants in neutral or alkaline soils. Many plants, such as blueberries, that prefer acidic soil are actually heavy iron feeders. Iron deficiency is particularly hard to identify, for the symptom drying up of young leaves—is common to many deficiencies.

Humus serves a crucial function in keeping iron in solution in soils. At neutral or slightly alkaline reactions, inorganic iron is chemically immobilized into insoluble compounds. Humus can form compounds with iron that render it available to plants even under alkaline conditions. Plants benefit indirectly when iron is supplied to soil microorganisms like azotobacter.

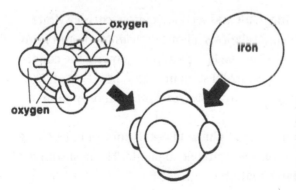

In chelation, ions of nutrients such as iron are surrounded by atoms from complex organic molecules that hold the nutrients in the soil and make them available to plants.

Azotobacter needs iron for its synthesis of nitrogen, but humus is necessary before azotobacter can assimilate iron.

Sufficient iron can be added to soil by composting with manure, crop residues, or dried blood. Foxglove stores large quantities of iron in its leaves and is another useful addition to compost piles. Seaweed and many garden and field weeds are good iron sources.

Manganese. Manganese is believed to be involved with the activity of oxidizing enzymes in plants. It also affects iron intake, vitamin formation, and photosynthesis. Plants deficient in manganese show a mottling of the tissue between veins. The veins themselves remain green and are sometimes surrounded by a band of green tissue. Leaves later turn white and fall off. These symptoms are most pronounced in legumes. Viruses, however, can produce the same appearance.

As with iron (as well as copper and zinc), manganese is most available under acidic conditions. Some very acidic soils may actually have manganese toxicity problems.

Copper. Copper occurs in greatest abundance in the growing parts of plants and is an essential catalyst for several enzymes. Copper deficiency appears in tips and end leaves in plants, especially in fruit trees. The tips of onion leaves die back when copper is deficient, and the skins of yellow onions become thin and pale. Copper may be deficient in muck soils, where it is bound up into extremely stable organic complexes.

Zinc. Zinc is essential for protein and starch synthesis and seed maturation. Zinc deficiency has been identified in citrus fruit, pecans, and corn. In a number of plants, the older leaves become discolored. Zinc is susceptible to being chemically immobilized by phosphorus, so excess phosphate fertilizer use can induce zinc deficiency.

Boron. Boron affects flowering, fruit and seed formation, carbohydrate and nitrogen metabolism, and water relations. Plants deficient in boron grow slowly; in severe cases the terminal bud, twig, or leaf dies. Among the conditions caused by boron deficiency are cracked stem in celery, heart rot and internal black spot in beets, corky spots in apples, and internal browning of cauliflower.

Deficiencies of boron are common in light, acidic soils subject to leaching, but excess lime can also make boron less available to plants. The best source of adequate boron nutrition is organic matter.

PLANT DISEASES

For a plant to be healthy, not only must it have suitable nutrition, water, air, heat, and light but it must be free of disease. Many plant diseases are caused by fungi and bacteria. It is true that these microorganisms are most likely to attack malnourished or weakened plants in preference to healthy ones. Still, microorganisms–including harmful ones–respond favorably to humus just as plants do. The answer to this dilemma lies in an as yet little-understood system of nature's checks and balances. Compost and humus promote the growth of both harmful and beneficial microorganisms. In addition, they promote the growth of bacteriophages, which destroy harmful bacteria. In the exceedingly complex soil ecosystem, harmful microorganisms–including wilts and smuts–seem to be brought under control when the life of the soil is in balance.

In *Humus*, Dr. Waksman states: "Plant deficiency diseases are usually less severe in soils well supplied with organic matter not only because of the increased vigor of the plants but also because of antagonistic effects of the various soil microorganisms which become more active in the presence of an abundance of organic matter."

Dr. Waksman and other authors have pointed out the omnipresence of soil organisms that produce antibiotic substances. It is quite probable that in the organic-amended soils, such organisms thrived and produced substances toxic to *Fusarium solani* f. sp. *cucurbitae*. In the field soil and sand-amended soil, the biological activity of such organisms must necessarily have been lower because of the limited nutritive conditions prevailing there.

Compost generally serves to suppress plant pathogens because it contains a rich diversity of beneficial microorganisms that act against plant diseases in two ways: As a general suppressive agent, beneficial organisms fill the ecological niche on plant leaves or roots that would otherwise be occupied by pathogens. They also produce antagonists to specific disease organisms, such as antibiotics or predatory fungi. Some compost organisms produce enzymes that break down cellulose and chitin, which are primary constituents of many plant pathogens, and in the process kill the pathogens.

While the high temperatures of thermophyllic composting kills many disease pathogens, it also kills many beneficial organisms. It is, however, possible to inoculate compost with the beneficials. Some research indicates that regular reinoculation of compost with specific fungi and bacteria that are known biocontrol agents is necessary to achieve consistent levels of disease suppression. The primary key to encouraging biocontrol organisms is to use a fully mature, well-stabilized compost.

Among the more exciting developments is the use of custom composts that suppress specific disease organisms. Dr. Harry Hoitink, professor of plant pathology at the Ohio Agricultural Research and Development Center of the Ohio State University, has pioneered the development of bark composts that suppress *Pythium* organisms responsible for damping-off and root rot. Some of this compost is marketed commercially to greenhouse producers who formerly drenched plants such as poinsettias, mums, and cyclamens with toxic fungicides.

German researcher Dr. Heinrich Weltzien at the University of Bonn also found that treating plants with liquid extracts of compost prevents attack by fungi that cause diseases such as blight and mildews. Late blight of tomatoes and potatoes, powdery mildew on grapes, and botrytis blight of beans are among the diseases that can be prevented using these extracts. This is not an effective treatment once the disease is established—it works only as a preventive.

The University of Florida Agricultural Experiment Station discovered that organic matter kills harmful nematodes. Reported researchers there: "Like practically all forms of animal life, nematodes have their enemies. Among the most common and efficient of these enemies are certain kinds of fungi that live in decaying vegetable matter. This doubtless accounts for much of the importance and advantages of a mulch."

Research has continued to support the value of compost for suppressing diseases such as *Pythium* and *Phytophthora* spp., *Botrytis cinerea* in strawberries, powdery mildew, and blight in potatoes. Dr. Deborah Neher at the University of Vermont and her associates have demonstrated the effectiveness of high-temperature composting of hardwood bark–based substrates to reduce the severity of blight on tomatoes and related crops, and to kill seeds of weeds like crabgrass.

Specialized compost mixes geared toward greenhouse and nursery producers that contain specific disease-fighting agents, such as *Rhizoctonia solani,* are now available commercially. Commercial products that contain beneficial, disease-suppressing organisms include seed treatments, compost inoculants, soil inoculants, and soil drenches.

Since Dr. Hoitink's pioneering research, scientists from all over the world have investigated and expanded on his work. Additional field research on the disease-suppressive benefits of compost tea preparations and vermicompost continues at universities and agricultural experiment stations, as well as among compost entrepreneurs. For more information on how best to use disease-suppressing composts, see Chapter 12.

PATHOGEN AND TOXICITY PROBLEMS

It would be unwise to assume that compost, in whatever form, is always good for plants. There is clear evidence that some pathogenic organisms, particularly viruses, can survive the composting process. Also, most bacterial pathogens must be subjected to prolonged high temperatures, or you can't count on killing them. For this reason, it is best to be cautious about composting wastes of plants related to your garden favorites. Tomatoes, potatoes, and peppers, for example, are all members of the same plant family and share many of the same diseases. Adding diseased tomato plants to your compost pile could transmit the pathogens to your peppers or to next season's tomato crop when the compost is applied. If you have disease problems in your garden, you're better off burning infested plants rather than risking infection of the next crop with your compost.

Researchers have also found extremely high levels of organic acids, mainly acetic acid, in incompletely decomposed composts. A study done in Belgium, using cress seeds germinated in samples of municipal refuse compost, found that it took 4 months for acetic acid to reach levels low enough to permit the seeds to germinate. The lesson here is to be sure that decomposition is complete before you use compost, or risk pickling your plants! Information on how to determine when your compost is mature enough can be found in Chapter 12.

Some persistent herbicides resist decomposition and will even pass through an animal's digestive system unchanged. This is a problem that has plagued a number of municipal and private compost producers (and their customers!) in recent times. Chemicals that have shown up in compost residues

🌱 **PREVENTIVE MEDICINE**

Help protect your plants from fungal blights and mildews by treating them with a compost extract spray. Mix one part well-rotted compost, preferably containing animal manures, with six parts water. Stir well and let it stand for about a week, then filter it through cheesecloth. Spray this liquid onto plants, or soak seeds overnight to prevent damping-off disease. Animal manures are thought to impart greater resistance because they contain phenols, compounds toxic to fungi, that accumulate on leaf surfaces. Most fungal organisms spread rapidly under moist, overcast weather conditions or when plants and soil remain wet for extended periods of time. Spray plants every 5 to 7 days when such conditions make infection likely.

around the United States include clopyralid, picloram, aminopyralid, and aminochlopyrachlor. Clopyralid is a long-lasting herbicide that is commonly used on turf and has surfaced in municipal composting facilities that compost lawn and leaf residues, and picloram is used to control broad-leaved weeds such as Canada thistle, commonly found in pastures. They can find their way into compost through grass clippings, hay, straw, and manure from animals that have grazed in pastures or eaten feed that contains them. Some states have banned the use of these herbicides, but the problem can be imported with hay and other livestock feed from places where they are permitted.

Residues of persistent herbicides as low as a 0.5 ppb (parts per billion) can damage sensitive plants such as beans, carrots, most flowers, and the tomato family. Most compost operations are careful to avoid taking in organic wastes or manure that may be contaminated, and they conduct germination tests on every batch to detect the presence of such plant-damaging chemicals.

Home composters should avoid taking in green waste from industrial areas, roadsides, power line rights-of-way, and similar areas that are routinely treated with herbicides. Make sure you know where your manure comes from, and inquire about herbicide use by farmers before accepting it. If you suspect herbicide contamination, contact your state department of agriculture or local extension office for advice on testing your compost.

COMPOST AND INSECT CONTROL

The observations of thousands of organic gardeners and farmers indicate that plants grown in a completely organic system, including the copious use of compost, are less likely to sustain insect attack and damage. Scientific experiments have borne out these observations.

The chemical approach to insect control has been to discover substances that will eliminate specific insect species, and then to apply them routinely during the growing season. The broad and deleterious ecological effects of this approach are well known. Organic control of insects, on the other hand, is based on manipulating the entire garden or farm ecology in such a way that all life-forms are in healthy balance. The predators of harmful insects are allowed to thrive, so insect damage—although not eliminated completely—causes no serious problem. Compost has a vital place in this organic system.

In the compost heap, insects are brought under control not only by microorganisms but also by the intense heat generated inside the heap. Any insect eggs will be destroyed by the heat, and microorganisms will then make short work of the remains. Often, the cool outer edges of the compost heap provide ideal conditions for insect multiplication. If you notice too many flies or sow bugs crawling over your heap, turn it so the insects and their eggs are thrust into the center of the heap, there to perish by heat and bacterial attack. Any heap that attracts more than a normal number of harmful insects should be covered with a thin layer of soil after each application of organic matter. With a little attention, no compost heap should become a breeding ground for the insects you are trying to bring into balance.

However, not all composting methods create the high temperatures necessary to destroy disease pathogens and weed seeds. If it's likely that you'll be composting diseased plant materials or lots of weeds, choose a hot-composting method. Composting methods and how much heat each generates are described in Chapter 8.

THE FRONTIERS OF COMPOSTING

The past 30 years have seen increasing recognition, among people from all walks of life, of the value of composting and the hope it holds for a world now overburdened with waste and climate chaos. The future of composting is bright, perhaps more so today than at any time since before World War II.

It was not until 1945 or so that our nation plunged headlong into a reckless energy binge, of which chemical agriculture was an integral part. At the same time, the revolution in plastics heralded an increase in disposable consumer goods and excess packaging, leading to the "throwaway society." A backlash of consumer spending followed the shortages of wartime, contributing to the burgeoning trash stream. After 40 years of prosperity, Americans woke up and discovered that we were running out of both fuel and places to put our growing mountain of trash—and despoiling a once-beautiful land in the process.

In the wake of the energy crisis of the '70s, a few pioneers pushed for more energy-efficient agricultural practices, in which composting played a major role. Municipal composting was promoted as an environmentally benign means of dealing with refuse as well as a source of valuable fertilizer for crop production. Unfortunately, this line of reasoning was frequently rejected because burying wastes in sanitary landfills was still generally cheaper than going to the trouble of composting them. Problems with some of the early designs for municipal composting systems further reduced cities' interest in large-scale composting. Financial performance suffered from the lack of a ready market for the finished product among farmers, most of whom remained convinced that chemical fertilizers were preferable.

It took the solid-waste crisis of the '80s to propel composting to prominence, not so much for its energy savings or value to soil fertility but as a means of reducing the volume of trash that has to be placed in landfills or incinerated. In the 1970s, according to the National Solid Wastes Management Association, some 20,000 landfills existed, and most were unlined dumps. As a result of stringent federal and state regulations, by 2012 there were slightly more than 1,900 municipal landfills. Tipping fees–the charges that waste haulers have to pay to deposit their loads–have been rising steadily. Nationwide, average tipping fees rose from about $9 per ton in 1985 to $44 a ton 15 years later. However, in more densely populated or heavily regulated states like New York, California, and Pennsylvania, tipping fees can frequently exceed $100 per ton and require long-distance transport of wastes to US Environmental Protection Agency–approved landfills.

At the same time, growing groundwater pollution prompted a toughening of environmental regulations, increasing the costs of disposing of wastes–primarily compostable ones that could potentially leach into water supplies. Incinerators, the most common alternative to landfills for trash, are often the source of air pollution problems. Also, the resulting ashes are hazardous wastes and must be disposed of accordingly. In 1989, the EPA issued regulations requiring municipalities to recycle 25 percent of their trash if they want a permit to build an incinerator.

FROM TRASH TO TREASURE

When communities all across the country recognized their predicament, composting along with recycling programs of all kinds–started looking like a very good idea indeed. By 1989, according to a *BioCycle* magazine survey, there were 986 programs to compost leaves and yard wastes, with 31 states reporting at least 1 such project–a 51 percent increase from the previous year. According to the EPA, in 2012 more than 19 million tons of yard trimmings were composted, representing almost a fivefold increase since 1990. However, while food waste accounts for slightly more of the total municipal waste stream, as of 2012 only about 2 percent was being recycled, compared with 23 percent of yard trimmings. We clearly still have a long way to go. Up to 75 percent of household garbage is derived from organic matter and, theoretically, can be composted. Restaurants, grocery stores, and institutions like colleges represent a significant portion of compostable waste generators. Even if the finished product were simply dumped into a landfill, composting would realize savings because the sheer bulk of the material would be reduced by almost half. Furthermore, it would no longer pose a toxic leachate problem, requiring expensive liners and test wells. Using the resulting compost to build healthy soil can be regarded as an added bonus—one that is increasingly recognized as another win-win as healthy soil microbiology works to store carbon drawn down by green plants from the atmosphere in a stable form.

Compost conserves energy because it supplies soil nutrients without calling on fossil fuel support. It saves energy because it can be made on the farm and in the garden, requiring no transportation from a factory. It saves energy because it is waste recycled via a very short route—as short as the distance from the kitchen to the backyard compost heap. Even the organic debris of an entire city can be recycled and returned to the land without leaving the metropolitan area.

The good news is that these concerns, combined with increased awareness of the problem of methane release from anaerobic decomposition taking place in landfills, has spurred increasing numbers of states and municipalities to take action. For example, the State of Vermont found itself with a single approved landfill to serve the entire state. In 2012, the state legislature, with pressure from environmental groups and local composting associations and businesses, unanimously passed a universal recycling law. Among other requirements, it phases out allowance for organic wastes to enter the landfill, so that by the year 2020 it will be illegal even for household food scraps to be dumped in the trash. Regional compost producers and institutional anaerobic waste-to-energy digesters have sprung into action to meet the challenge of collecting and recycling formerly landfilled wastes, returning the end product to the soil through a statewide "close the loop" program. Vermont's law has served as a model for other states, and by the end of 2016, 10 states and municipalities had some form of ban on food scraps going to landfills.

MUNICIPAL COMPOSTING PROGRAMS

Leaves and yard wastes—tree trimmings, grass clippings, and so forth—are easy to keep separate from other household garbage and relatively simple to compost, and so they represent the earliest and still most common community composting option. Leaves and yard waste also constitute a large share of the municipal trash stream, especially in the fall. On average, about 14 percent of the municipal waste stream nationwide consists of yard waste. Municipal yard waste and leaf-composting programs have become commonplace, and as of 2012, at least 24 states or municipalities had banned the disposal of green waste in landfills or incinerators.

Wellesley, Massachusetts, was among the first towns to institute leaf-composting programs in the early '70s, spurred by the closing of its incinerator for failing to meet air emission standards. At first the townspeople just decided to dump their leaves separately, but then they began windrowing and turning the piles regularly with a front-end loader. After acquiring a compost screener in 1989, the town did so well selling compost that it started soliciting debris from landscapers in hopes of tripling its compost production. The city of Davis, California, has contracted with a waste management company to pick up leaves and yard waste for composting since 1972.

New Jersey became a leader in statewide commitment to recycling in general. Among other incentives, the state has given grants to communities to purchase vacuum trucks to collect leaves raked to curbside by residents on specified days in the fall. Montgomery County, Maryland, also uses vacuum trucks to collect residential leaves and, in 1989, began collecting grass clippings, left in biodegradable plastic or paper bags, on a weekly basis. They have found that the clippings combine well with partly composted leaves from the previous fall. After experimenting with different ratios, they found that two parts leaves to one part grass clippings resulted in faster decomposition, with no odor problems.

Municipalities such as Seattle are now routinely collecting food scraps for composting, distributing special bins for use in curbside pickup programs. According to EarthShare, "Seattle isn't the only city that wants your old food scraps. Over 150 communities in the US now offer some form of curbside compost collection." San Francisco has an ambitious goal of eliminating any trash from landfills or incinerators by 2020, and by the end of 2017 was already composting or recycling 80 percent of its trash. New York City's enormous Department of Sanitation has a goal of zero waste going to landfills by 2030, and has now begun curbside compostables pickup, reaching an estimated 3.3 million residents in 2017.

New York, Seattle, and other cities are also providing residential food-scrap drop-off sites, as well as community compost centers and urban farms where educational materials and composting workshops are offered to local residents, along with various types of compost bins and accessories at reduced cost.

Collecting and composting yard wastes and food scraps is only part of the picture. Having a plan to dispose of the finished compost is essential to a successful town composting program. Many cities give it away to local residents but sell it to landscape and nursery businesses. Some use it in their own public works programs for parks and roadside plantings. New York, besides using its compost to improve the soil in the city's numerous parks and green spaces, offers community gardeners, street tree stewards, and other nonprofit groups free pallets of bagged compost on request.

A valid concern about composted yard waste products is the possible presence of harmful residues from the variety of pesticides and herbicides that are applied to lawns, trees, and shrubs. As noted in Chapter 4, residues of some persistent herbicides have caused problems for municipal as well as commercial compost makers, leading to more rigorous protocols for sourcing and testing raw materials that may pose risks. Concentration of heavy metals, particularly lead, is another potential hazard posed by municipal leaf compost. The removal of lead from most gasolines has reduced lead emissions from vehicles, thereby reducing the amount of lead absorbed by plant leaves. Additional research into metal accumulation by leaves is still needed, as they are increasingly recycled into home vegetable gardens.

Another obstacle to municipal composting efforts is the public perception of composting as smelly and unsightly, which generates opposition to placement of facilities. Cornell researchers have demonstrated that compost sites can make good neighbors. "We've found that the bad odors can be controlled at a properly run composting facility, and composting can generate good odors instead–the smells people associate with a forest on a wet day," says Dr. Tom Richard, one of the Cornell scientists. This demonstration project conducted in Westchester County also included an economic analysis that shows composting is by far the cheapest means of waste disposal. Says Dr. Richard, "As landfills and incinerators continue to escalate in cost, the economic advantages of composting become increasingly apparent."

A COMPOST BIN IN EVERY YARD

While municipal composting is a good idea, wouldn't it be even better for households to compost their own organic wastes, eliminating the need for a whole municipal service structure? This is exactly the line of thinking pursued in King County, Washington, which includes the city of Seattle. The citizens of Seattle have led the way in recycling awareness, recycling up to 25 percent of their waste even before the city set its ambitious goal of recycling 60 percent of its garbage by 1996.

Seattle's backyard composting program developed in three stages. Starting in 1980, the city adopted a composting strategy and set up a few neighborhood composting demonstration sites. Reports Carl Woestendiek, the city's recycling specialist, "Residents were asked to bring their leaves and grass clippings to a neighborhood site and volunteers would do the composting. The program was actually too successful—we had more yard waste than our volunteers could handle." However, this project reached only people who were already interested in composting, and it relied on volunteer labor for most of the station maintenance. After a while, volunteer enthusiasm declined, and waste started piling up.

In 1985, the city contracted with Seattle Tilth Association, a nonprofit organization formed to promote ecological gardening and farming, to design the Master Composter program. Modeled after the successful and widespread Master Gardener program, it first trains interested citizens in composting theory and methods, then has them serve as neighborhood resource people to bring this information to the public. Says Woestendiek, "Our aim is not to teach a few how to compost perfectly, but rather to teach many people how to produce usable compost." According to the *Master Composter Resource Manual*, "by networking with community groups, promoting [their] program through the media, and working with people on a one-on-one basis, [they] hope to make composting a common household practice."

Within the first 5 years, hundreds of people had completed the Master Composter course statewide. The program consists of 36 hours of formal training, 24 hours of internship, and 40 hours of community outreach time. Those who finish the course receive a pitchfork, a compost thermometer, and a training manual, along with a mandate to teach as many neighbors as they can how to compost. This may involve giving presentations to schools and community groups, holding open houses at their own compost sites, distributing literature, and going to people's homes to help with composting problems. Alumni of the program receive extensive support in the form of informational literature, portable displays, a slide show, and compost demonstration sites. Anyone with questions can call a compost information hotline.

Seattle's program soon expanded to include all of King County and progressed to a new level–distributing low-cost compost bins and information about how to use them. The Backyard Composting Program distributed more than 16,000 compost bins to county residents in 1989, at a price of $8.75 each, including delivery. The bins, manufactured by the county from fall-down western cedar, a by-product of the northwest milling industry, were distributed in kit form. The possibility of providing the bins to residents free of charge was considered but rejected, according to project manager Cheryl Waters, because "if people are willing to pay even a small price for a bin, they will be more likely to set it up and continue to use it."

Seattle's model has been shared far and wide, and by 2017 there were more than 500 Master Composter training programs throughout North America and beyond. Master Composter certification is offered by state extension programs, including Cornell Cooperative Extension and the University of Vermont. New York City, as well as numerous other urban centers, offers Master Composter training and home composting classes. Various nonprofit organizations, such as the Rodale Institute in Pennsylvania and ECO City Farms in Maryland, provide composting training for home gardeners as well as educators, institutions, and farmers.

COMMUNITY COMPOSTING

The Washington, DC–based Institute for Local Self-Reliance (ILSR) has taken the lead in promoting the concept of community composting through its Neighborhood Soil Rebuilders program. In addition to a comprehensive "train the trainer" program to guide community organizers through the process of creating neighborhood composting programs, they offer conferences and webinars aimed at sharing information and ideas for successful composting businesses, cooperatives, and social enterprises.

A newly developed *Hierarchy to Reduce Food Waste and Grow Community* document lays out in simple graphics a policy structure from most-desired to least-desired options for reducing, recycling, or finally disposing of food wastes. According to ILSR staff, "composting can be small scale and large scale and everything in between, but too often home composting, onsite composting, community scale composting, and on-farm composting are overlooked. Anaerobic digestion systems come in different sizes as well." Citing the EPA's 2015 partnership with the US Department of Agriculture that aims to establish a domestic goal to reduce food loss and waste by half by the year 2030, ILSR notes that "the agency's hierarchy remains an important guideline for how this goal is to be met: prevent food waste, feed hungry people, feed animals, and recover via industrial uses and anaerobic digestion." However, they note that the EPA's hierarchy does not differentiate between industrial-scale municipal and industrial composting operations and those that are more dispersed, neighborhood- and farm-based enterprises. "We believe size matters," states ILSR's webpage, and therefore "ILSR supports the development of a diverse and distributed food waste reduction and recovery infrastructure. We hope local and state governments will consider using our hierarchy as a policy framework."

Toward this end, ILSR works with groups and individuals interested in establishing worker-owned cooperatives and social enterprises to provide community-scale composting services to diverse constituencies. A recent webinar offered information on both of these business models. Facilitated by Brenda Platt, ILSR codirector, the webinar featured two dynamic speakers. Eric Lombardi was a national spokesperson for the GrassRoots Recycling Network, the first US zero-waste organization, and helped found the Zero Waste International Alliance. Under his direction, a small Denver-based nonprofit called Eco-Cycle became the largest zero-waste social enterprise in America. Boston's Lor Holmes is general manager of CERO (Cooperative Energy, Recycling, and Organics), a worker-owned company founded by African American and Latino entrepreneurs from Roxbury and Dorchester. In less than a year, CERO raised more than $350,000 via nearly 100 community investors to launch its worker-owned food-scrap collection enterprise in the Boston area and began operations in 2014. In 3 years, CERO created seven full-time living-wage jobs and diverted more than two million pounds of organic "waste" from landfill and incineration, using it instead to revitalize soil and support urban agriculture.

The recent Frederick Compost Summit organized by ILSR brought together local regulators, farmers, stakeholders, and citizens to discuss existing challenges, such as zoning and unclear county regulations, that hamper the ability of this Maryland county's large number of farmers to compost. Held at Fox Haven Learning Center, which is also an ecological retreat, organic farm, and wildlife sanctuary, presenters included two graduates of ILSR's Neighborhood Soil Rebuilders (NSR) training course, Lacey Walker and Phil Wescott. After completing the course, they took their knowledge back to Frederick County and organized the Frederick Compost Workgroup to engage both local government and the community. Thanks to their advocacy, the county has now identified source-separated organics collection and decentralized community-scale composting as two of three priority waste-management options requiring more detailed analysis.

ILSR also partnered with the Highfields Center for Composting in Hardwick, Vermont, to produce a community composting manual, *Growing Local Fertility*, in 2014. Highfields got its start as the Highfields Institute in 1994, when farmer Tod Delaricheliere began learning to compost his dairy manure and experimented with different recipes using locally available resources. His neighbors took notice and recognized that he was improving his soil and saving money at the same time. This was also a time when Hardwick was becoming the center of an agricultural revolution, as related in the book *The Town That Food Saved* by Ben Hewitt.

Highfields Center for Composting was created in 1999 to spread the word about composting to farmers around Vermont. A year later, Tom Gilbert, local farmer and soil enthusiast, took the helm as executive director. Traveling around Vermont educating farmers, Tom started thinking, "Why should composting be limited to farms when everyone is part of the food cycle?" With the help of some young "agripreneurs," the organization expanded to the state capital of Montpelier, partnering with the Central Vermont Waste Management District on a program that sought to tackle the challenges of community composting in a rural area. Thus was born Highfields' signature Close the Loop! program, which aimed to create community composting projects in several Vermont regions in order to capture food waste from vegetable growers, restaurants, ski areas, and schools to "close the loop" on local food systems.

The Highfields team helped design and establish several composting operations around Vermont and also developed its own Research and Education Compost Site in neighboring Wolcott. In addition to maintaining a food-scrap collection route and producing thousands of cubic yards of excellent compost, Highfields initiated an ambitious research program in collaboration with soil scientists, established a commercial-scale vermicomposting operation, and conducted compost heat recovery trials with different designs and recipes. An all-star advisory committee was assembled, including such luminaries as Dr. Will Brinton of Woods End Laboratories, Dr. Jean Bonhotal of Cornell, Dr. Deborah Neher of the University of Vermont, *BioCycle* editor Nora Goldstein, Vermont Compost Company creator Karl Hammer, and organic dairy farmer and author Jack Lazor, among others.

Perhaps Highfields' crowning achievement was its collaboration with environmental and organic farming advocates to help the Vermont legislature to pass its landmark legislation, the Universal Recycling Act, in 2012. This law has served as a national model and has set Vermont on track toward becoming the first in the nation to require recycling of all organics by 2020.

Despite some fund-raising success—including a Kickstarter campaign for the compost heat recovery project—income from compost sales, consulting fees, and contracts never allowed Highfields to attain viability as a social enterprise. Following the loss of Tom Gilbert's visionary leadership after he stepped down to start his own farm, and on the eve of publication of *Growing Local Fertility* with ILSR in 2014, Highfields was forced to close its doors. Tom went on to create Black Dirt Farm, picking up the former Highfields food-scrap collection program and purchasing the vermicompost system, continuing to help close the loop in his home community in Vermont's Northeast Kingdom. In its 15 years or so of operation, Highfields served as a powerful compost inoculant in Vermont and nationally, stirring up a heap of awareness about the need for community-based composting.

COMPOSTING HAZARDOUS WASTES

Hazardous wastes present an even more troublesome problem for financially pressed municipalities, and there is increasing interest in the possibility of composting hazardous organic compounds. Research conducted by W. W. Rose and W. A. Mercer in the late 1960s demonstrated that composting could degrade materials such as diazinon, parathion, dieldrin, and DDT. Since then, work has been done on composting as an option for treating oily waste. Most of this research has focused on aerobic decomposition processes, but recent studies have shown that certain chlorinated compounds, such as polychlorinated biphenyls (PCBs), need an anaerobic phase in order to break down.

In describing hazardous waste treatment, Dr. Clarence Golueke cautions that "much research is needed before composting is accepted as a practical and safe option. For example, there is the question of whether or not decomposition simply proceeds to an intermediate product that is equally or even more toxic than the original waste." There is also the danger that composting could be seen as a panacea for hazardous waste disposal problems, leading to a dampening of efforts to reduce the manufacture and use of these substances.

The field of bioremediation is emerging rapidly and gaining attention as oil spills and toxic contamination resulting from flood events increase in frequency. Most closely related to composting is the use of mushrooms to absorb and transform dangerous pollutants, known as mycoremedation. For example, oyster mushrooms are commonly used to consume oil spills, and white rot fungi have been used to break down pesticides as well as pulp and paper wastes. Researchers have found promising results using mushrooms to degrade such toxins as polycyclic aromatic hydrocarbons (PAHs), polychlorinated biphenyls (PCBs), polycyclic chlorine polymers (PCPs), TNT, neurotoxins, and synthetic dyes, as well as for water filtration and airborne pollutants. Mushroom visionary Paul Stamets uses oyster mushroom mycelia in burlap sacks as a gray-water filter. Professional mycologist Tradd Cotter suggests that urban chicken owners can cultivate mushroom mycelia in the chicken coop as a way of eliminating "fowl" odors and consuming any human pathogens such as E. coli or salmonella.

Carbon sources such as sawdust, straw, corncob, and corrugated cardboard can feed the fungi and speed up decontamination. Fungal mycelia–the hairlike threads that permeate the growing medium and eventually produce a fruiting body that we recognize as a mushroom–do the real work of detoxification. Different species can secrete powerful enzymes that are capable of decomposing a wide range of organic compounds, even highly toxic wastes that are deadly to most soil microorganisms. Once the mycelia have done their work and fruited, the resulting material can then be safely composted. Tradd Cotter recommends using vermicomposting for these materials to ensure that any pathogens or remaining contaminants have been neutralized.

BIOTHERMAL ENERGY AND COMPOST HEAT RECOVERY

In the process of turning unwanted trash into soil-building humus, compost organisms are capable of generating a considerable amount of heat. One ton of decomposing material gives off about as much heat as 10 gallons of number 2 fuel oil. Dubbing it "biothermal energy," a few innovators are working on using the heat of composting to warm homes and greenhouses. Although such applications for biothermal energy are new, gardeners have warmed their hotbeds with the biothermal energy of decomposing horse manure for decades.

One of the most intriguing models for biothermal energy use is detailed in *Another Kind of Garden*, by Jean and Ida Pain. Living in the south of France, they were able to provide most of their household heat by circulating coils of water pipe through huge piles of chipped slash and green brush. As the brush decomposed, its heat was absorbed by the water and piped through ordinary household radiators. In spring, their heat source was ready to use to rebuild the worn-out soils in their district. They also experimented with tapping the methane gas sometimes released by the composting process. In countries such as India, this methane is called biogas and is commonly used for family cooking needs. When organic materials decompose anaerobically in a landfill, biogas can build up to dangerous levels and must be burned off or otherwise released to prevent explosions.

Landfill gas, as it's known, is increasingly becoming a power source, as electrical utilities install methane generators to capture and burn the methane from landfills to produce electricity. However, unlike biogas or methane generators on farms or municipal waste treatment sites, the organic digestate produced does not become available to be returned to the soil.

In addition to heat and, under low-oxygen conditions, methane, active compost produces significant amounts of carbon dioxide. Because plants need both heat and carbon dioxide, several attempts have been made to combine composting with greenhouses. The most well-documented of these was built by Bruce Fulford at New Alchemy Institute on Cape Cod, Massachusetts. This small prototype, measuring 12 by 48 feet, was carefully monitored as a potential source of income for small farmers.

The New Alchemy researchers found that compost alone was not reliable as a heat source in New England but that it could supplement conventional or solar heat systems. Its primary usefulness, according to researcher Mark Schonbeck, is that "you can get root zone heating by having germination pads directly above the composting chamber." Ammonia gas given off by the compost created another stumbling block. Although plants need the nitrogen, which comprises most of the ammonia molecule, too much ammonia is toxic. This was solved by inserting a peat moss filter in the ducts used to vent heat throughout the greenhouse. Tomatoes ripened more quickly in the carbon dioxide–rich atmosphere of the composting greenhouse, and New Alchemy's research showed that potential financial returns were enough to justify the cost of building the structure.

One note of caution is that newly emerging research into the impact of elevated carbon dioxide levels on plant composition points to some cause for concern. The research shows that while plants may grow faster and produce more bulk under high CO_2 conditions, they contain a lower concentration of essential nutrients, such as protein, and more sugars and other carbohydrates as a result. This finding suggests that the rise in CO_2 resulting from unbridled fossil fuel consumption, surpassing 400 ppm in 2017, could be a factor in the decline in the nutrient density of crop plants that has been observed by multiple researchers over the past 40 years.

Jean Pain's work in the 1970s has inspired a new generation of compost heat-recovery developers in the 21st century. The compost-power network bills itself as a nonprofit educational networking organization dedicated to expanding the use of regenerative soil-building compost heat-recovery systems. Compost Power founder Gaelen Brown developed a small-scale compost-powered water heater using a sophisticated heat exchange technology that expands on the original "Pain mound" technique to improve the efficiency of heat capture.

Researchers at the University of New Hampshire worked with Brian Jerose of Agrilab Technologies to test the potential for capturing heat from compost in a static-pile aerated-compost system. Instead of forcing the air through the pile, Matt Smith and John Aber found that drawing the air through the pile using a suction system resulted in greater ability to capture heat and allowed a composting facility to use this method on several active piles simultaneously. In their 2014 report outlining their methods, they note that optimizing "heat recovery from a compost pile requires not only negative aeration, but the capture of the energy within the compost water vapor, which accounts for 63 percent of the energy balance of a pile." They also found that using the energy to heat water, rather than simply directing the heated air to a desired location, was the easiest way to use the heat captured. They used Agrilab's isobar system for heat exchange, which is based on a simple refrigerant process similar to those used for heat pumps and refrigerators.

The Agrilab system has been further developed for multiple applications, most recently through installation of a system at the Foster Brothers Farm in Middlebury, Vermont. This farm has pioneered the use of "cow power" to feed electricity into Vermont's grid from a cow manure–based methane generator, and now the Fosters are also making aerated compost with heat captured using Agrilab's isobar technology. In a 2017 interview, Bob Foster explained that he reuses the heat to both speed the composting process and keep the 70-by 80-foot compost bagging facility at a comfortable temperature for workers, and said the farm has reduced propane use and cut the time required for compost to mature from 3 months to 1. As Agrilab Technologies fine-tunes the system, he expects that additional compost-generated heat could allow the farm to run a year-round greenhouse.

COMPOSTING TOILETS AND HUMANURE

USDA soil scientist F. H. King, who traveled to Asia in the early 20th century, made note of the scrupulous collection of human "night soil" by Chinese peasants, a practice that contributed to the sustainable soil fertility of this region over the course of 4,000 years. While the advent of modern sanitation has been lauded as the source of the dramatic improvement in public health since King wrote, overreliance on outlandish quantities of precious fresh water to dispose of our waste stream has contributed to a worsening crisis of water pollution, not to mention wasting valuable nutrients that should be returned to the land to restore depleted soils.

Innovations, such as use of biological filtration systems to treat sewage, pioneered by scientists such as Dr. John Todd and his associates at Ocean Arks International, can help reclaim this wastewater but do little to recycle the valuable nutrients contained in human excrement to return to agriculture. Municipal sewage sludge, which is almost universally mixed with runoff from stormwater and various forms of industrial waste, presents its own drawbacks, even when composted (as we will see in Chapter 13).

Author Gene Logsdon, in his own irreverent style, writes about the possibility that we may adapt our culture to embrace the need for composting our own manure in his 2010 book, *Holy Shit*, saying, "If we are forced to start saving water and manure, we could easily get used to the idea of taking fifteen minutes or so every day to manage our wastes by way of dry toilets and composting rather than making them disappear down the flush toilet." He goes on to point out that there is now a World Toilet Day and a World Toilet Summit, which has called for the end of the flush toilet.

The simplest dry-composting toilet design is that popularized by Joseph Jenkins in his widely referenced *The Humanure Handbook*. A 5-gallon plastic bucket may be placed in an enclosed container and positioned under a toilet seat with ample supplies of dry leaves, shredded paper, or sawdust to "flush" the excrement deposited therein. This receptacle is then removed when it gets filled, and its contents brought to a compost site. Various authors have attested to the sanitary conditions and absence of odors present in such arrangements. This is only workable in more rural areas, but as Logsdon notes, "If human manure becomes as valuable as fertilizer in the United States as it has been in Asian countries for centuries, manure pickup could become as routine as trash pickup."

Various composting toilets are available for purchase, some of which are similar to the Jenkins model and require frequent emptying into an outdoor compost site. These are generally best suited to rustic campsites, off-grid cabins, and mobile applications. More substantial models can include heating units, fans, and stirring devices that permit the material to fully decompose within a more generous chamber, with the finished compost removed through a door at the bottom. These are suitable for installation in a home in lieu of a flush toilet, and they either rest entirely on the floor with an elevated seat or must be installed with the composting chamber in a basement area. Designs for home-built composting chambers can be found that provide either a detached outhouse-style facility or one that more closely resembles the traditional bathroom appliance. These may be built with two chambers that can each accommodate a year's worth of deposits, so that once full, the material can fully decompose before being removed to use in the garden.

It is often suggested that composted humanure should not be used for food crops, since some human pathogens can survive the composting process; Jenkins, among others, disputes such warnings, and attests to good health after decades of using his humanure compost on the family food garden. Logsdon takes a more cautious approach, recommending allowing the humanure to sit for at least a year and maybe two, just to be safe. It is good to question the scientific as opposed to the cultural basis for avoiding contact with anything that has ever touched human excrement.

Some research has recently been conducted on the value of human urine as a foliar fertilizer when collected and diluted. Though urine is a valuable source of nitrogen and lacking in microorganisms when it is excreted, collecting it separately from feces can be challenging (at least for females), and storage for any period of time is sure to generate unpleasant odors.

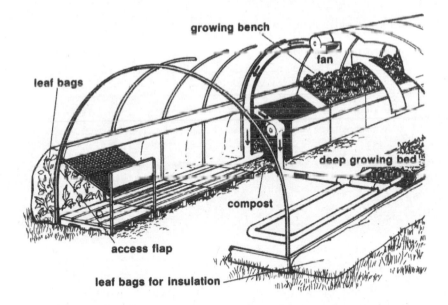

The composting greenhouse tested at the New Alchemy Institute uses compost piles beneath the benches as a source of root zone heat and carbon dioxide.

INDIVIDUAL INITIATIVES

Compost and composting are now a major part of our solid-waste policy. In order to recycle organic wastes to the fullest possible extent, we must concentrate on municipal composting, the recycling of industrial wastes, and the intelligent use of sewage sludge. More information about these processes appears in Chapter 13. They are the boldest lines of composting's new frontier.

The responsibility for maintaining governmental and industrial participation in composting, however, continues to rest with individuals, families, and community organizations, all working to remind these larger entities of their environmental obligations. The efforts of home composters may extend only as far as the backyard or may reach to the entire community or even to the state or national legislature. At any level, such efforts are important in turning around our country's solid-waste and energy policies, and, closer to home, all can provide rich additions to our farms and gardens, usually at no cost.

MATERIALS FOR COMPOSTING

Materials for composting are all around you. Many gardeners need look no further than the home grounds for a sufficient supply. Kitchen wastes, lawn clippings, weeds and plant debris, dog and cat hair–nearly anything that once lived (and is thus organic) is a candidate for the compost heap.

After you have exhausted the home supply and still don't have all the materials you would like, you can plan a series of foraging expeditions, beginning as close to home as possible and ranging out as far as you must in order to fulfill your requirements.

Manure should be the first item on your list, since it is by far the most important ingredient in any heap. If you try, you can get it free for the hauling or at a token fee at poultry farms, riding stables, feedlots, even zoos and wild game farms–any place that holds large numbers of animals in concentration. Even a friend with one horse and no garden can supply all the manure you'll need for a backyard pile.

Your chances of getting manure at a family farm are not as good, since farmers will probably want their manure for their own fields. Even if you seem to have all the home materials your compost heap can use, try to find a source of manure. Its tremendous bacteria content will bring your heap into biological and chemical balance and aid the rapid reduction of all the other materials.

But you don't have to stop with manure expeditions. In town, you can scavenge at grocery stores, city agencies, factories and mills, restaurants, and many retail operations. Ranging farther into the country, you can find materials in fields and along roadsides, streams, and ponds; at farms and orchards; at sawmills and canneries. Nearly any organic gardener can locate ample composting materials by going no farther than 5 miles from home. The farmer, of course, must make composting an integral part of his or her soil management plan, utilizing every scrap of home material and adding green manure crops as necessary. Even the organic farmer–especially one who has few animals or cultivates a small but intensive area–might need to look for supplementary materials. The materials listed in this chapter can be of use to both gardeners and organic farmers seeking to enhance their composting operations.

WHERE TO BEGIN

Begin, of course, at home. Are you discarding any organic matter at all? Newspapers? Tea bags? Clippings from the children's haircuts? Dishwater? With the exception of human and pet excreta (addressed later in this chapter), you can use everything. Before foraging, be sure that your home recovery program is 100 percent effective.

Once you venture outside your own yard, the best place to start is with friends, neighbors, and relatives. Some diligent composters offer to cart away kitchen scraps after every social call. This is often a valuable community service for people who would like to compost their wastes but for one reason or another are not able to do so. Recycled plastic pails with tight-fitting lids, such as those used for wallboard compound, make excellent containers for storing a week's worth or more of goodies. A layer of peat moss or sawdust on the bottom helps absorb moisture and odors. You can offer to pick up the full pail regularly and leave a fresh, empty one in its place.

Your expeditions away from home can continue with a trip through the business directory of the phone book. Go through it slowly, listing all possible sources of materials. Your search might end when you find that you can pick up manure at the local riding stable every Saturday morning and vegetable trimmings from the neighborhood supermarket every Tuesday and Friday afternoon. After your routine is established, it usually operates like clockwork.

Here is a partial list of away-from-home materials. You will come across others in your expeditions—but do consider these for starters.

Farms and orchards. These can provide spoiled hay, corn silage, eggshells, manure of every kind, feathers, barnyard litter, spoiled fruit, spent mushroom soil, whey from dairy operations, and orchard litter.

Factories and mills. Apple pomace is available from cider mills. Other possible compostables include cannery wastes of all kinds; shredded bark, sawdust, and wood shavings from lumber mills and carpentry shops; botanical drug wastes from pharmaceutical firms; cement dust; cocoa bean hulls (good mulch); coffee chaff from coffee wholesalers; cottonseed meal; felt wastes; agricultural frit from glass factories; grape pomace from wineries and spent hops from breweries; granite dust from cutting operations; leather dust;

The search for a variety of composting materials should begin at home.

lignin from paper mills; spoiled meal from flour mills; peanut shells; slag from steel plants; spice marc (spent) from spice packers; tanbark from tanneries; tankage from meat-processing plants and slaughterhouses.

Stables and feedlots. Manure and stable litter of all kinds are valuable compostables.

Retail stores. You can get vegetable trimmings from supermarkets and shops, hair from barbers and salons, pet hair from grooming parlors, food wastes from restaurants, coffee grounds from cafés, shredded paper store offices, plant wastes from florists, and sawdust from carpentry shops and lumber supply houses.

Roadsides, fields, and waterways. Rural road and power line maintenance crews who cut brush and trees will often deliver loads of wood chips to your site. Old leaves, weeds, and water plants from streams, lakes, and ponds may be plentiful. A note of caution: Many native plants, even those viewed as weeds, are endangered species that are protected by law. This is especially true of plants growing near oceans or in wetlands; such areas often contain fragile ecosystems that should not be disturbed. In gathering materials in fields and wild areas, be aware of your ecological responsibility to avoid robbing natural areas of their native plants.

REGIONAL MATERIALS

Gardeners in certain parts of the country can avail themselves of materials abundant in their regions. New Englanders can look for sawdust, dairy manure, and maple syrup wastes. Those along seacoasts can find greensand, fish scraps, and seaweed. Southwestern gardeners should look for cannery wastes, mesquite, olive residues, grape pomace from wineries, and citrus wastes. Southerners may have access to cotton gin trash, Spanish moss, peanut shell ashes, tung oil pomace, sugarcane trash, molasses residue, castor pomace, tobacco stems, rice hulls, and water hyacinth plants.

In collecting materials for your heap, not only will you be adding to your own soil's fertility and structure but you will also be contributing to the recycling of wastes that might otherwise become pollutants in the environment. Many communities now have or are planning composting facilities for at least part of their trash. If yours is one of them, they probably make finished compost available free or at low cost to gardeners. Chapter 13 has more information about using municipal compost. If your town has not yet pursued this option, it may offer free delivery of leaves, shredded tree trimmings, and other compostable municipal wastes.

Supermarkets and restaurants may be happy to contribute their organic wastes to you, since it lowers their disposal costs. Increasingly, such large organic waste generators are required to separate out compostable material to keep it out of landfills. Most important, however, these materials, instead of being dumped, buried, or burned, will find their way back to the soil.

MATERIALS TO AVOID

Although nearly any organic material can contribute to good compost, there are some that should be avoided, and others should be used only in limited amounts. First, you want your heap to be balanced among green matter, animal wastes, manure, and soil. If you build your heap of 80 percent tankage from the local meat-packing plant, not only will you have a putrid mess, but you will attract every stray dog, cat, and raccoon within a 5-mile radius. A truckload of grape pomace or a ton of wet hops from the brewery will be equally hard to handle, as will be the neighbors if your heap's odor wafts their way. Strive, then, for a commonsense balance in the materials you select, and be sure to add a layer of soil over the heap every time you add materials that might cause odor or attract vermin.

Human feces should not be used unless they have been properly treated and permitted to age sufficiently. Even then, concerns about disease pathogens make it best to avoid such material or to use it strictly for ornamentals. Urine alone can be used quite safely, however. See Chapter 5 for a discussion of humanure use.

Wastes from pet dogs, cats, and birds should not be used on the compost pile. Although dog manure is as rich in nutrients as other manures, it is more difficult and less pleasant to handle than the mixed bedding and manure of cattle and horses. In addition, it may carry organisms parasitic to humans. Special composters designed exclusively for dog droppings offer pet owners a safe alternative.

Cat manure is even more hazardous, especially to pregnant women and small children. Cat droppings may contain *Toxoplasma gondii*, a one-celled organism that, when transmitted to a pregnant woman, may infect her unborn child, causing brain and eye disease. *Toxocara cati* is a roundworm, also common in cat feces, that causes similar problems in children. Keep the contents of the litter box away from children and the compost pile.

Bird droppings have been similarly indicated as potential disease sources. Since they are most often mixed with bedding and dropped birdseed from the bottom of the cage, bird droppings will also tend to introduce unwanted weeds into your compost.

Materials that will not decompose readily–large pieces of wood, oyster and clam shells, large quantities of pine needles, rags, brush, cornstalks, heavy cardboard–should not be used in large amounts unless they are shredded first.

Large amounts of highly acidic materials such as pine needles and oak leaves should not be used without the addition of enough limestone to neutralize the acid. For acid-loving crops, however, you might wish to build acidic compost by the deliberate use of these materials.

Be very careful about diseased plants–you may be better off burning them and adding the ashes to your compost than risking inoculating your whole garden with them. Weeds can generally be composted, but be careful to ensure hot composting temperatures if they have produced seed. A few species, such as quack grass and Canada thistle, reproduce readily from the tiniest bit of surviving rhizome and should be avoided entirely.

Don't use large amounts of grease and oil, since they not only attract animal pests but also inhibit the biochemical processes necessary to successful composting. The amount of grease and oil from a normal household will cause no problem. However, carting home tubs of spent grease from the local potato chip factory is unwise.

Do not use toxic materials. There is little sense in trying to build an organic soil by including pesticide-treated wastes in the compost heap. Plant debris from roadsides might have been subject to a broad, potent, and persistent herbicide applied by the highway department. Similarly, green waste from municipal parks may have been treated with pesticides and herbicides used in grounds maintenance. Be careful in choosing materials.

MATERIALS FOR ENRICHMENT

There are many substances you can buy to increase your compost's N-P-K content or control its pH. Although it is not necessary to add these materials to the heap, many gardeners find it worth the expense to ensure a high nutrient level in their compost.

Among the materials and products available at garden centers and through mail-order outlets are bagged manure, vermicompost, dried blood, bonemeal, limestone, cottonseed meal, greensand, hoof and horn meal, tobacco wastes, seaweed, peat moss, and other natural products that are valuable to the heap because of their nutrient levels or ability to correct pH. All will be considered later in this book.

Many people add lime to their compost to increase its pH. This is not often necessary or beneficial, and it is not a good idea if you are composting manure, since the lime reacts with the nitrates in the manure to drive off ammonia. If lime is needed, apply it directly to the soil or mix it with the finished compost for potting mixes. The microbes inhabiting your compost heap can often benefit from the calcium in lime, but other forms of calcium, such as eggshells or any marine animal (oyster, crab, clam) shells, pulverized as finely as possible, will serve just as well. Bonemeal and wood ashes are also rich in calcium. Avoid all of these materials if you want compost for acid-loving plants such as rhododendrons, camellias, and blueberries, in which case you may want to use acidic peat instead of soil in your heap.

Rock or colloidal phosphates are excellent materials for enriching the mineral content of your compost. Microbial action makes their nutrients more readily available than they would be if they were added directly to the soil. They also contain significant amounts of calcium and micronutrients. Other rock powders such as granite dust and greensand, both sources of potassium and micronutrients, are similarly made more available to plants when first consumed by compost organisms.

Specific nutrients can be added by using plants that are especially rich in those elements in your compost. Seaweeds, such as the kelps, are rich in potassium and are good sources of such elements as iodine, boron, copper, magnesium, calcium, and phosphorus. If available locally, seaweed should certainly be added to the compost heap. The water hyacinths that grow so abundantly in the rivers of the South are rich in many of the elements that are more apt to be deficient in the soil. Leaves, discussed more thoroughly later in this chapter, are a teeming source of micronutrients that are not found in upper layers of soil; use them in compost whenever possible.

Refer to the lists beginning on page 122 for other materials that are particularly high in nitrogen, phosphorus, and potassium.

ACTIVATORS

A compost activator is any substance that stimulates biological decomposition in a compost pile. There are organic activators and artificial activators. Organic activators are materials containing a high amount of nitrogen in various forms, such as proteins, amino acids, and urea, among others. Some examples of natural activators are manure, garbage, dried blood, compost, humus-rich soil, and urine.

Artificial activators are generally chemically synthesized compounds such as ammonium sulfate or phosphate, urea, ammonia, or any of the common commercial nitrogen fertilizers. These materials are not recommended.

There are two ways in which an activator may influence a compost heap: (1) by introducing strains of microorganisms that are effective in breaking down organic matter and (2) by increasing the nitrogen and micronutrient content of the heap, thereby providing extra food for microorganisms.

Those who follow the practices of biodynamic agriculture consider certain activators, made according to precise instructions, to be essential for producing the highest-quality compost. These preparations are used in minute quantities as part of a holistic approach to working with soil, plants, and the energies of nature. The biodynamic method is explained more fully in Chapter 8.

Claims have sometimes been made that special cultures of bacteria will hasten the breakdown of material in a compost heap and also produce a better quality of finished compost. Products are manufactured that are reported to be effective in improving the action of a compost heap.

Most independent tests, however–including those conducted at the Rodale Institute–indicate that there is no benefit to be gained from the use of an activator that relies solely on the introduction of microorganisms. It seems that microorganisms will quickly multiply to the limit that their environment will permit. Since all the necessary microorganisms are already present in manure, soil, and other composting materials, there is no benefit to be gained from introducing strains in the form of an activator product. The best activator is a layer of finished compost from the previous heap or a generous amount of healthy topsoil.

Biochar, a form of charcoal created by heating carbonaceous material under conditions of low oxygen, is often touted as an all-around elixir for stimulating soil biology. There is increasing evidence that mycorrhizal fungi in particular are more abundant in biochar-amended soils, where their mycelia find hospitable conditions of moisture and aeration. The large amount of surface area offered by biochar particles provides an ideal environment for microbial colonization.

Commercial biochar-based products have proliferated in recent years. Quality of the raw input, particle size, and process controls are all variables that determine the effectiveness of the product. According to David Yarrow, a midwestern "carbon-smart" farm consultant, a potent inoculant can be obtained by mixing some good-quality compost with biochar consisting of different-size particles, a full complement of micronutrients, and enough water to keep it moist but not soggy. A sugar source such as molasses is sometimes added as a way to jump-start bacterial growth. This well-blended mixture should sit undisturbed as long as possible to allow a full diversity of microbes to colonize the material. Most often used to restore depleted soils, such concoctions can also be of value in boosting microbial populations in compost that may be lacking in manure or other highly biologically active ingredients.

Nitrogen Activators

The cause of most compost heap "failures" is a lack of nitrogen. Almost invariably, a heap that doesn't heat up or decay quickly enough is made from material that is low in nitrogen. Nitrogen is needed by the bacteria and fungi that do the work of composting, to build protoplasm and carry on their life processes.

In experiments conducted at the Rodale Institute, it was shown that increasing additions of bloodmeal (a high-nitrogen activator) produced associated increases in the temperature of the pile, indicating increasing bacterial activity. In the tests, 3 pounds of bloodmeal in a 31-pound pile produced the best results.

Good nitrogen activators besides bloodmeal (which is expensive when purchased commercially at garden centers) include tankage, manure, bonemeal, and alfalfa meal. Human urine, which contains about 1 percent nitrogen, also makes an excellent compost activator. Just how much you should add to the heap depends on the nature of the material you are composting.

Low-nitrogen materials such as straw, sawdust, corncobs, and old weeds should have at least 2 or 3 pounds of nitrogen supplement added per 100 pounds of raw material. If plenty of manure, grass clippings, fresh weeds, and other high-nitrogen materials are available to be mixed in with the compost, no nitrogen supplement will be necessary.

COMMON MATERIALS

Here is a list of the more common—and some not-so-common—materials that can be used in composting.

Alfalfa

Alfalfa is a perennial herbaceous legume grown as livestock feed and as a green manure or cover crop. Alfalfa grows almost everywhere in the United States and is widely available as hay, meal, or dehydrated feed pellets. Its nitrogen content and absorbency make it an excellent addition to the compost pile.

In combination with leaves and/or household garbage, alfalfa serves as a good compost stimulant and activator; its 12:1 carbon/nitrogen (C/N) ratio helps bring the pile's overall C/N ratio into the desired 25:1 to 30:1 range. While expensive when sold as hay, alfalfa is moderately priced in the form of dehydrated pellets or meal, and these products can be purchased at most feed-stores. Farmers and feedstores may also have rotted or spoiled bales, unsuitable as animal feed, that they will gladly give you.

Apple Pomace

Anyone who presses his or her own cider produces heaps of this sweet pulp. Yellow jackets, hornets, and bees love to zero in on the residues, so it's best to get the pomace into a working compost heap as soon as possible. Fresh pomace is wet and heavy and should be mixed well with dry leaves, hay, or other absorbent matter.

While low in nitrogen, pomace does contain valuable amounts of phosphoric acid and potash. Large numbers of seeds are also present in pomace; these storage organs contain reserves of phosphorus and nitrogen, adding to the nutrient value of the pomace.

If you collect pomace from commercial presses, look into the source of their apples and the pesticides applied to the fruit. Apple skins may contain residues of metallic sprays, especially if such sprays are used heavily. Spray residues can build up to toxic levels when large amounts of pomace are used.

Bagasse

Bagasse is the waste plant residue left from the milling of sugarcane. Gardeners in the Deep South may have access to quantities of this valuable addition to the compost heap. (See also "Sugar Wastes" on page 117.)

Banana Residue

The skins and stalks of this tropical fruit contain abundant amounts of phosphoric acid and potash. Banana skins decompose rapidly, a sign that the microbes of decay are well supplied with nitrogen. Banana skins are usually a staple in kitchen scraps, and their use in a compost heap will guarantee lots of bacterial activity. Incorporate banana skins into the core of your compost pile, or cover them quickly with organic matter to avoid attracting flies.

Basic Slag

This industrial by-product, formed when iron ore is smelted to make pig iron, is most commonly found in steelmaking areas. The smelting process uses large amounts of limestone and dolomite that combine with impurities in the ore, rising as a sludge that coats the surface of the molten metal. Skimmed off, cooled, and hardened, the resultant slag contains numerous minerals also found in the soil—calcium, magnesium, silicon, aluminum, manganese, sulfur, and iron—plus trace amounts of boron, chromium, copper, molybdenum, potassium, sodium, strontium, tin, vanadium, zinc, and zirconium. The exact percentage of these minerals depends on variations in the smelting process. Basic slag provides calcium (in the form of calcium silicate), magnesium, and slow-release phosphate. Often used as a liming agent, it makes other essential nutrients more accessible and protects plants from potentially toxic elements such as manganese and aluminum.

The "Composition of Slag" table on page 92 shows the main elements found in slag, the compounds in which they most often occur, and the average range of each mineral.

Packaged slag has been pulverized into a fine black powder so it can be used as a soil builder in gardening and farming. The material is alkaline and is popular as a liming agent. Tests show that slag is better for this purpose than lime because of its greater store of minerals.

Since slag is made up of finely pulverized but insoluble particles, it can be applied liberally to soil or a compost heap with no fear of overuse. It won't burn plants or roots. Beans, peas, clover, vetches, alfalfa, and other leguminous crops will benefit from its application. Slags vary in content, so check the analysis before using them. Avoid slags with low or nonexistent amounts of nutrients and minor elements. Don't use slags containing excessive amounts of sulfur.

COMPOSITION OF SLAG

MATERIAL	COMPOUND	PERCENTAGE
Lime	CaO	38–45
Magnesia	MgO	4–9
Silica	SiO_2	33–39
Alumina	A1A	10–14
Manganese oxide	MnO	0.2–1.5
Iron oxide	FeO	0.2–0.7
Sulfur	S	1.0–2.0

Beet Wastes

Residues from sugar beet processing are commonly used for livestock feed, though they will compost readily. The nitrogen content averages 0.4 percent, potassium content varies from 0.7 to 4.1 percent, and phosphoric acid content ranges from 0.1 to 0.6 percent. Dried beet pulp is also available at many feedstores. Organic farmers cannot use sugar beets as livestock feed, since virtually all of the sugar beets produced in North America are genetically modified varieties. However, genetically modified plant materials can be used as compost feedstock. (See "GMO Wastes," page 99.)

Bonemeal

A slaughterhouse by-product, the pulverized residue of bones is, along with rock phosphate, a major source of phosphorus for the farm and garden. Bonemeal also contains a large percentage of nitrogen, though the content of both minerals depends on the age and type of bones processed. Raw bonemeal usually contains 20 to 25 percent phosphoric acid and 2 to 4 percent nitrogen. Steamed bonemeal, the more commonly available variety, has up to 30 percent phosphorus and 1 to 2 percent nitrogen. Steamed bonemeal is finer than raw bonemeal, so it breaks down more rapidly in the soil or compost heap.

Bone black is charred bone that has been used as a filter for sugar refining. Bone black contains about 1.5 percent nitrogen, 30 percent phosphoric acid, and many micronutrients.

Bonemeals are most effective when mixed with other organic matter and added to well-aerated soils. They will exert an alkalizing effect because of their lime content, so match their use to your soil's pH characteristics. Use them moderately in composting to avoid the volatilization of nitrogen to ammonia.

Buckwheat Hulls

Buckwheat is a cereal crop grown mainly in the northeastern United States and in Canada. Popular among organic farmers and gardeners as a green manure and bee forage crop, it grows well in even marginal soils. Buckwheat hulls, left after processing of the grain, are lightweight and disk shaped. They make good additions to the compost heap, though many gardeners prefer to use them as mulch. The hulls absorb water easily, stay in place once applied (a layer 1½ inches thick will suffice), and look like a crumbly loam.

Castor Pomace

Castor pomace is the residue left after the oil has been extracted from the castor bean. It is widely used as an organic fertilizer in place of cottonseed meal, because the latter is a valuable feed. The nitrogen analysis of castor bean varies from 4 to 6.6 percent, while phosphoric acid and potash have been found to be 1 to 2 percent, with greater variation occurring in the phosphorus content.

Where animal matter is unavailable, compost can easily be made with castor pomace and other plant matter. Moisten the pomace and spread it over the green matter in semiliquid form. The finer the plant matter, the quicker the bacterial action.

Citrus Wastes

Gardeners living near factories producing orange and grapefruit products should make use of this easily composted residue, though dried citrus pulp is also available in bulk from some feedstores. The nitrogen content of these materials varies according to the type of fruit and the density of the skin. The thicker the peel, the more nitrogen it contains.

Orange skins contain about 3 percent phosphoric acid and 27 percent potash (surpassed only by banana skins, with 50 percent potash). Lemons are higher in phosphorus but lower in potash than oranges. Grapefruits average 3.6 percent phosphoric acid, and their potassium content is near that of oranges.

You may use whole waste fruits (culls) in the compost pile, although their nutrient content will be lower due to the high water content. Citrus wastes will break down faster if shredded (the bagged, dried pulp sold as animal feed comes in dime-size chips) and mixed with green matter and a source of nitrogen and bacteria like manure, lawn clippings, or garden soil.

Unfortunately, citrus crops are routinely sprayed by commercial growers. If the spray program is moderate, the chemicals should break down during the composting process without causing harm. To be absolutely sure of what you're adding to your compost, use only fruits and fruit wastes from organic growers.

Cocoa Bean Shells

These residues from chocolate factories are available in bulk from garden supply houses, but because they make such an attractive mulch, cocoa bean shells rarely find their way into the compost heap. They are rich in nutrients, though, and benefit the soil however they're used. Cocoa shell dust has 1.5 percent phosphorus, about 1.7 percent potassium, and 1 percent nitrogen—a high analysis of the latter, considering the woody nature of cocoa.

If the shells themselves have been treated to extract caffeine and theobro-mine, the residues will have about 2.7 percent nitrogen, 0.7 percent phosphoric acid, and 2.6 percent potassium. Untreated raw shells show a higher nutrient content. Pressed cocoa cake has also been offered as fertilizer. It's higher in nitrogen, has less potassium than shells, and has a phosphorus content of nearly 0.9 percent. The nitrogen content of cake will vary according to its processing.

If you can locate a source of oil-free and theobromine-free cocoa wastes, you'll have a useful product for mulching acidic soils. The extraction process uses lime, so the shells will help raise the pH while adding moisture-retentive organic matter. Cocoa shells are also weed-free and odorless.

To use them as mulch, spread the shells in a layer 1 inch deep. They are light brown, look nice around shrubs, evergreens, and flowerbeds, and offer excellent drought-proofing and insulative properties. Shells used in compost piles should be shredded or pulverized.

Coffee Wastes

Earthworms seem to have a particular affinity for coffee grounds, so be sure to use these leftovers on the compost pile, in your worm box, or as a mulch. The grounds are acidic and can be used by themselves around blueberries, evergreens, and other acid-loving plants. Mix the grounds with a little ground limestone for plants needing alkaline or neutral soil.

The nutrient content of coffee residues varies according to the type of residue. Grounds have up to 2 percent nitrogen, 0.33 percent phosphoric acid, and varying amounts of potassium. Drip coffee grounds contain more nutrients than boiled grounds, though the potassium content is still below 1 percent. Other substances found include sugars, carbohydrates, some vitamins, trace elements, and caffeine.

Coffee processing plants sell coffee chaff, a dark material containing over 2 percent nitrogen and potassium. Chaff is useful either as a mulch or in compost.

Apply your coffee grounds immediately, or mix them with other organic matter. They hold moisture extremely well. Left standing, they will quickly sour, inviting acetobacters (vinegar-producing microbes) and fruit flies.

Corncobs

These residues used to be available in large amounts from mills, but modern combines now shred the stalks and expel the cobs right back into the field. Cobs contain two-thirds of the nutrients found in the corn kernel, but they must be shredded before composting or their decay will take years. Let the cobs age in open piles for several months, then grind them with a shredder or lawn mower.

Cobs have superior moisture retention and make effective mulches when spread 3 to 4 inches deep. Shredded cobs may also be used as a seed-starting medium. In long-standing, no-turn piles, unshredded cobs mixed with leaves and other dense materials will provide aeration and discourage caking and matting.

Cottonseed Meal

Cottonseed meal is made from cottonseed that has been freed from lints and hulls and deprived of its oil. Since cottonseed cake is one of the richest protein foods for animal feeding, relatively little is available for use as fertilizer. Although it is a rich source of nitrogen, it may also contain high levels of pesticide residues. This is because cotton, as a nonfood crop, receives heavy applications of pesticides, some of which may accumulate in the seeds. Unless you have access to meal from organically grown cotton, you may choose to avoid cottonseed meal in favor of another nitrogen source for your compost pile. Organic farmers may use conventional cottonseed meal as a fertilizer if it has been tested for pesticide residues and determined to be free of such prohibited substances. (See "GMO Wastes," page 99.)

Cottonseed meal is commonly used to increase soil acidity for acid-loving specialty crops, but other materials, such as pine needles and peat moss, will serve the same purpose. Cottonseed meal has a nitrogen content of around 7 percent. Its phosphoric acid content is between 2 and 3 percent, while potash is usually 1.5 percent.

Dried Blood

Dried blood is a slaughterhouse by-product. It is high in nitrogen, about 12 percent, but its phosphorus content varies from 1 to 5 percent. Dried blood is used mainly as an animal feed, though most garden shops carry it for use as a fertilizer. The cost per pound can be quite high because it is tied to the price of meat. Dried blood can be applied directly to the soil around plants, but it should be kept several inches away from the stems to avoid burning. Dried blood may be used in compost heaps. Sprinkled over layers of moist organic matter, its high nitrogen content stimulates decay organisms, especially when added to carbon-rich materials.

Felt Wastes

Check hat factories for discarded hair, wool, and felt. These materials may contain up to 14 percent nitrogen and will aid in making rapid, high-heat compost. Such wastes are quite dry, however, and will decompose slowly or pack down unless they are thoroughly moistened and mixed with bacteria-rich ingredients like manure or green matter.

Fish Scraps

Gardeners near oceans or fish-processing plants can usually truck home loads of this smelly stuff. It is well supplied with nitrogen and phosphorus (7 percent or above for each nutrient) and also contains valuable micronutrients like iodine. But, like all fresh residues, fish scraps easily turn anaerobic and are highly attractive to rodents, flies, and other scavengers.

Fish scraps must be handled carefully in the garden, either buried (covered with at least 4 inches of soil) or composted in properly built heaps enclosed by sturdy bins or pens. The trick is to use generous amounts of bulky, high-carbon materials such as shredded brush, straw, or sawdust to balance the high nitrogen and moisture of the fish, to increase aeration, and to discourage packing down.

Composting fish scraps in a pit is somewhat easier (once you've dug the pit, of course). Mix them with organic matter or soil and cover them with enough dirt to discourage flies. The pit must also be enclosed by a sturdy fence or wall and topped with a scavenger-proof frame or lid.

Fish scraps present difficult challenges to the composter on any scale, but offer ample benefits when used with reasonable care and attention to providing adequate carbon and air. Dr. William F. Brinton, of Woods End Research Laboratories in Maine, has successfully demonstrated fish waste composting, with minimal odor problems, using a farm- or industrial-scale windrow method.

Crab meal is becoming a popular organic-approved fertilizer readily obtained through garden supply stores. Besides serving as a good source of nitrogen, phosphorus, calcium, and essential micronutrients, crab shells are high in chitin, which suppresses some plant pathogens and parasitic nematodes as it decomposes under bacterial action.

Garbage

Americans routinely throw away mountains of valuable food scraps, setting them out on the curb or grinding them up in disposals and flushing them into overworked municipal sewage systems. Yet kitchen scraps are truly a neglected resource, containing 1 to 3 percent nitrogen along with calcium, phosphorus, potassium, and micronutrients. The material is free, available in quantity every day, and relatively easy to handle.

Kitchen scraps may be dug directly into the garden (see "Trench and Post-hole Composting" on page 177). Alternatively, they may be composted in heaps or pits. You can conveniently save household garbage until you are ready to layer it into a new or existing compost pile. Use a plastic bucket with a tight-fitting lid, and each time you add garbage, cover it with a layer of sawdust or peat moss to absorb moisture and odors. When adding kitchen scraps to your compost pile, mix them well with absorbent matter like dead leaves or hay to offset the wetness. Use a predator-proof enclosure, and be sure to keep all scraps well into the pile's core, covering them thoroughly with dirt or additional materials to discourage flies.

Chop or shred all large pieces of matter (potatoes, grapefruit rinds, eggshells, and so on) to hasten decomposition. Meat scraps, fat, or bones should be used with caution in compost piles, for these materials take too long to fully break down and are most attractive to scavenging animals.

GMO Wastes

An extremely difficult issue is that of organic wastes derived from genetically modified organisms (GMOs). Corn, soybeans, canola, potatoes, rice, cotton, alfalfa, and sugar beets now could all possibly be GMOs, which are not permitted to be used to produce an organic product, according to the National Organic Program. However, waste products from crops like corn and alfalfa may be used as fertility inputs. Research is still inconclusive as to how completely the composting process breaks down the genetically altered DNA, and there are no definitive limits (at least in the United States) for GMO contamination in an organically grown product. In the case of wastes of crops that may be GMOs (e.g., spoiled corn silage), it is best to make sure that the material was not grown from genetically modified seed. There is, however, no clear evidence that GMOs in the feedstocks will remain in the finished compost.

Gin Trash

Gin trash is another by-product of the cotton industry. Once burned and discarded, these leaf and stem wastes are now being composted and returned to the soil. While cotton wastes contain many valuable nutrients and fibrous organic matter, their effect on soil health may not always be beneficial, depending on the type of cotton and the state in which it was produced. In some states, including Texas and Oklahoma, arsenic compounds may be applied as a defoliant and desiccant. Significant residues of this carcinogen are left in the gin trash, making it an undesirable addition to the compost pile. Normal arsenic levels in the soil run about 5 parts per million, but gin wastes may contain 40 times that amount.

Although arsenic acid may no longer be used in cotton production, organic forms of arsenic are still legal for use as a defoliant. Home composters who have access to gin trash should consider its source and the production methods used in their state before making gin trash a part of their composting program. Because of the timing of arsenic applications, contamination of the seeds does not occur; arsenic residue is not a concern with cottonseed meal. (See "Cottonseed Meal" on page 96.) In some parts of Texas and California, gin trash from organically produced or "eco-grown" cotton may be available. If you have cotton gins in your area, check with their operators to find out about the types of cotton crops they handle.

Granite Dust

Granite dust is a natural source of potash that is superior to the chemically treated potash sold as commercial fertilizer. Granite dust or granite meal has a potassium content of between 3 and 5 percent, contains micronutrients, is inexpensive, and will leave no harmful chemical residues. Unlike chemically treated sources of potash, granite dust is slow acting, releasing its nutrients over a period of years. It may be used in the compost pile or added to soil or sheet compost. Use it liberally directly on the soil, applying 10 pounds to 100 square feet when spreading. Choose a windless day for application, and wear a dust mask.

Grape Wastes

Wineries produce these residues of skins, seeds, and stalks by the ton during the pressing season. Vineyards also accumulate large amounts of grapevine pieces after annual pruning. While the nutrient content of grape wastes isn't that high, the sheer bulk of organic materials involved benefits the soil by promoting aeration and microbial activity.

The residues of pressing will be wet and mushy and should be mixed with absorbent plant matter. Additional nitrogen in the form of manure or high-protein green matter may be necessary if you desire rapid, hot compost. The prunings are tough and must be chopped into pieces 3 to 6 inches long, or shredded, if they are to break down in a season.

Grass Clippings

This is one compostable—a true "green manure"—that most gardeners can produce or obtain in abundance. Even if you don't have your own lawn, your fellow citizens do; in suburban areas they'll leave bags of clippings conveniently lined up along the curbsides for your harvesting every garbage collection day.

Freshly gathered green clippings are exceedingly rich in nitrogen and will heat up on their own if pulled into a pile, but because of their high water content, they will pack down and become slimy. This can be avoided by adding grass clippings in thin layers, alternating with leaves, garbage, manure, and other materials, thus preventing them from clumping together. If you discover a mass of matted clippings when you turn your compost, just break it up with a garden fork or spade and layer the pieces back into the pile. Grass clippings and leaves can be turned into finished compost in 2 weeks if the heap is chopped and turned every 3 days. You can profitably mix two parts grass clippings with one part manure and bedding for a relatively fast compost, even without turning.

Clippings that have been allowed to dry out will have lost much of their nitrogen content but are still valuable as an energy source and to absorb excess moisture. Clippings make an excellent mulch in the vegetable or flower garden or around shrubs and trees. As a mulch, clippings look neat and stay in place, and only a light layer (3 to 4 inches) is needed to choke out weeds and seal in moisture.

If you have extra grass clippings on hand later in the season, use them as a green manure. Simply scatter them in an area that has already been harvested and turn them in immediately, along with any previously applied mulch. The fresh clippings decompose quickly in the soil and stimulate microbial activity by providing abundant nitrogen. More mulch should be added to the surface over winter to prevent exposure of bare soil to the weather. Additionally, you can use clippings as a green manure before planting a late crop, but give the soil a week or 10 days to stabilize before planting. When used this way, grass clippings greatly improve the physical condition of heavy-textured soils.

Not all grass clippings should be removed from the lawn; when left after mowing, their nutrients enrich the lawn itself, without the application of chemical fertilizers. However, most lawns do not need as much enrichment as a full growing season's clippings will provide. Collecting grass clippings also helps reduce weed growth by removing weed seeds from the lawn.

There is one environmental caution about grass clippings. Many homeowners use various "weed and feed" preparations or any of a half-dozen herbicides in striving for an immaculate lawn. The most troublesome of these chemicals is 2,4-D, a weed killer that has caused birth defects in lab animals and may be carcinogenic.

Although this systemic, rapid-action plant hormone attacks broad-leaved plants like dandelions, literally causing them to grow themselves to death in hours, 2,4-D doesn't affect grasses. The narrow-bladed leaves do absorb traces of the hormone but not enough to harm them. Much more 2,4-D remains as a residue in broad-leaved plants, though even this should theoretically be broken down by soil microbes in a week. But beware of grass clippings that may have spray adhering to them from a fresh application. If used as a mulch, such clippings could cause herbicide damage to your garden plants—most of which are broad-leaved.

Ask your neighbors or whomever you gather clippings from what they used on their lawns. (If several mowings and some rains have occurred since the last application of herbicide, the clippings should be clear of 2,4-D residue.) Use your own clippings if you have them, and look around for natural lawns showing a healthy crop of dandelions—a sign that the landowner wisely avoided using herbicides.

🌿 LETTING THE CLIPPINGS FALL

Leaving grass clippings on your lawn some of the time provides the grass with natural fertilizer and saves work. It is recommended in Grasscycling, a lawn care plan designed by the Professional Lawn Care Association of America. The low-maintenance lawn care plan is based on the highly successful Don't Bag It program originally developed in Texas. Leaving clippings does not cause thatch buildup, as was once believed. Thatch is made up of dead roots, leaf sheaths, and rhizomes, not clippings. If you mow with a regular lawn mower, don't let the grass grow more than 1½ inches between mowings, and mow the grass only when it is dry. Even so, the clippings can be messy.

Mulching mowers eliminate the mess by chopping the clippings into fine fragments after they cut the grass. The fragments fall down into the lawn, where they decompose rapidly and release nutrients. Mulching mowers can also shred a few fallen leaves on the lawn while you are mowing and can be used to prepare piles of leaves for composting.

Mulching lawn mowers chop grass clippings into fine bits that break down quickly to return nutrients to the lawn.

Greensand

Greensand is an iron-potassium silicate that imparts a green color to the minerals in which it occurs. Being an undersea deposit, greensand contains traces of many (if not all) of the elements that occur in seawater. Greensand has been used successfully for soil building for more than 100 years. It is a fine source of potash.

Greensand contains from 6 to 7 percent of plant-available potash, but it is released very slowly when applied directly to the soil. Incorporating greensand into your compost improves the availability of its potassium and micronutrients. Good glauconite deposits also contain 50 percent silica, 18 to 23 percent iron oxides, 3 to 7.5 percent magnesia, small amounts of lime and phosphoric acid, and traces of more than 30 other elements useful to higher plant life. Unlike wood ashes, another frequently used source of potash, greensand does not have an alkalinizing effect.

Hair

Between 6 and 7 pounds of hair contain as much nitrogen as 100 to 200 pounds of manure. Like feathers, hair will decompose rapidly in a compost pile but only if well moistened and thoroughly mixed with an aerating material. Hair tends to pack down and shed water, so chopping or turning the pile regularly will hasten decay. Most barbershops or hair salons will be happy to supply you with bags of hair (though they may think your request is strange unless you explain).

Hay

Farmers often have spoiled hay available free or at low cost to gardeners. Hay is an excellent source of carbon for compost and also contains significant amounts of potassium, especially if it includes legumes such as alfalfa, clover, or vetch.

Hay is sometimes best used as mulch, especially around fruit trees. However, unless it was cut early, before seed heads began to form, it poses the hazard of introducing weed seeds into your garden. High-temperature composting will kill most weed seeds. To ensure that high enough temperatures (above 140°F/60°C) are reached, you should chop or shred the hay first, especially if it has matted in the bales. This can be done by spreading out the sections and running a lawn mower back and forth over them. You should alternate layers of nitrogenous materials such as manure with the shredded hay, to stimulate rapid heating. Make sure the materials are moist enough by giving each layer a good sprinkling. If high enough temperatures are not reached within a couple of days, the pile should be turned and re-layered with an additional nitrogen source.

Hoof and Horn Meal

There are many grades of hoof and horn meal. The granular form breaks down with some difficulty unless kept moist and well covered; it also tends to encourage the growth of maggots because it attracts flies. Finely ground horn dust, which gardeners use for potting mixtures, is quite easily dissolved. The nitrogen content is from 10 to 16 pounds per 100-pound bag, or as much as a ton or more of manure, while the phosphoric acid value is usually around 2 percent. If available, this is a very handy source of nitrogen for gardeners with small compost heaps, because it can be easily stored, is pleasant to handle, and is less costly than other forms of bagged organic nitrogen.

Hops

Hops are viny plants grown and used for making beer. (Hops impart the characteristic bitter flavor.) Spent hops, the wastes left after the brewing process, are an excellent garden fertilizer, containing (when dry) 2.5 to 3.5 percent nitrogen and 1 percent phosphoric acid. They do have a strong odor when wet and fresh, but this dissipates rapidly.

Wet hops may be spread directly on the garden in fall or spring just as you would apply manure. Turn the matter under, mixing it with the top 4 to 5 inches of soil. Wet hops heat up rapidly, so keep them several inches away from plant stems to burning. This tendency to heat up is, of course, desirable in making compost. Be sure to balance the sogginess of spent hops with absorbent matter.

Spent hops make a good mulch when dry. They resist blowing away and will not easily ignite if a lighted match is tossed onto a pile. (Many other mulch materials burn easily.) A layer of dry, spent hops will break down slowly, staying put for 3 years or more.

Another brewery waste to inquire about is the grain left over from the mashing process. When wet, this material contains almost 1 percent nitrogen and decays rapidly. Brewers' grains are also in high demand for livestock feed.

Incinerator Ash

Incinerator ash, if available, can be a fine source of phosphorus and potash for the compost heap. Its phosphorus content depends upon what was burned but averages 5 or 6 percent; its potassium content is from 2 to 3 percent. As with many compostable materials, the source of the ash should be considered before it is added to the compost pile. Ash from apartment-building incinerators may be acceptable, depending on the materials burned. It is best to avoid municipal incinerator ash, most of which is considered hazardous waste because the heavy metals and other toxic substances found in municipal solid waste often become more concentrated and soluble when burned.

Leather Dust

Available as a by-product of leather processing and as a commercial fertilizer from garden shops, leather dust contains from 5.5 to 12 percent nitrogen. Phosphorus is also present in considerable amounts.

Leather dust is often contaminated with the heavy metal chromium, used in the tanning process, and is for this reason prohibited for use by organic farmers. Unless you have a source that produces leather dust with low or no levels of heavy-metal contaminants, it is best to refrain from using it on your compost or on soil in which food crops will be grown.

Leaves

Leaves are a valuable compostable and mulch material abundantly available to most gardeners. Because trees have extensive root systems, they draw nutrients up from deep within the subsoil. Much of this mineral bounty is passed into the leaves, making them a superior garden resource. (See the table "Composition of Fallen Leaves" on page 107.) Pound for pound, the leaves of most trees contain twice the mineral content of manure. The considerable fiber content of leaves aids in improving the aeration and crumb structure of most soils.

Many people shy away from using leaves in compost because they've had trouble with them packing down and resisting decay. Leaves don't contain much nitrogen, so a pile of them all alone may take years to decay fully. But most leaves can be converted to a fine-textured humus in several weeks (or, at most, a few months) if some general guidelines are followed.

- Add extra nitrogen to your leaf compost since leaves alone don't contain enough nitrogen to provide sufficient food for bacteria. Manure is the best nitrogen supplement, and a mixture of five parts leaves to one part manure will break down quickly. If you don't have manure, nitrogen supplements like dried blood, alfalfa meal, and bonemeal will work almost as well. In general, add 2 cups of dried blood or other natural nitrogen supplement to each wheelbarrow load of leaves.
- Don't let your leaves sit around too long and dry out. As leaves weather, they lose whatever nitrogen content they may have had. This, combined with the dehydration of the cells, makes them much more resistant to decomposition than when used fresh.
- Grind or shred your leaves. A compost pile made of shredded material is easily controlled and easy to handle.

If you don't have a shredder, you can adapt various other devices to leaf shredding. Many people use a rotary mower for shredding. A mower that is not self-propelled is best and easiest to control. Two people can work together very nicely, one piling up leaves in front of the mower and the other running it back and forth over the pile. A leaf-mulching attachment on the blade will cut the leaves more finely, but sometimes it is not necessary. You will be surprised how many leaves you can shred this way in 30 minutes or so.

Of course, some people use a mower with a mulching attachment to cut up leaves right on the lawn. This does not make them available for compost or mulch somewhere else—like the garden—where they are more essential.

If you have so many leaves that you can't compost all of them—or if you don't have the time to make compost—you can make leaf mold. Leaf mold is not as rich a fertilizer as composted leaves, but it's easier to make and is especially useful as mulch.

A length of snow fencing or woven wire fencing placed in a circle makes the best kind of enclosure for making leaf mold. Gather leaves in the fall and wet them thoroughly; then tamp them down in the enclosure. Leaves are slightly acid. If your plants don't need an acid mulch, add some limestone to the leaves before tamping them down.

These leaves will not break down over the winter into the kind of black, powdery leaf mold found on the forest floor, but by spring or summer they will be broken up enough to serve as a fine mulch. Some people, including nursery operators who require fine potting soil, keep leaves "in cold storage" for several years. When they come for their leaves, they find black, crumbly humus.

Leaf mold is ordinarily found in the forest in a layer just above the mineral soil. It has the merit of decomposing slowly, furnishing plant nutrients gradually, and improving the soil structure as it does so. Leaf mold's ability to retain moisture is amazing. Subsoil can hold a mere 20 percent of its weight in water; good, rich topsoil will hold 60 percent; but leaf mold can retain 300 to 500 percent of its weight.

Freshly fallen leaves pass through several stages, from surface litter to well-decomposed humus partly mixed with mineral soil. Leaf mold from deciduous trees is somewhat richer in such mineral foods as potash and phosphorus than that from conifers. The nitrogen content varies from 0.2 to 5 percent.

COMPOSITION OF FALLEN LEAVES

NAME	CALCIUM	MAGNESIUM	POTASSIUM	PHOSPHORUS	NITROGEN	ASH	pH
Ash, white	2.37	0.27	0.54	0.15	0.63	10.26	6.80
Beech, American	0.99	0.22	0.65	0.10	0.67	7.37	5.08
Fir, balsam	1.12	0.16	0.12	0.09	1.25	3.08	5.50
Hemlock, eastern	0.68	0.14	0.27	0.07	1.05	—	5.50
Maple, red	1.29	0.40	0.40	0.09	0.52	10.97	4.70
Maple, sugar	1.81	0.24	0.75	0.11	0.67	11.85	4.30
Oak, white	1.36	0.24	0.52	0.13	0.65	5.71	4.40

If you keep poultry or livestock, use your supply of leaves for litter or bedding along with straw or hay. Leaf mold thus enriched with extra nitrogen may later be mixed directly with soil or added to the compost pile.

A lawn sweeper is a good tool to use for collecting leaves. It is easier than raking and often does a better job. Handheld leaf vacuums are also available at most lawn and garden stores.

Many municipalities are now composting leaves and yard wastes instead of dumping them into landfills. If your community has such a program, you can send in your surplus leaves with a good conscience and probably pick up finished compost in return.

Limestone

Limestone is an important source of calcium and, when dolomitic limestone is used, magnesium. It is commonly applied to raise the pH of acidic soils and may sometimes be appropriate when composting very acidic materials such as pine needles. However, compost made from a good variety of materials should have a pH near neutral without the addition of lime. Moreover, it is unwise to use lime with fresh manure or other nitrogenous materials, as it reacts chemically to drive off ammonia gas and thus loses some of the valuable nitrogen.

If your soil is acidic, it is best to apply lime to it directly, rather than through compost. Any reliable soil test will tell you how much lime is needed. If you live in a humid region, lime should be applied every 3 or 4 years, preferably in the fall so it will become available first thing in the spring. Use a grade fine enough to pass through a 100-mesh screen. In drier climates, where soil pH is naturally neutral or higher, liming is rarely necessary. You may want to use some lime for making potting soil with your compost—use about 1 tablespoon for 20 quarts of soil mix.

Most vegetables and garden plants prefer a slightly acidic to neutral pH, so laboratory liming recommendations generally strive for a pH of 6.5 to 6.8 (a pH of 7 is neutral). Some vegetables—legumes such as beans, peas, and alfalfa, for example—do better with slightly alkaline soil, while many berries prefer acidic conditions. Organic matter in the soil tends to buffer the effects of pH extremes by making nutrients available to plants regardless of soil pH. Lime, therefore, should be used to supplement soil improvement through the addition of compost.

Manure

Manure is the most valuable ingredient in the compost pile. For a full discussion of using manure in composting, see Chapter 7.

Molasses Residues

The wastes from sugar refining are obviously rich in carbohydrates, but they also contain some mineral nutrients. Naturally occurring yeasts in the compost will ferment these sugars rapidly. Dry molasses is often available from feedstores.

Olive Wastes

Olive pits contain phosphorus, nitrogen, and some lignin (a woody substance related to cellulose). But the pits must be ground or chopped before composting, or they'll take years to decay. Pulpy olive wastes vary in nutrient density. One analysis showed the pomace (what's left after oil extraction) having 1.15 percent nitrogen, 0.78 percent phosphoric acid, and 1.26 percent potassium. The pulp is oily and should be well mixed with other organic matter.

Paper

Many kinds of paper, even those with colored inks, can be used for compost or mulch. You can save a lot on trash collection costs, and keep the valuable carbon for your soil, by recycling paper through your compost. Although the colored inks contain various heavy metals, one study found that their concentration is low enough to be negligible, even when glossy magazines are used as a garden mulch. If only a few colored-ink items are mixed in with newsprint, there should be no cause for concern.

The secret to using paper successfully is to shred or chop it as finely as possible. Matted layers of newspaper, like hay and grass clippings, will halt the composting organisms in their tracks. Various tools will work for this process, including shredders used for brush. If you don't have a lot of paper, a sharp machete will chop it adequately. And don't forget the office paper shredder–you may even be able to recycle preshredded office paper from local businesses. Dairy farmers in various regions are being encouraged to use newspaper, which they shred using silage-making equipment, as bedding for their animals. The newspaper is very absorbent and makes an excellent compost medium when mixed with manure.

Shredded paper should be incorporated into your compost in layers, alternating with garbage or other wet materials. Because it is almost pure cellulose, it requires a concentrated nitrogen source to stimulate decomposition, but once broken down it creates a high-quality humus that will improve the tilth of any soil.

Peat Moss

This naturally occurring fibrous material is the centuries-old, partially decayed residue of plants. Widely sold as a soil conditioner, mulch, and plant propagation medium, peat's major advantages are its water retention (it is capable of absorbing 15 times its weight in water) and fibrous bulk. Dry peat will help loosen heavy soils, bind light ones, hold nutrients in place, and increase aeration. But while its physical effects on soil are valuable, peat isn't a substitute for compost or leaf mold. Expensive, relatively low in nutrients, and acidic, peat is best used as a seed-flat and rooting medium or as a mulch or soil amendment for acid-loving plants.

If a distinctly acidic compost is needed for certain plants, substitute peat for the soil in your compost pile. (See "Soil," page 116.) Peat compost is beneficial for camellia, rhododendron, azalea, blueberry, sweet potato, watermelon, eggplant, potato, and tomato plants–all of which prefer acidic soil conditions.

Pea Wastes

Feeding pea shells and vines to livestock and getting the waste back as manure is an excellent recycling method. Otherwise, pea wastes can be rapidly composted since they are rich in nitrogen when green. Dry vines should be shredded or chopped before or during composting, to hasten decay. Diseased vines should be burned and the ashes returned to the soil. (Pea ash contains almost 3 percent phosphoric acid and 27 percent potassium.)

Pet Wastes

As discussed earlier in this chapter, the wastes of dogs, cats, and birds are potential carriers of organisms that may cause disease in humans. Such materials should not be included in the home compost pile. Wastewater from aquariums, however, contains a certain amount of algae and organic matter that can be beneficial to plants. Use aquarium water to add moisture to your compost heap or for watering plants.

Phosphate Rock

Phosphate rock is a mainstay in organic gardens and farms because of its value as a soil and compost pile amendment. While its chemical composition varies according to the source, phosphate rock generally contains 65 percent calcium phosphate or bone phosphate of lime. A diversity of other compounds and micronutrients important to plant development is also present.

Phosphate rock is a naturally occurring mineral, however; don't confuse it with superphosphate. The latter has been treated with sulfuric acid to increase its solubility. But many micronutrients are lost due to this processing, and the increase in the availability of sulfur stimulates the presence of sulfur-reducing bacteria in the soil. These organisms attack sulfur and also ingest a fungus that normally breaks down cellulose in the soil. Besides encouraging this microbial imbalance, superphosphate can leave harmful salts in the soil. Furthermore, within a few days superphosphate will react chemically with calcium and other soil nutrients to become indistinguishable from the less-soluble rock powder.

Phosphate rock creates no such problems. It's slow acting, which makes nutrients available to plants for many years after a single application. Applied alone to vegetable or flower gardens, 1 pound to every 10 square feet of growing area will suffice for 3 to 5 years. It may be sprinkled lightly over succeeding layers in a compost heap to add nutrients to the finished product. It is valuable when combined with manure and other nitrogenous materials, since it prevents loss of nitrogen in the form of ammonia. The nutrients in rock phosphate are more readily available to plants when it is added via compost, having first been incorporated into the bodies of countless microorganisms.

Worldwide phosphate deposits are rapidly being depleted, and some experts suggest that we are in a time of "peak phosphorus." For this reason, it is best to look toward recycling of phosphorus through the return of organic wastes and manure to the soil. Phosphorus runoff from farm fields poses a similar threat to nitrogen runoff, causing algae blooms and other problems in surface waters. By encouraging high fungal soil organisms and stimulating mycorrhizal growth in your compost, you can maintain adequate phosphate nutrition for crops without contributing to extraction of an increasingly scarce resource.

Pine Needles

Pine needles are compostable, although they will break down rather slowly because of their thick outer coating of a waxy substance called cutin. Pine needles are also acidic in nature, and for this reason they should not be used in large quantities, unless compost for acid-loving plants is desired. For best results, shred the needles before adding them to the heap.

Evergreen needles have been found to be effective in controlling some harmful soil fungi, such as *Fusarium* spp., when used as a mulch or mixed directly into the soil.

Potato Wastes

Potato peels are common components of kitchen scraps. They provide a valuable source of nitrogen (about 0.6 percent as ash) and minor elements for the compost pile. Rotted whole potatoes, chopped or shredded, are worthwhile compost pile additions. The tubers contain about 2.5 percent potash, plus other minerals. Use the potato vines, too; they can be either composted or dug back into the soil. The vines, when dry, contain approximately 1.6 percent potash, 4 percent calcium, and 1.1 percent magnesium, plus sulfur and other minerals.

Rice Hulls

Often considered a waste product, rice hulls have been found to be rich in potash and to decompose readily, increasing humus content, when worked into the soil. The hulls make an excellent soil conditioner and a worthwhile addition to the compost heap. They also make a good, long-lasting mulch that does not blow away.

Gardeners in the Texas–Louisiana Gulf Coast area can often get ample amounts of this material from rice mills; occasionally it is free. Some mills make a practice of burning the hulls, and the residue from this operation contains a high percentage of potash, making it especially valuable as a composting material.

Sawdust

Sawdust is often useful in the compost heap, although it is better used as a mulch. Some gardeners who have access to large quantities use it for both, with equally fine results. In most areas, lumberyards will occasionally give sawdust free for the hauling. Sawdust is very low in nitrogen. One of the objections against using sawdust is that it may cause a nitrogen deficiency. However, many gardeners report fine results from applying sawdust as a mulch to the soil surface without adding any supplementary nitrogen fertilizer. If your soil is of low fertility, watch plants carefully during the growing season. If they become light green or yellowish in color, side-dress with an organic nitrogen fertilizer such as alfalfa meal, bloodmeal, compost, or manure. Regular applications of manure tea will also counteract any slight nitrogen deficit.

Some people are afraid that the continued application of sawdust will sour their soil—that is, make it too acidic. A comprehensive study made from 1949 to 1954 by the Connecticut Agricultural Experiment Station of sawdust and wood chips reported no instance of sawdust making the soil more acidic. It is possible, though, that sawdust used on the highly alkaline soils of the western United States would help to make the soil neutral, a welcome effect.

When used for compost, sawdust is valuable not only as a carbon source but as a bulking agent, allowing good air penetration in the pile. This is true only of sawdust that comes from sawmills or chain saws; the fine material that results from sanding can become packed and anaerobic. Although sawdust is slow to break down, the larger bits you may find remaining in finished compost will not present problems when added to your soil and will improve the texture of heavy soils. Wood wastes such as sawdust also stimulate fungal colonization, helping to extract phosphorus from otherwise unavailable soil reserves.

Seaweed

Coastal gardeners can gather different types of seaweed by wandering the shoreline. Look for kelp (laminaria), bladder wrack (also called fucus), sea lettuce (ulva), and other varieties. Gardeners elsewhere can buy dried, granulated seaweed (kelp meal) or liquid concentrate. All these seaweed variants are rich in many types of micronutrients and are a boon to plants, soil health, and the compost pile.

Compared with barnyard manure, seaweed in general has a similar organic content. The proportions, however, vary–seaweed has more potassium than manure but has less nitrogen and phosphorus. Seaweed is perhaps most valued for its micronutrient content. An analysis of the seaweed most commonly used in seaweed meals and extracts identified the presence of some 60 elements, including all those important for plant, animal, and human health.

Use wet, fresh seaweed quickly because it deteriorates rapidly when piled haphazardly. Exposure to the elements will quickly leach out many of seaweed's soluble minerals. Dig the seaweed under, or mix it with nitrogenous and absorbent materials for rapid composting. Bacteria feast on the alginic acid found in the leaves, which makes seaweed an excellent compost pile activator. If composted with manure that is rich in litter, seaweed aids the speedy decay of the straw; very little nitrogen is lost, and all the other elements are preserved. Decay occurs rapidly.

If you have only a small amount of seaweed, chop it and soak it overnight in a gallon of hot water (160° to 180°F/71° to 82°C). Sprinkle this mixture over successive layers of the compost pile. The liquid can also be used as a fertilizer and as a seed-soaking solution.

Kelp meal can be used as an activator in compost, since its rich micronutrient composition stimulates microbial growth. Seaweed extract can be used to feed plants directly through their leaves, and may also be applied to compost in the course of moistening the layers. When used as a foliar feed, plant growth is also stimulated by seaweed's content of cytokinins and other plant growth hormones.

Sewage Sludge

Sewage sludge is the solid residue left after organic wastes and wastewater have been chemically, bacterially, or physically processed. Depending on how it is processed, sludge may contain up to 6 percent nitrogen and from 3 to 6 percent phosphorus.

Activated sludge is produced when sewage is agitated by air rapidly bubbling through it. Certain types of very active bacteria coagulate the organic matter, which settles out, leaving a clear liquid that can be discharged with a minimum amount of pollution. The resulting sludge is usually heat-treated before being offered as a soil amendment.

Digested sludge is formed when the solid matter in sewage is allowed to settle without air agitation, the liquid is drained off, and the sludge is fermented anaerobically. The conventional anaerobic digestion system takes from 15 to 30 days at 99°F (37°C) from the time the sewage reaches the sedimentation tank until the digested solids are pumped into filter beds for drying. The dried material is either incinerated or used for soil improvement.

Until recently, most sewage sludge was incinerated, buried in landfills, or dumped offshore. Now there's an increasing interest in using this potentially valuable material as a soil conditioner. This would be ideal if the residue were composed solely of the remains of human waste, but that isn't the case. Since industrial wastes are often treated in the same sewage plants as household wastes, sewage sludges are often contaminated with heavy metals that, when regularly incorporated into the soil, can build up to toxic levels.

All municipal sludge must be composted at high temperatures before it can be safely used as a garden fertilizer. Even then, avoid using it for edible crops, especially roots and leafy greens, since some viruses can survive hot composting temperatures. Any municipal solid-waste composting operation should provide information on metals and other toxic compounds in its products if it offers them for sale to the public; most states prohibit distribution of uncomposted sludge to the public.

As restrictions on sewage waste disposal make it more difficult and costly, an increasing number of cities are establishing sludge composting programs. Gardeners who have access to the products of such programs should ask questions and get detailed answers about the content of the sludge, its chemical analysis, and how it has been processed. Unless you're absolutely sure of the chemical content of your community's sludge, don't apply it near or on food crops or anywhere that runoff might contaminate a garden, an orchard, or a well. See Chapter 13 for more information about municipal sludge composting.

Sewage sludge, composted or not, is prohibited for use as a fertilizer by organic farmers. See Chapters 8 and 12 for discussions of the rules governing compost and other permitted fertility inputs for organic farming under the USDA's National Organic Program.

Soil

While not a necessity, soil is a valuable component in compost making. The thin (1/8-inch) layer called for in Indore heaps contains billions of soil organisms that consume plant, animal, and mineral matter, converting it to humus. Soil also contains minerals and organic matter, so it acts like an activator when added to compostables. You can achieve much the same results using finished compost saved from a previous batch.

Thin layers of dirt in the compost heap work to absorb unstable substances produced by fermentation, thereby slowing their loss to the atmosphere. And when the pile is built, a topping of several inches of topsoil will stop heat and water from leaving the pile. Don't add too much soil, however, or the finished compost will be quite heavy.

Other than your own property, sources for soil include nearby woods, fields, building excavations, and mud from streams and ponds free of industrial or agricultural pollution. Don't use pond or stream mud directly in your soil; it will have the same effect as adding raw manure. Mud is also easier to handle if you dry it before composting, by mixing it with layers of absorbent plant wastes.

Straw

Although straw will add few nutrients to the compost heap, it is widely used because it is readily available and adds considerable organic material. It is unsurpassed as an aerating medium, as each straw acts as a conduit for air to circulate throughout the pile.

The fertilizer value of straw is, like that of all organic matter, twofold: It adds carbon material and plant food to the compost. The carbon serves the soil bacteria as energy food, while the plant food becomes released for growing crops. Where straw is used as mulch, incorporate considerable amounts of nitrogen (preferably in the form of manures) so that the bacteria that break down the straw into humus do not deplete the soil of the nitrogen needed by growing plants.

If used in quantity, the straw should be cut up. Long pieces of straw mixed with other materials that hold water or composted with ample amounts of barnyard manure offer no trouble, though heaps cannot be turned easily. Straw compost must therefore be allowed to stand longer. For quicker compost, weigh down the material with a thicker layer of earth. This also preserves the moisture inside the heap.

If a large straw pile is allowed to stay outside in the field, it will eventually decay at the bottom into a crumbly substance. Such material is excellent for compost making and mulching. Some of the fungi it contains are of the types that form mycorrhizal relations with the roots of fruit trees, evergreens, grapes, roses, and so on, and a straw mulch will therefore benefit these plants not only as a moisture preserver but as an inoculant for mycorrhizae.

The nitrogen value of straw is so small that it need not be accounted for in composting. The mineral value of straw depends on the soils where the crops were grown. (See the table "Typical Analyses of Straws" on page 118.)

Sugar Wastes

The most plentiful sugar-processing residue is burned bone, or bone charcoal, which is used as a filtration medium. Called "bone black" when saturated with sugar residues, this substance contains 2 percent nitrogen, more than 30 percent phosphorus, and a variable potassium content. Raw sugar residues, also known as bagasse, have over 1 percent nitrogen and over 8 percent phosphoric acid.

Tanbark

Tanbark is plant waste that remains following the tanning of leather. Its residues are shredded, heaped, and inoculated with decay-promoting bacteria. Thus composted, tanbark is sold in bulk as mulching material. Analysis shows nitrogen at 1.7 percent, phosphorus at 0.9 percent, and potassium at 0.2 percent; minor amounts of aluminum, calcium, cobalt, copper, iron, lead, magnesium, molybdenum, zinc, and boron are also present. Like peat, tanbark makes an excellent mulch but is generally too expensive to use extensively in compost.

TYPICAL ANALYSES OF STRAWS (%)

STRAW	CALCIUM	POTASH	MAGNESIUM	PHOSPHORUS	SULFUR
Barley	0.4	1.0	0.1	0.1–0.5	0.1
Buckwheat	2.0	2.0	0.3	0.4	?
Corn stover	0.3	0.8	0.2	0.2	0.2
Millet	1.0	3.2	0.4	0.2	0.2
Oats	0.2	1.5	0.2	0.1	0.2
Rye	0.3	1.0	0.07	0.1	0.1
Sorghum	0.2	1.0	0.1	0.1	0.2
Wheat	0.2	0.8	0.1	0.08	0.1

Source: Kenneth C. Beeson, US Department of Agriculture

Tankage

Tankage is the refuse from slaughterhouses and butcher shops, except blood freed from the fats by processing. Depending on the amount of bone present, the phosphorus content varies greatly. The nitrogen content varies usually between 5 and 12.5 percent; the phosphoric acid content is usually around 2 percent, but may be much higher.

Tankage, because it is usually rich in nutrient value, is especially valuable to the compost pile. However, it is also in demand as a feed additive and so is available only sporadically. Because it is an animal waste, tankage does require special care in composting. Your compost must be kept in a secure, enclosed container, safe from four-legged scavengers. Use a good supply of high-carbon materials such as leaves, hay, or sawdust to absorb odors, with a layer of soil over each layer of tankage.

Tea Grounds

Useful as a mulch or for adding to the compost heap, one analysis of tea leaves showed the relatively high content of 4.15 percent nitrogen, which seems exceptional. Both phosphorus and potash were present in amounts below 1 percent.

Tobacco Wastes

Tobacco stems, leaf waste, and dust are good organic fertilizer, especially high in potash. The nutrients contained in 100 pounds of tobacco wastes are 2.5 to 3.7 pounds of nitrogen, almost 1 pound of phosphoric acid, and from 4.5 to 7 pounds of potassium.

Tobacco leaves are "stripped" for market in late fall, leaving thousands of stalks. Some farmers use their stalks to fertilize their own fields, chopping up the stalks and disking them into the soil. Some stalks are available for gardeners, however, and tobacco processing plants bale further wastes for home use.

These wastes can be used anywhere barnyard manure is recommended, except on tobacco, tomatoes, potatoes, and peppers because they may carry some of the virus diseases of these crops, especially tobacco mosaic virus.

Compost tobacco wastes, or use them in moderation in mulching or sheet composting mixed with other organic materials. They should not be applied alone in concentrated amounts as a mulch—the nicotine will eliminate beneficial insects, earthworms, and other soil organisms as well as harmful ones.

Water Hyacinth

Southerners who lack sufficient green matter for compost can often find quantities of the water hyacinth (*Eichhornia crassipes*) growing in profusion in Southern streams. This plant is considered a serious menace to agriculture, fisheries, sanitation, and health in the South and other parts of the world where it grows with remarkable rankness. For best results, shred and mix it with partially decomposed "starter material" such as soil or manure.

Weeds

Weeds can be put to use in the compost pile. Their nitrogen, phosphorus, and potash content is similar to other plant residues, and large quantities can provide much humus for the soil. Weed seeds will be killed by the high temperatures in the compost pile, and any weeds that sprout from the top of the heap can be turned under. Be careful not to allow weeds to grow and set seed on your finished compost. Weeds can even be used for green manure, as long as they will not be stealing needed plant food and moisture. Some produce creditable amounts of humus, make minerals available, and conserve nitrogen.

There are certain weeds that you are better off burning or piling separately from your garden compost, since they are extremely vigorous and hard to kill. This applies primarily to weeds that reproduce through underground stems or rhizomes, such as quack grass, johnsongrass, bittersweet, and bishop's-weed.

Wood Ash

Wood ash is a valuable source of potash for the compost heap. Hardwood ashes generally contain from 1 to 10 percent potash, in addition to 35 percent calcium and 1.5 percent phosphorus. Wood ashes should never be allowed to stand in the rain, as the potash would leach away. Use wood ashes cautiously—it is not uncommon for home gardeners to create difficult nutrient imbalance problems by applying too much wood ash. It is a strong alkalinizing agent and also increases soil salinity. You should use it in the garden only if a soil test indicates acidic soil and a lack of potassium.

Wood ashes can be mixed with other fertilizing materials or side-dressed around growing plants. Apply no more than 2 pounds per 100 square feet. Avoid contact between freshly spread ashes and germinating seeds or new plant roots by spreading ashes a few inches from plants. Be similarly sparing with wood ashes in your compost—use no more than a dusting on each layer, if you must. Manure and hay are also rich in potassium, and they do not pose the dangers of wood ashes.

Wood Chips

Like sawdust and other wood wastes, wood chips are useful in the garden. In some ways, wood chips are superior to sawdust. They contain a much greater percentage of bark and have a higher nutrient content. Since they break down very slowly, their high carbon content is less likely to create depressed nitrogen levels. They do a fine job of aerating the soil and increasing its moisture-holding capacity, and they make a fine mulch for ornamentals. Wood chips promote fungal growth, including mycorrhizae, which improves stable humus, aggregation, and the water-holding capacity of your soil.

Generally, the incorporation of fresh chips has no detrimental effect on the crop if sufficient nitrogen is present or provided. Better yet, apply the chips ahead of a green manure crop, preferably a legume; allow about a year's interval between application and seeding or planting of the main crop. Other good ways to use wood fragments are as bedding in the barn, followed by field application of the manure; as a mulch on row crops, with the partially decomposed material eventually worked into the soil; and adequately composted with other organic materials. Well-rotted chips or sawdust are safe materials to use under almost any condition.

Wool Wastes

Wool wastes, also known as shoddy, have been used by British farmers living in the vicinity of wool textile mills since the industrial revolution in the early 19th century. The wool fiber decomposes when in contact with moisture in the soil and, in the process, produces available nitrogen for plant growth. Generally, the moisture content of the wool wastes is between 15 and 20 percent. It contains from 3.5 to 6 percent nitrogen, 2 to 4 percent phosphoric acid, and 1 to 3.5 percent potash.

🌱 C/N RATIOS AND NUTRIENT ANALYSES

The following tables and lists provide information about the carbon/nitrogen ratios and relative nutrient contents of a variety of organic materials. The presence of a material in this section does not necessarily mean it is ideal for composting; neither does exclusion of a material mean that it cannot be composted. As mentioned at the beginning of this chapter, the best materials for composting may be those that are in close proximity to the compost pile.

Many items are listed as ash; however, it is not recommended to reduce organic matter to ash. These materials are most valuable as compost pile additions in their natural conditions. Burning organic matter also eliminates moisture, and the carbon it contains is sent into the atmosphere instead of feeding soil life. The only organic matter you should consider burning would be diseased plant materials or noxious weeds. Be aware that most municipalities place restrictions on burning, especially at certain times of the year.

Since nearly all organic material contains some amount of nitrogen, phosphorus, potassium, and micronutrients, you don't need to obsess over including all the plant nutrients in your compost pile. If you incorporate a good variety of materials into your compost, the necessary nutrients will be there. As mentioned in Chapter 4, compost not only provides nutrients, it also makes soil nutrients more available to plants. Only in instances where soil analysis indicates a significant nutrient deficiency should much effort be given to boosting levels of a certain nutrient in your compost.

CARBON/NITROGEN RATIOS OF BULKY ORGANIC MATERIALS

For discussion of carbon/nitrogen ratios in composting, see Chapter 8.

MATERIAL	RATIO
Vegetable wastes	12:1
Alfalfa hay	13:1
Seaweed	19:1
Rotted manure	20:1
Apple pomace	21:1
Legume shells (peas, soybeans, etc.)	30:1
Leaves	40–80:1
Sugarcane trash	50:1
Cornstalks	60:1
Oat straw	74:1

MATERIAL	RATIO
Chaff and hulls (various grains)	80:1
Timothy hay	80:1
Paper	170:1
Sugarcane fiber (bagasse)	200:1
Sawdust	400:1

Natural Sources of Nitrogen

The materials listed below are grouped into representative classifications of organic matter; each group is ordered from highest nitrogen concentration to lowest. For specific nitrogen analyses, see the table "Percentage Composition of Various Materials" starting on page 127.

Manure

Rabbit manure

Sewage sludge

Chicken manure

Human urine

Swine manure

Sheep manure

Horse manure

Cattle manure

Animal Wastes (other than manures)

Feathers

Felt wastes

Dried blood

Crabs (dried, ground)

Silkworm cocoons

Tankage

Fish (dried, ground)

Silk wastes

Shrimp heads (dried)

Crabs (fresh)

Fish scraps (fresh)

Wool wastes

Jellyfish (dried)

Lobster refuse

Shrimp wastes

Eggshells

Mussels

Milk

Oyster shells

Meal

Cottonseed meal

Gluten meal

Bonemeal (raw)

Wheat bran

Bonemeal (steamed)

Bone black

Oats (green fodder)

Corn silage

Plant Wastes

Tung oil pomace

Castor pomace

Tea grounds

Peanut shells

Tobacco stems

Coffee grounds

Sugar wastes

Seaweed (dried)

Plant Wastes

Olive pomace

Brewery wastes

Cocoa shell dust

Grape pomace

Potato skins (raw)

Pine needles

Beet wastes

Seaweed (fresh)

Leaves

Raspberry leaves

Apple leaves

Peach leaves

Oak leaves

Pear leaves

Cherry leaves

Grape leaves

Pea (garden) vines

Grasses

Cowpea hay

Vetch hay

Soybean hay

Pea forage

Alfalfa	Timothy hay
Red clover	Salt marsh hay
Clover	Kentucky bluegrass hay
Millet hay	Immature grass

Natural Sources of Phosphate (other than phosphate rock or bonemeal)

The following phosphate sources are listed in order from highest phosphorus content to lowest. For specific phosphorus analyses, see the table "Percentage Composition of Various Materials" starting on page 127.

Shrimp wastes	Tankage
Sugar wastes (raw)	Castor pomace
Fish (dried, ground)	Rapeseed meal
Sludge (activated)	Wood ashes
Lobster and crab refuse	Cocoa shell dust
Wool wastes	Chicken manure
Dried blood	Rabbit manure
Banana residues (ash)	Silk mill wastes
Apple skins (ash)	Sheep and goat manure
Orange skins (ash)	Swine manure
Peapods (ash)	Horse manure
Cottonseed meal	Cattle manure
Hoof and horn meal	

Natural Sources of Potash

The materials in each group below are listed in order from highest potassium content to lowest. For specific potash analyses, see the table "Percentage Composition of Various Materials" starting on page 127.

Natural Minerals

Greensand

Granite dust

Basalt rock

Hay Materials

Millet hay

Cowpea hay

Vetch hay

Soybean hay

Alfalfa hay

Red clover hay

Kentucky bluegrass hay

Pea forage

Timothy hay

Winter rye

Immature grass

Salt marsh hay

Pea (garden) vines

Straw

Buckwheat straw

Oat straw

Barley straw

Rye straw

Sorghum straw

Cornstalks

Wheat straw

Leaves

Cherry leaves

Peach leaves

Raspberry leaves

Apple leaves

Grape leaves

Pear leaves

Oak leaves

Manure

Pigeon manure

Chicken manure

Duck manure

Rabbit manure

Swine manure

Horse manure

Sheep or goat manure

Cattle manure

Miscellaneous

Banana residues (ash)

Peapods (ash)

Cantaloupe rinds (ash)

Wood ash

Tobacco stems

Cattail reeds or water lily stems

Molasses wastes

Cocoa shell dust

Potato tubers

Wool wastes

Rapeseed meal

Beet wastes

Castor pomace

Cottonseed meal

Potato vines (dried)

Vegetable wastes

Olive pomace

Silk mill wastes

PERCENTAGE COMPOSITION OF VARIOUS MATERIALS

The presence of a C, N, or O in the C/N column indicates whether a material's effect on compost would be carbonaceous (C), nitrogenous (N), or other (O). Rock powders, for example, do not affect the C/N ratio and are designated O. C/N ratios of ashed materials represent their effects when fresh; when ashed, they are similar to rock powders.

MATERIAL	NITROGEN	PHOSPHORIC ACID	POTASH	C/N
Alfalfa hay	2.45	0.5	2.1	N
Apple fruit	0.05	0.02	0.1	N
Apple leaves	1.0	0.15	0.4	N
Apple pomace	0.2	0.02	0.15	N
Apple skins (ash)	—	3.0	11.74	N
Banana residues (ash)	—	2.3–3.3	41.0–50.0	N
Barley (grain)	1.75	0.75	0.5	N
Barley straw	—	—	1.0	C
Basalt rock	—	—	1.5	O
Bat guano	5.0–8.0	4.0–5.0	1.0	N
Beans, garden (seed and pods)	0.25	0.08	0.3	N

MATERIAL	NITROGEN	PHOSPHORIC ACID	POTASH	C/N
Beet wastes	0.4	0.4	0.7–4.1	N
Bloodmeal	15.0	1.3	0.7	N
Bone black	1.5	—	—	O
Bonemeal (raw)	3.3–4.1	21.0	0.2	O
Bonemeal (steamed)	1.6–2.5	21.0	0.2	O
Brewery wastes (wet)	1.0	0.5	0.05	N
Buckwheat straw	—	—	2.0	C
Cantaloupe rinds (ash)	—	9.77	12.0	C
Castor pomace	4.0–6.6	1.0–2.0	1.0–2.0	N
Cattail reeds and water lily stems	2.0	0.8	3.4	O
Cattail seed	0.98	0.39	1.7	C
Cattle manure (fresh)*	0.29	0.25	0.1	N
Cherry leaves	0.6	—	0.7	N
Chicken manure (fresh)*	1.6	1.0–1.5	0.6–1.0	N
Clover	2.0	—	—	N
Cocoa shell dust	1.0	1.5	1.7	C
Coffee grounds	2.0	0.36	0.67	N
Corn (grain)	1.65	0.65	0.4	N
Corn (green forage)	0.4	0.13	0.33	N
Corncobs (ground, charred)	—	—	2.0	C
Corn silage	0.42	—	—	N
Cornstalks (green)	0.75	—	0.8	C
Cottonseed hulls (ash)	—	8.7	23.9	C
Cottonseed meal	7.0	2.0–3.0	1.8	N
Cotton wastes (factory)	1.32	0.45	0.36	C
Cowpea hay	3.0	—	2.3	N
Cowpeas (green forage)	0.45	0.12	0.45	N
Cowpeas (seed)	3.1	1.0	1.2	N
Crabgrass (green)	0.66	0.19	0.71	N
Crabs (dried, ground)	10.0	—	—	N
Crabs (fresh)	5.0	3.6	0.2	N
Cucumber skins (ash)	—	11.28	27.2	N
Dried blood	10.0–14.0	1.0–5.0	—	N
Duck manure (fresh)*	1.12	1.44	0.6	N

MATERIAL	NITROGEN	PHOSPHORIC ACID	POTASH	C/N
Eggs	2.25	0.4	0.15	N
Eggshells	1.19	0.38	0.14	O
Feathers	15.3	—	—	N
Felt wastes	14.0	—	1.0	N
Field beans (seed)	4.0	1.2	1.3	N
Field beans (shells)	1.7	0.3	1.3	C
Fish (dried, ground)	8.0	7.0	—	N
Fish scraps (fresh)	6.5	3.75	—	N
Gluten meal	6.4	—	—	N
Granite dust	—	—	3.0–5.5	O
Grapefruit skins (ash)	—	3.6	30.6	O
Grape leaves	0.45	0.1	0.4	N
Grape pomace	1.0	0.07	0.3	N
Grass (immature)	1.0	—	1.2	N
Greensand	—	1.5	7.0	O
Hair	14.0	—	—	N
Hoof and horn meal	12.5	2.0		N
Horse manure (fresh)*	0.44	0.35	0.3	N
Incinerator ash	0.24	5.15	2.33	O
Jellyfish (dried)	4.6	—	—	N
Kentucky bluegrass (green)	0.66	0.19	0.71	N
Kentucky bluegrass hay	1.2	0.4	2.0	C
Leather dust	11.0	—	—	N
Lemon culls	0.15	0.06	0.26	N
Lemon skins (ash)	—	6.33	1.0	O
Lobster refuse	4.5	3.5	—	N
Milk	0.5	0.3	0.18	N
Millet hay	1.2	—	3.2	C
Molasses residue from alcohol manufacture	0.7		5.32	N
Molasses waste from sugar refining	—	—	3.0–4.0	N
Mud, freshwater	1.37	0.26	0.22	N
Mud, harbor	0.99	0.77	0.05	N

MATERIAL	NITROGEN	PHOSPHORIC ACID	POTASH	C/N
Mud, salt	0.4	—	—	N
Mussels	1.0	0.12	0.13	N
Nutshells	2.5	—	—	C
Oak leaves	0.8	0.35	0.2	N
Oats (grain)	2.0	0.8	0.6	N
Oats (green fodder)	0.49	—	—	N
Oat straw	—	—	1.5	C
Olive pomace	1.15	0.78	1.3	N
Orange culls	0.2	0.13	0.21	N
Orange skins (ash)		3.0	27.0	O
Oyster shells	0.36	—	—	O
Peach leaves	0.9	0.15	0.6	N
Pea forage	1.5–2.5	—	1.4	N
Peanuts (seed/kernels)	3.6	0.7	0.45	N
Peanut shells	3.6	0.15	0.5	C
Peapods (ash)	—	3.0	9.0	N
Peas, garden (vines)	0.25	—	0.7	N
Pear leaves	0.7	—	0.4	N
Pigeon manure (fresh)*	4.19	2.24	1.0	N
Pigweed (rough)	0.6	0.16	—	N
Pine needles	0.5	0.12	0.03	C
Potato skins (ash)	—	5.18	27.5	N
Potato tubers	0.35	0.15	2.5	N
Potato vines (dried)	0.6	0.16	1.6	C
Powder works wastes	2.5	—	17.0	O
Prune refuse	0.18	0.07	0.31	N
Pumpkins (fresh)	0.16	0.07	0.26	N
Rabbitbrush (ash)	—	—	13.04	C
Rabbit manure	2.4	1.4	0.6	N
Ragweed	0.76	0.26	—	N
Rapeseed meal	—	1.0–2.0	1.0–3.0	N
Raspberry leaves	1.45	—	0.6	N
Red clover hay	2.1	0.5	2.1	N
Redtop hay	1.2	0.35	1.0	C

MATERIAL	NITROGEN	PHOSPHORIC ACID	POTASH	C/N
Rock and mussel deposits from sea	0.22	1.78	0.09	O
Roses (flowers)	0.3	0.1	0.4	N
Rye straw	—	—	1.0	C
Salt marsh hay	1.1	0.25	0.75	C
Sardine scraps	8.0	7.1	—	N
Seaweed (dried)	1.1–1.5	0.75	4.9	N
Seaweed (fresh)	0.2–0.4	—	—	N
Sheep and goat manure (fresh)*	0.55	0.6	0.3	N
Shoddy and felt	8.0	4.2	—	N
Shrimp heads (dried)	7.8	10.0		N
Shrimp wastes	2.9	10.38	0.09	O
Siftings from oyster shell mounds	0.36	1.14	1.0	N
Silk mill wastes	8.0	1.82	1.08	N
Silkworm cocoons	10.0	1.9	0.3	N
Sludge	2.0	2.5–4.0	0.6	N
Sludge, activated	5.0	—	4.96	O
Smokehouse fire-pit ash	—		1.0	C
Sorghum straw		—	1.2–2.3	N
Soybean hay	1.5–3.0	0.2	0.25	N
Starfish	1.8	4.99	18.0	C
String bean strings and stems (ash)	—			
Sugar wastes (raw)	2.0	8.0		C
Sweet potatoes	0.25	0.1	0.5	N
Swine manure (fresh)*	0.6	0.45	0.5	N
Tanbark ash	—	0.34	3.8	C
Tanbark ash, spent	—	1.75	2.0	C
Tankage	3.0–11.0	2.0–5.0	—	N
Tea grounds	4.15	0.62	0.4	N
Timothy hay	1.2	0.55	1.4	C
Tobacco leaves	4.0	0.5	6.0	N
Tobacco stems	2.5–3.7	0.6–0.9	4.5–7.0	C
Tomato fruit	0.2	0.07	0.35	N

MATERIAL	NITROGEN	PHOSPHORIC ACID	POTASH	C/N
Tomato leaves	0.35	0.1	0.4	N
Tomato stalks	0.35	0.1	0.5	C
Tung oil pomace	6.1	—	—	N
Urine, human	0.6	—	—	N
Vetch hay	2.8	—	2.3	N
Waste silt	9.5	—·	—	N
Wheat bran	2.4	2.9	1.6	C
Wheat (grain)	2.0	0.85	0.5	N
Wheat straw	0.5	0.15	0.8	C
White clover (green)	0.5	0.2	0.3	N
Winter rye hay	—	—	1.0	C
Wood ash	—	1.0–2.0	6.0–10.0	O
Wool wastes	3.5–6.0	2.0–4.0	1.0–3.5	N

*Dried manures are up to 5 times higher in nitrogen, phosphoric acid, and potassium.

7

USING MANURE

Manure, the dung and urine of animals, is the most important single ingredient in the compost heap. It is difficult, although not impossible, to make a good compost pile without it. The use of manure as a soil amendment and fertilizer is a time-honored tradition that can be traced from the earliest written words through modern agricultural texts. While one would hesitate to ascribe miraculous properties to such a lowly substance, there are few materials that are as beneficial to composting as manure. Gardeners who compost by the earthworm pit method find manure to be an almost essential ingredient. It is also important to any rapid composting method that requires a high-nitrogen, high-bacteria heat-up material.

Gene Logsdon, affectionately known as "the contrary farmer," wrote a whole book in praise of manure, complete with amusing anecdotes, scientific findings, and cultural wisdom. In speculating that manure is becoming a "hot commodity" once again in order to keep the world from starving, Logsdon reminds us that Asian civilizations survived for thousands of years in part because "Every scrap of animal waste, human waste, and plant residue was scrupulously collected and reapplied to the land. So precious was manure that Chinese farmers stored it in burglarproof containers."

On a broader scale, manure is a resource that we have been wasting at a fearsome rate. Some observers have estimated that between mismanagement and misuse, less than 20 percent of the nutrients in manure ever find their way back to agricultural lands. Considering that there are more than 175 million farm animals in the country and that a single hog, for example, will produce more than 3,000 pounds of manure annually, the aggregate waste is horrendous. Composting is the best way to reclaim the nutrients and organic matter in manure.

The most common domestic sources of manure are horses, cattle, goats, sheep, pigs, rabbits, and poultry. The dung consists of undigested portions of foods ground into fine bits and saturated with digestive juices in the alimentary tract. Dung contains, as a rule, one-third of the total nitrogen, one-fifth of the total potash, and nearly all of the phosphoric acid voided by the animals. But it is because of the large bacterial population—as much as 30 percent of its mass—that manure is so valuable in the compost heap. The addition of manure provides the necessary bacteria that will quickly break down other materials.

The urine contains compounds from the digested portion of the foods and secretions from the animal body. Urine usually contains about two-thirds of the total nitrogen, four-fifths of the total potash, but very little of the phosphoric acid voided by the animal. Because they are in solution, elements in urine become available much more quickly than the constituents found in dung. Urines are especially valuable as activators in converting crop residues into humus.

The value of animal manure varies with the food eaten by the animal, the age of the animal, and the physical condition and health of the animal. The richer the animals' food is in elements essential to plant growth, the more valuable the manure. The manure of animals fed on wheat bran, gluten meal, and cottonseed meal, for instance, will be richer than that from animals fed straw or hay without grains. Likewise, the manure of young animals that are forming bones and muscles from their foods will be poorer in nutrients than the manure of mature animals.

MANURE'S CONTRIBUTIONS TO THE SOIL

The value of manure as a soil additive varies according to the products an animal produces. Milk, for example, contains considerable amounts of nitrogen, phosphorus, and potassium, while wool holds a large store of nitrogen. Using manure is not entirely without hazards—in the Southwest, where soils tend to be highly alkaline, additions of urine can contribute to toxic salt levels—and manure should be applied with caution around salt-sensitive plants.

The way manure is handled affects its eventual benefits to the soil. In rotting, manure loses some of its nitrogen content. Studies by the US Environmental Protection Agency have found that within 4 days manure can lose half its fertilizing value if it is left lying in a thin pile on the ground. Bedding should be composted when fresh for best results. Even short-term storage wastes nutrients.

The values of manure and fertilizers in general have been, in the past, based on the relative amounts of nitrogen, phosphoric acid, and potash they contain. While these are major elements that doubtless affect the values of manure to a greater extent than the proportion of any other constituents, it is misleading to make a direct comparison between farm manures and chemical fertilizers based solely on the relative amounts of N-P-K. Soil needs continual replenishment of its organic matter to convert into humus, and humus plays an important role in making nutrients available to the higher plants. (See the table "N-P-K, Organic Matter, and Moisture Content of Various Manures" on page 137.)

There is a difference between fresh manure and rotted manure. Assuming that fresh manure is a normal mixture of urine and feces, fresh manure differs from rotted manure in several ways.

- Moisture loss during the composting process results in higher concentrations of plant nutrients in rotted manure. One ton of fresh manure may lose half its weight in moisture as it rots.
- The nitrogen in the composted manure has been fixed by microorganisms, while nitrogen in fresh manure is mostly soluble.
- The solubility of phosphorus and potash is greater in composted manure. If leaching during composting can be prevented, there is no change in the total amount of phosphorus and potassium. Precautions must be taken to prevent the loss of nitrogen in the composting process, however.

Manure in the compost heap decomposes in definite stages. These may be briefly outlined as follows:

1. **Decomposition of urinary nitrogen.** Ammonia in the urine is lost unless the manure is kept moist and compact or the nitrogen is fixed through the addition of a phosphorus source such as phosphate rock.

2. **Decomposition of insoluble nitrogen.** Next, the insoluble nitrogen contained in the solid parts of the excrement breaks down with the formation of ammonia.

3. **Conversion of soluble into insoluble nitrogen.** Ammonia and other soluble compounds of nitrogen are used in considerable amounts as food for the bacteria in manure and are stored in their bodies in insoluble form. This nitrogen becomes available when the bacteria die and decompose.

4. **Formation of free nitrogen.** Under certain conditions, ammonia and nitrates are decomposed; free nitrogen is formed and escapes into the atmosphere.

5. **Decomposition of nitrogen-free compounds.** The fibrous parts of the manure, made up largely of cellulose, lignin, and other complex carbohydrates, are eventually broken down. Carbon in the form of carbon dioxide and hydrogen in the form of water escape into the atmosphere. These elements escape in such amounts that the pile's bulk is reduced by one-quarter to one-half its original size.

OUT OF BALANCE

The greatest virtue of the traditional family farm in America is that it is a self-contained unit with a balanced complement of crops and livestock. Livestock eat farm-produced grains and grasses, and the land on which these crops are raised is enriched by the animals' manure. A farmer who manages animal manure wisely can return to the soil 70 percent of the nitrogen, 75 percent of the phosphorus, and 80 percent of the potash removed by the crops grown to feed the animals.

Large-scale livestock operations have tended to ignore the balance achieved by the family farm. Animals are raised on huge tracts of ranch and pastureland and fattened in feedlots where their nitrogen-rich manure causes ecological imbalance instead of contributing to soil fertility. More than 2 billion tons of manure are produced annually in the United States, yet little of this vast store of nutrients is returned to the soil. Much of it falls on ranges and in poorly managed feedlots where it is lost to agriculture. Stricter environmental standards and increasing concern about groundwater pollution resulting from feedlot runoff have created incentives to recycle feedlot wastes.

However, in at least one highly publicized project, the alternative being touted is burning the manure to produce electricity. Even farmers who do attempt to return manure to their fields lose much of its value through misunderstanding and mismanagement.

N-P-K, ORGANIC MATTER, AND MOISTURE CONTENT OF VARIOUS MANURES (%)

KIND OF ANIMAL MANURE	NITROGEN	PHOSPHATE	POTASH	ORGANIC MATTER	MOISTURE
Rabbit	2.4	1.4	0.6	33	43
Chicken	1.1	0.8	0.5	25–45	55–75
Sheep	0.7	0.3	0.9	32–34	66–68
Horse	0.7	0.3	0.6	22–26	74–78
Steer	0.7	0.3	0.4	17	83
Cattle	0.6	0.2	0.5	17	83
Duck	0.6	1.4	0.5	25–45	55–75
Pig	0.5	0.3	0.5	14	86

USING MANURE TO ADVANTAGE

Animal manure by itself is not a completely balanced fertilizer, either chemically or biologically. There may be too much urine and too little cellulose, or vice versa. When manure is added directly to the soil, it generally releases highly soluble nitrates that behave similarly to chemical fertilizers, as well as ammonia, which can burn plant roots and interfere with seed germination. When composted first, manure's imbalances can be rectified and the manure itself can be digested and used more quickly than if added alone.

The use of urine-soaked bedding or litter in the compost pile is an especially wise practice. The litter catches urine that would otherwise be lost. Urine has a high nitrogen content, so extra high-carbon material (in addition to the bedding) should be used. In other words, compost manure and bedding with plenty of coarse, dry vegetable material—weeds, plant debris, and so on. Adding rock phosphate stabilizes nitrogen and prevents its volatilization as ammonia, as well as boosting the phosphorus content of your compost. Also, by covering your compost pile with black plastic, a layer of straw, or other protection, you can prevent nutrients from being leached out by rain.

Manure is often full of weed seeds that can be killed by the high temperatures in composting. The high temperatures will also kill pathogens that may be present in livestock manure. This is especially important when using manure from grain-fed cattle or sheep, as well as animals routinely fed or treated with antibiotics, as is the case with most conventional livestock operations. Manure from organic and grass-fed animals has been shown to pose little or no risk of virulent human pathogens such as the potentially deadly E. coli O157:H7.

Chicken Manure

Chicken manure is the "hottest" of all animal manures, meaning that it is the richest in nitrogen, phosphorus, and potassium. Fowls do not excrete urine separately, as mammals do. Chicken droppings must be composted or incorporated with a high-carbon mulch or cover crop before use, or they will burn any plants with which they come into contact. Accumulation of raw chicken manure from large factory chicken farms–both broilers and layers–is a huge environmental problem in places like the Chesapeake Bay watershed. Many chicken farmers use some type of absorbent organic material for litter in their henhouses, such as leaves, shredded straw, wood shavings, ground corncobs, or ground cornstalks. By continually adding to the litter under roosts to catch droppings, they are able to control odors that can cause respiratory problems in chickens as well as discomfort to people. It also helps conserve the nitrogen content of the manure, which is stabilized by microbial workers rather than being released in the form of ammonia. Some large chicken farmers, including organic operations such as Pete and Gerry's in Monroe, New Hampshire, compost their chicken manure on-site and sell it to local farmers and gardeners. Avoid cleaning out old poultry house contents, since dry chicken manure (as well as turkey and pigeon manure and bat manure, called guano) is a common incubation site for the spores of a human respiratory disease.

Horse Manure

Horse manure is richer in nitrogen than cattle or swine manure and, like chicken droppings, is called a hot manure. It is also much more prone to fermentation or "fire-fanging," a fairly rapid oxidation that destroys nutrients. Some farmers water horse manure to prevent fire-fanging, but leaching can occur if too much water is added. When using horse manure in the compost pile, mix it with other manures or with large quantities of high-carbon materials, and add moisture. Horse owners tend to bed their animals extremely well, so stable manure is often largely wood shavings or straw with a small amount of manure mixed in. In these cases, horse manure can be combined with other manures to correct the carbon/nitrogen ratio. Horse manure also prevents the harmful action of denitrifying bacteria.

Swine Manure

Pig and hog manure are highly concentrated but less rich in nitrogen than horse manure. Most commercial hog producers store their manure as a liquid slurry that is mostly water. It is best used when mixed with other manures or with large quantities of vegetation. It ferments relatively slowly. Hog farmers in the southern hemisphere often use the manure slurry to feed biogas digesters to produce gas for cooking and to generate electricity. The remaining digestate can then be composted or spread directly on fields.

Sheep Manure

Sheep manure is another hot manure. Like horse manure, it is quite dry and very rich.

Cattle Manure

Cattle manure is moister and less concentrated than that of other large animals. Because of its high water and low nitrogen contents, it ferments slowly and is commonly called a cold manure. Because of their complex digestive systems, cows and other ruminants produce manure that is especially rich in beneficial microorganisms.

Rabbit Manure

Rabbit manure is even higher in nitrogen than some poultry manures, and it contains a large percentage of phosphates. It decomposes easily and requires no shredding. Because the nitrogen level is so high, however, it should be used in small quantities. Some rabbit producers use litter in their rabbit cages and add this to the compost pile to conserve the rabbits' urine. Earthworm pits set directly under wire rabbit cages offer another sensible use of rabbit manure. The worms quickly turn the raw manure into fully composted castings, and the rabbit raiser can have an extra source of income through earthworm sales.

FINDING MANURE

The best places for the home gardener or homesteader to get manure are those where there are high concentrations of animals and no fields to fertilize. These include riding academies and stables, feedlots, dairies, and poultry farms. Dog and cat manures should be avoided–they carry diseases that can be particularly dangerous to young children. Some gardeners go so far as to contact zoos or to visit local fairgrounds or circus grounds after the animals have left town. Bill Bricker, an enterprising gardener from Augusta, Georgia, actually created a small compost business using, among other ingredients, manure from a local cricket farm. Sometimes, one will be asked to pay a modest sum for manure, but often it comes free for the hauling. Some commercial composting operations are paid to "dispose" of manure. The urban gardener with a very small plot can probably afford to buy commercially prepared manure, already composted, screened, and bagged. Small-scale homesteaders might raise a few chickens, a pony, ducks, geese, or a few pens of rabbits and will certainly use every scrap of manure produced by these animals. They may, however, still wish to supplement this supply by making some arrangement to haul manure from a nearby dairy or poultry farm.

When you buy or haul away manure from those who have no use for it, you are not only helping your own garden but also helping to solve what is becoming a major ecological problem caused by the concentration of livestock and poultry in areas with little or no ground available for the disposal of wastes. Operators of large livestock production units are interested in disposing of much waste at minimal expense; they often dump wastes on small parcels of land where high concentrations of salts result in nutrient imbalance in soil, excessive nitrate accumulation in plants, and leaching to groundwater. In the long run, it would be in our best interests to deconcentrate stock and poultry production–break up the animal factories–to regain the ecological balance that existed when farms were small and diversified. In the meantime, any manure you can remove from these concentrated lots and use in home composting is all to the good. Be aware, however, that manure being held at such farms may be sprayed with larvicides to control fly populations. It may also contain residues from antibiotics or other livestock medications. The presence of such substances can counteract the benefits of manure in your compost by suppressing important microbial populations and introducing potentially hazardous chemicals.

Feedlots, stockyards, and other large commercial stock facilities are gradually finding manure a usable, even profitable, by-product of their enterprise. They process bagged, dried manure and manure compost for gardeners and make it available through garden and hardware stores. The quality of these products can vary considerably—see Chapter 13 for information to help you evaluate them. The Chicago stockyards were among the first to compost and sell their manure, at one time processing 20 tons of manure and bedding per load in huge digesters that used injected air to fuel and speed bacterial activity. More information on commercial-scale composting can be found in Chapter 13.

MANURE TEA

Another use for manure, apart from composting, is for manure tea, or liquid manure. To make this useful organic fertilizer, place one or two shovelfuls of fresh or dried manure in a permeable bag—burlap works well, but perforated plastic or mesh will also do. The finer the holes in the bag, the less likely it is that weed seeds from the manure will get into your tea. Tie the bag closed,

Manure tea, a valuable liquid fertilizer, can be made by steeping a permeable bag of livestock manure in a drum of water. The resulting tea may be sprinkled on the compost pile or diluted for use as plant food.

then place it in a barrel or other large container filled with water. Make sure the bag is submerged. Allow your "teabag" to steep for about a week.

Manure tea can be used at full strength for periodic feedings, or dilute it and use it to water plants. Do not apply undiluted manure tea directly onto your plants—it could injure them. At full strength, manure tea poured over the layers of green and dried material in a compost pile not only provides needed moisture but also distributes bacteria and nitrogen to all parts of the pile. Manure tea may not be applied to any organic crop under the National Organic Program regulations. Organic farmers who want to use manure tea can apply it to hayfields or cover-cropped areas, but not to crops for human consumption within 120 days of harvest.

SUBSTITUTES

If you absolutely can't find or afford manure for your pile, be sure to use a high-nitrogen substitute. Among the best of these are bloodmeal, cottonseed meal, tankage, shoddy, hoof or horn meal, fish and shellfish scraps, hair (if time for decomposition is allowed), or wool wastes. Leguminous vegetable meals such as alfalfa and soybean, sold as livestock feed, are excellent nitrogen sources. Freshly cut weeds, grass, or other plants or their leaves or stems are high in nitrogen, but this nitrogen is released quickly and they cannot be depended upon as the source for all the nitrogen needed in a pile. Check Chapter 6 for more information on these materials.

METHODS

There are quite a few ways to let nature make compost for you—under the ground, above the ground; in bins, boxes, pits, bags, and barrels; in strips, in sheets, in trenches; in 14 months or 14 days; indoors or outdoors. Nearly all stem from the famous Indore method developed by Sir Albert Howard, and they all (except for anaerobic methods) have the same basic requirements. All composting methods aim simply to meet the needs of the microorganisms that do all the work of turning raw organic matter into humus. Those basic needs are air, moisture, energy food (carbon) and protein food (nitrogen) in the right proportions, and warmth. Any method involving a pile also needs to be a minimum size or critical mass so that high enough temperatures can be maintained. Beyond that, you will want to ensure that there is a culture of the right organisms ready to get started. (See the table "Solving a Heap of Problems" on page 181.)

Although innumerable refinements are possible, as long as you keep these basic requirements in mind, you can improvise a variety of ways to achieve the desired goal: the creation of moist, fragrant, fertile humus. Let's examine those requirements in greater depth, since neglect of any one can result in disappointment and frustration.

AIR

It is possible to make compost without air, or anaerobically, through the activities of a different type of microorganism. However, most home composting systems are aerobic and so require adequate air to be available throughout the pile. Aerobic bacteria are thought to be more beneficial to the soil.

There are various techniques for ensuring aeration, the most common and obvious being to turn the pile at regular intervals. The more frequent the turning, the faster the raw materials decompose, since air is most often the limiting factor in this process. Compost tumblers achieve the same effect with much less effort—you need only rotate the drum every day, and the compost can be finished within 2 weeks. Commercially available and homemade barrel composters are discussed more fully in Chapter 10.

Some gardeners avoid laborious turning by finding clever ways to introduce air into static piles. Municipal-scale composting operations sometimes use large blowers to force air through their windrows via a network of perforated pipe. This technique can be adapted to a smaller scale by burying perforated drainpipe at intervals within the pile. Natural convection is sufficient to circulate air through such a pile.

You can also induce greater air circulation by building a bin with a bottom lined with hardware cloth and raised a foot or so off the ground. The wire must be stretched tightly and attached securely to the bin's frame to support the weight of the pile, which can reach several tons in a large heap. Plastic sheets placed on the ground under the bin can be used to catch any liquids that drain out; these can be poured back onto the pile for more efficient use of nutrients.

Another time-honored trick for good aeration involves layering poles into the heap and withdrawing a few every day or so during the major heat buildup. You can also stick the pile with the tines of a pitchfork to open air

Lengths of perforated pipe, placed at intervals within the compost heap, allow air to reach the pile's interior and reduce or eliminate the need to turn the pile.

channels. There is even a tool on the market that has a small umbrella-like mechanism: You insert it into the pile, open the blades, and twirl it around to make an air pocket.

Sunflower stalks have soft centers that rot out quickly to create organic "pipes" for aerating a compost pile. A well-ventilated heap can be formed by using a 2- to 4-inch layer of sunflower stalks as a base, then topping that with 12 inches of compostable materials, followed by ¼ inch of soil. Add a few more stalks, another layer of moistened compostables, and another ¼ inch of soil. Continue this layering until the pile is about 4 feet high, finishing it with a 2-inch layer of soil.

Jerusalem artichoke stalks are also effective aerators, but cornstalks do not rot out easily and cannot be used for air channeling.

If you are in no hurry, a static pile built on a base of brush or other coarse materials will have enough aeration to allow materials to gradually decompose. In this case, it is especially important to layer in materials that are fluffy enough to allow air to penetrate. Shredding, grinding, or chopping ingredients such as leaves, hay, or paper will prevent the formation of impermeable mats. The finer the materials can be cut, the more quickly they will decompose, since small pieces are more accessible to microbial colonization.

MOISTURE

Good compost will be about as damp as a moist sponge. When a handful is squeezed, no drops of moisture should come out. Too little moisture slows down decomposition and prevents the pile from heating up. Microorganisms need a steamy environment. Too much moisture, signaled by a foul odor and a drop in temperature, drives out air, drowns the pile, and washes away nutrients.

It is important to consider drainage when building your pile. If you live in a humid climate, select a site that drains easily so the pile never sits in a pool of water–the organic matter will wick up the excess moisture and create anaerobic conditions. In arid climates, it may be helpful to sink the pile into a shallow pit to trap moisture.

A pile containing a great deal of hay can also be a problem. Country folks know how a haystack sheds water–a well-made haystack keeps the bulk of the hay dry through winter rains. If you are using hay, counter this water-resistant tendency by limiting the hay layers to 6 or 8 inches and wetting each layer thoroughly as you build the pile. Hay that is shredded is less of a problem, especially when combined with wet materials such as cow manure or kitchen scraps. To control the moisture in an exposed heap, cover it with a few inches of hay, which should help shed rain. Some gardeners cover their compost with black plastic and remove it during selected rains.

Be especially careful to check the moisture content when turning the pile–the turning process itself releases moisture. If the pile is soggy, you can add more absorbent materials such as leaves or dried grass clippings. If it is dry, give it a good sprinkling every 6 to 8 inches.

CARBON/NITROGEN RATIO

Decomposers need carbon for energy and nitrogen for growth, and it is the composter's job to supply both kinds of materials in roughly the proportions the microorganisms prefer. The ideal C/N ratio for composting is between 25:1 and 30:1, with carbon being the higher number. Precision is unnecessary–with a little experience, you will acquire a feel for the best combinations.

Carbonaceous materials are generally brown or yellow, dry, coarse, and bulky compared with nitrogenous materials, which tend to be green, succulent, gooey, and dense. High-carbon materials are almost always plant materials such as straw, cornstalks, sawdust, and leaves. Nitrogenous materials more often include animal by-products, although it is quite possible to make compost without use of any materials derived from animals. Examples of high-nitrogen materials are grass clippings, alfalfa meal, bloodmeal, and poultry manure. A few materials, such as fresh clover, most kitchen garbage, and manure mixed with bedding, already have C/N ratios in the ideal range. You can find information about the C/N ratios of various materials in the tables at the end of Chapter 6.

The carbon materials contribute mass to the pile and give rise to the organic gums abundant in humus. Nitrogen is necessary to stimulate microbes to reproduce as rapidly as possible. However, even materials that contain very little nitrogen will break down over time, but they will never reach the temperatures needed for hot composting. If there is too much nitrogen in relation to carbon, nitrogen will be lost as ammonia, easily detected by its smell. This generally lasts only a day or two, until the material stabilizes. In the worst case, excess nitrogen may cause the pile to become putrefied and anaerobic, usually because carbonaceous materials also contribute to proper aeration.

Some composting guides recommend adding synthetic nitrogen carriers such as urea or sodium nitrate as activators. This is never necessary and is a bad idea because these materials can disrupt microbe populations. Moreover, their manufacture consumes vast quantities of natural gas. If you need a concentrated nitrogen source, there are many naturally derived alternatives available commercially—refer to Chapter 6 for a listing.

WARMTH AND CRITICAL MASS

Bacteria become dormant when the temperature drops below 55°F (13°C). If properly built, a compost pile's interior will stay well above that temperature even in freezing weather. Northern composters sometimes insulate their piles with leaves, straw, or hay, even to the point of building an enclosure of hay bales to keep things cooking. Decomposition will slow during the winter months, but a pile built in fall and kept covered should be reasonably finished by spring.

To achieve optimum hot-composting temperatures (140°F/60°C) in any season, a minimum pile size is required. Otherwise, the heat generated by the initial organisms quickly dissipates before the pile can reach the right temperature for thermophilic organisms. A pile must be at least 3 feet in each dimension to provide the necessary critical mass. For best heating, try for a heap 4 or 5 feet square on the bottom, rising to 4 feet high. Dr. Clarence Golueke, author of *Biological Reclamation of Solid Wastes*, says that in a pile this size, less than half the material (that part right in the middle) is exposed to the highest temperatures. Temperature decreases toward the outside of the pile. When turning, shovel the undigested materials from the outside portions of the pile into the middle. This often causes a second heating as this material gets a chance to decompose in the heart of the heap.

For continuously composting household, yard, and garden waste while maintaining optimum pile size, a "wandering compost pile" is effective. Starting with minimum dimensions of 3 feet high by 3 feet wide by 3 feet deep, this type of heap "wanders" as fresh ingredients, such as kitchen refuse (minus meat or animal fat), are tossed onto the sloping front face and finished compost is sliced from the back. By screening the finished compost as it is removed and using the larger particles to cover additions to the front of the pile, newly added materials are seeded with the necessary microorganisms.

INOCULATION

Bacteria and fungi are certain to be among the unseen inhabitants of whatever materials you include in your compost, but they may not be the right mix of the right types for optimal composting. The more diverse your compost ingredients, the more likely you are to include a good balance of bacteria and fungi. Different materials, such as wood waste, may serve to encourage fungal over bacterial proliferation, which is known to produce a more stable and spongelike form of humus. The best way to inoculate your pile with the right

finished compost

fresh ingredients

While continuously composting household, yard, and garden waste, a "wandering" compost pile moves as new materials are added to the sloping front face and finished compost is sliced from the other end.

cultures is simply to sprinkle a thin coating of good topsoil or finished compost, saved from a previous batch, over each layer of materials that you add.

As noted in Chapter 6, there are various useful methods for creating homemade compost inoculants, much as a sourdough bread or yogurt culture may be maintained in a more concentrated brew that includes the ideal nutrient source for the desired microbes. While biochar is a popular medium for propagating beneficial fungi, some composters use nutrient-rich substrates to culture effective microorganisms (EM) through an anaerobic fermentation process. Recipes generally include various plants and herbs as well as molasses or other sugar sources, resulting in high populations of lactic acid bacteria, yeasts, actinomycetes, and photosynthesizing bacteria. Bokashi, as this fermentation method is sometimes known, is especially valued for producing custom batches of compost tea to stimulate the right kinds of organisms to revitalize depleted soils.

EM alone has not been shown conclusively to benefit agricultural soils or crop health. However, a long-term study conducted at China Agricultural University showed that application of EM in combination with compost significantly increased wheat straw biomass, grain yield, and straw and grain nutrition compared with traditional compost and control treatment.

CHOOSING A METHOD

The choice of a method of composting is an important decision for the gardener, one that must take into account many factors: the space and constructions available, the total need for compost in terms of the area under cultivation and the rate of use, the time to be given to the project, the human and mechanical energy available, the equipment owned or obtainable, the materials at hand or easily procurable, and special crop needs. Methods that meet the requirements of compost organisms form a continuum: from quick, hot composting that requires effort and attention, to slow, cool techniques that are less trouble. Mulching and sheet composting also involve low temperatures and are slower still to contribute much humus to the soil. Each method has its advantages and drawbacks, as well as its stalwart advocates and detractors. (See the table "Hot Versus Cool: Compost Pros and Cons" on page 151.) All involve acquiring a sensitivity to the well-being of compost's microscopic laborers, which is as much an art as a science. The time needed for a quick compost to be ready to use is generally less than 8 weeks, and may be as little as 2. This speed is achieved by keeping aeration levels high, either by passing air through a static pile or, more commonly, by frequent turning. If we liken composting to a combustion process, it is clear that the more air there is available, the hotter the compost will be. You can tell if compost is working properly by monitoring its temperature; turn it again as soon as the temperature drops. A thermometer is helpful but not essential for this process. Many composters simply shove their arms into the pile to see how hot it is, but those of more delicate sensibilities (or arms) can insert a metal rod for a few minutes and feel the end when it is withdrawn. If it feels hot to the touch, you're in the ballpark. The object is to maintain the temperature in the thermophilic range–113° to 158°F (45° to 70°C)–until decomposition is complete and heating can no longer occur.

Some Like It Hot

The advantages of hot composting relate mainly to its fast turnover. Even in cooler climates, you can process six or more batches in a season. If you have a big garden and limited room for composting, this is the way to go. It's also the most effective way to build fertility when you're just starting out in a new location. The other major advantage to this method is its temperature. Few weed seeds and pathogens can survive thermophilic temperatures, especially if they are maintained for several weeks. This gives you more leeway to compost materials that should otherwise be avoided. However, it's best to avoid composting materials that may carry diseases or weed seeds until you are sure of your hot-composting skills.

The major disadvantage of quick composting, with the exception of static piles that use forced aeration, is the labor involved. Not everyone is enthusiastic enough–or able–to be out there turning the compost every few days, especially if the pile is much larger than a 3-foot cube. This is also a less forgiving process than others; if the moisture level or carbon/nitrogen ratio is wrong, you have to make adjustments. Another drawback is that the whole pile must be built at once. If your compost pile is also your household garbage disposal system, kitchen wastes must be stored up until you're ready to start a new pile.

HOT VERSUS COOL: COMPOST PROS AND CONS

PROS	CONS
Hot	
• Produces finished compost quickly	• Is labor intensive
• Uses space efficiently	• Requires careful control of moisture and C/N ratio
• Builds fertility quickly for new garden locations	• Must be built all at once, requiring storage of kitchen wastes until it's time to start a new pile
• Kills most weed seeds and pathogens	• Conserves less nitrogen
	• Produces compost with reduced ability to suppress soilborne diseases
Cool	
• Needs little maintenance	• Allows nutrient loss through extended exposure to elements
• Spares disease-suppressing microbes	• May take 6 months to 2 years to produce finished compost
• Conserves nitrogen	• Fails to kill pathogens or weed seeds
• Allows materials to be added a little at a time	• Needs balanced carbon and nitrogen, as well as wet and dry materials, as you add to the pile
	• Produces compost with more un-decomposed bits of high-carbon materials

Hot composting conserves less nitrogen than cooler methods, since extra nitrogen is required to stimulate fast bacterial growth and some inevitably drifts off in the form of ammonia. However, a cool pile that sits in the rain for over a year also loses much of its nitrogen content. Finally, studies at the Ohio Agricultural Research and Development Center have shown that compost produced at high temperatures has less ability to suppress soilborne diseases than does cool compost. This is because the beneficial bacteria and fungi that attack pathogens cannot survive the higher temperatures.

Note that compost used by organic farmers has to comply with the National Organic Program requirements. The NOP requires compost that is made with manure to be hot composted. The rules stipulate that an organic producer can use composted plant and animal materials that start with a C/N ratio ranging from 25:1 to 40:1. If the process uses an in-vessel or static

aerated pile system, the materials must stay at a temperature of between 131°
and 170°F (55° and 77°C) for 3 days. If it is a windrow system, the materials
must stay in this temperature range for 15 days, during which time the pile
must be turned at least five times. Vermicomposting at lower temperatures is
also accepted, although the regulations include additional stipulations for
this process.

If this process isn't followed, or is not fully documented, the compost has
to be used in the same way as raw manure, which cannot be used less than
120 days in advance of harvesting a crop for human consumption whose edible portion may come into contact with soil. This regulation is intended to
ensure that no human pathogens can contact the crop.

A Cool Alternative

Some compost professionals tend to turn up their noses at slow, cool methods,
deriding them as "let it happen" compost. However, if you have the space but
not the time or stamina to work with your compost, this is the easiest
approach to take. Compost made in this manner will still heat up at first, but
not to the levels of hot compost–120°F (49°C) is a maximum. The mesophilic
organisms will carry most of the burden of humus making, which will occur
in 6 months to 2 years, depending on climate, materials used, and aeration
conditions.

The advantages and disadvantages of cool composting mirror those of hot
composting: It involves less work but longer lag time until the compost is finished. It fails to kill pathogens or weeds but spares disease-suppressing
microbes. It conserves nitrogen but must be protected from the elements longer. It has the advantage of allowing you to add materials a little at a time until
you have a critical mass. The drawback to this is that you must be careful to
balance carbon and nitrogen as well as wet and dry materials as you go. Otherwise, you can create anaerobic conditions or unpleasant smells. It's often helpful to keep a supply of dry high-carbon materials on hand to layer in when you
spread household garbage; remember to sprinkle some soil on top each time
you add fresh materials.

There is fierce debate regarding which method produces humus of a
higher quality. Although cool compost generally results in more undecomposed bits of high-carbon materials, these can easily be screened out and

🌱 **A SPECTRUM OF METHODS BY TEMPERATURE**

The composting methods described in this chapter cover the range of temperatures from hot (thermophilic) to cool (mostly mesophilic) and beyond. The list below shows the methods in temperature order from hot to cool, along with page numbers indicating where each method is discussed.

California method (page 156) (hot)

City people's method (page 163) (hot)

Compost tumblers (page 165) (hot)

Johnson-Su bioreactor (page 166) (hot)

Raised bins (page 166) (cool end of hot spectrum)

Movable compost for raised beds (page 169) (hot or cool)

Windrows and piles (page 171) (hot or cool)

Biodynamic composting (page 160) (cool or hot)

Indore method (page 153) (cool)

Ogden's step-by-step composting (page 168) (cool)

Pit composting (page 169) (cool)

Mulch and sheet composting (page 172) (beyond the cool end)

Trench and posthole composting (page 177) (beyond the cool end)

Anaerobic composting (page 178) (beyond the cool end)

added into the next pile. Whichever method you choose, the process is really a variation of Sir Albert Howard's Indore method.

THE INDORE METHOD

The Indore process consists of a systematic use of traditional procedures. When Howard first put the system into practice, he used only animal manures, brush, leaves, straw or hay, and sprinklings of chalk or earth. The material was piled in alternating layers to make a 5-foot-high stack, or it was placed in a pit 2 or 3 feet deep. The original procedure was to use a layer of

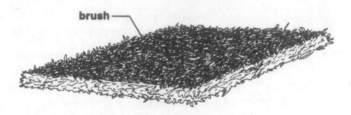

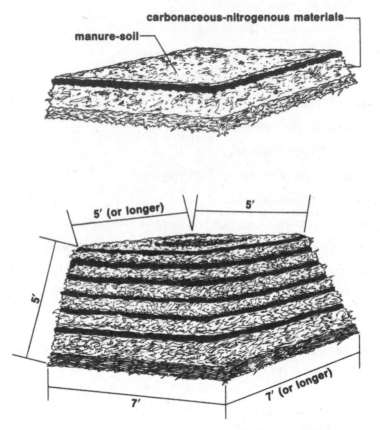

In the Indore method, a layer of brush forms the base of the pile. It is followed by a layer of green or dry vegetable matter, then a layer of manure and a sprinkling of soil. The layers are repeated until the pile is 5 feet high.

brush as a base and to heap green or dry vegetable material over it in a 6-inch layer, followed by a 2-inch layer of manure and a sprinkling of soil. The order of layers was repeated until the desired height of 5 feet was reached.

The general proportions were, by volume, three to four parts of vegetable matter to one part of animal manure. Howard advised spreading limestone or chalk between layers along with earth. In his work with village or large farm-scale projects, he suggested 5-foot-high piles, measuring 10 by 5 feet, or wind-rows of any practical length, 10 feet wide.

Later in the history of the Indore method, composting with night soil (mixed human urine and feces), garbage, and sewage sludge was done. These materials were layered with high-carbon organic material such as straw, leaves, animal litter, and municipal trash.

The piles were turned, usually after 6 weeks, and again after 12 weeks. Two turnings were the general practice, but the exact timing of these turnings varied. Occasionally, additional turnings were given to control flies, though the more common practice was to cover the pile with a 2-inch layer of compacted soil when flies or odors were a problem. The liquor draining from the composting mass was, in some variations of the early Indore process, recirculated to moisten the pile.

Harold B. Gotaas, in *Composting: Sanitary Disposal and Reclamation of Organic Wastes*, suggests that the early Indore process stacks were aerobic for a short period after piling and after each turn, but anaerobic otherwise.

The chief advantage to the Indore method as originally practiced is that it can be practiced on a fairly large scale without the need for either mechanization or a great amount of labor. According to Dr. Golueke, although many successful large-scale modified Indore composting efforts use windrows, composting of garden and kitchen waste by the Indore method is done best in bins or pits.

Modifications

The Indore process has been used widely in India where it is most frequently seen today in a modification called the Bangalore method. The process is also employed in Malaysia, China, Sri Lanka, South Africa, Costa Rica, East Africa, and other parts of the world. In general, Indore modifications have emphasized the use of night soil, sewage sludge, garbage, or green matter as substitutes for manure. They have also sought higher temperatures through increased frequency of turning and by substituting turning for covering as a means of fly control. Mechanized Indore windrows are now used in some countries.

Another adaptation of the Indore method uses only animal bedding and fresh green plant matter. A sheet of black plastic covers and confines the pile to increase heat and reduce leaching. The total process takes about 3 weeks, and no turning is necessary.

THE UNIVERSITY OF CALIFORNIA METHOD

The composting method developed at the University of California in the early 1950s is probably the best known and the most clearly articulated of the rapid-return or quick methods. It is similar to earlier methods recommended by modifiers of the Indore method, to those practiced in mechanical digester units in Europe and America, and to those described and advocated by Harold B. Gotaas of the World Health Organization in his 1935 book *Composting*. Whereas the Indore method may be described as falling on the cool end of the compost spectrum, the California method aims for more heat and faster

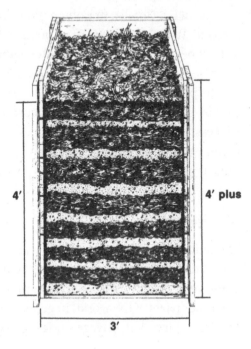

The minimum dimensions of a bin for the California method should be 3 feet by 3 feet, with a height of 4 to 6 feet.

decomposition. The California method has been used in the windrow composting of municipal wastes where shredding of materials, planned adjustment of the C/N ratio, regular and frequent turning for aeration, and control of moisture content are practiced. Municipal composting differs from garden composting in the nature of its materials and in the quantity of its product. Paper and ash that are present in municipal compost require specific adjustments, and so do factors resulting from the bulk of the material, such as compaction and overheating due to self-insulation.

The California method as it applies to the home gardener's individual needs may be summarized this way: (1) Raw material of proper composition and in a suitable condition must be provided, and the pile should be built all at one time; (2) a bin is needed to contain the material; and (3) a set procedure must be followed in setting up the contents of the bin.

According to Dr. Golueke, the C/N ratio of the material should be 25 to 30 parts of carbon to 1 part of nitrogen. The home gardener may achieve this by using green garden debris or garbage for the nitrogen and dry garden debris for the carbon matter. A high C/N ratio can be lowered (in favor of nitrogen) through the use of manures. See Chapter 6 for more information about the C/N ratios of various materials.

For home gardeners who wish to adjust the C/N ratio of their piles, Dr. Golueke recommends "trial and error, coupled with good judgment." He suggests layering dry and green materials in 2- to 4-inch-deep layers. Paper, he says, is an ineffective absorbent, while high-cellulose or woody materials offer carbon in a resistant form and therefore require additional nitrogen material to balance them at the early stages of the process. High-carbon material acts as an absorbent in the pile and gives it structure.

A minimum volume of 1 cubic yard will usually ensure self-insulation, but greater volume may be required in cold weather. The minimum floor dimensions of the bin should be 3 feet square, and the height of material inside the bin should not exceed 6 feet or be less than 4 feet. A bin may be constructed from wood and hardware cloth, wood alone, or concrete. It may be covered with a screen to discourage flies. Although not essential, a double-bin system allows you to turn the pile by transferring the materials from one bin to the other. (Bins are discussed in more detail in Chapter 10.)

Material to be composted should be reduced in size to pieces of 6 to 8 inches, though in garden composting all you really need to do is chop any thick flower stalks and vegetable vines. Shredding with a power shredder is ideal but not essential. Ground material composts faster than coarse, high-cellulose material.

Turning is essential to the California method, for it provides aeration and prevents the development of anaerobic conditions. The more frequent the turning (so long as it is not done more than once a day), the more rapidly the method works. If you have a single bin, turning the pile requires you to remove the front of the bin and fork out the contents, beginning with the top layer and keeping track of the original location of the material. When you return the contents, make sure that the material from the outer layers (top and sides) of the pile ends up in the interior of the new pile. The same result can be achieved in a single operation if you construct a double bin. The material should be fluffed as it is forked, and it should be so thoroughly mixed that the original layers are indistinguishable. In the course of the composting process, every particle of the pile should at one time or another have been exposed to the interior heat of the pile.

Turning schedules are not absolute, and by varying the turning frequency, the compost-making process may be extended to a month or even more, or reduced to as little as 12 days. The suggested schedule for 12-day compost is this: (1) Turn on the 3rd day after starting the pile; (2) turn again on the 3rd day after the first turning (skip a day); and (3) make the third and final turn on the 9th day after setting up the pile.

On the 12th day, following this schedule, the compost will be complete and ready for use, although it can benefit from further ripening.

The best way to monitor the decomposition process is by noting the course of the temperature changes in the heap. This may be done with a hotbed thermometer placed inside the pile about 12 inches from the surface. (A string on the end of it will aid in retrieval, for if the pile is working, it will be too hot to dig around in.) The temperature will rise from 110° to 120°F (43° to 49°C) within 24 to 48 hours after the process begins and to 130°F (54°C) or higher within 3 to 4 days. When the temperature sinks back to 110°F (43°C), the compost will be ready for use.

Over the years, we have found that home composters tend to be either too casual or too compulsively pseudoscientific and precise in their composting operations. The most important human ingredients in the process are good judgment and common sense. Use your nose and eyes to determine the cause of any failures you have, and be intelligent about making adjustments of C/N ratio, moisture, and aeration until you achieve satisfactory results.

Modifications

Most of the common modifications of the California system are easily antici-pated within the system itself. Schedules, as we have noted, can be adjusted. An experiment performed at the Rodale Institute, for example, followed a 14-day schedule with turnings on the 4th, 7th, and 14th days. This experiment started with proportioned but thoroughly mixed ingredients (the mixing was done during the grinding). All material was ground. Sprinklings of dried blood or cottonseed meal were used for nitrogen when manure was scarce or absent.

One variation of the California method emphasizes a second shredding after the 2nd week in a 2-week process, when a thorough turning has been given after 1 week. The second shredding is followed by sifting. Residue is removed to be used as mulch.

Another, more substantial, modification of the California method is becoming increasingly popular. As might be anticipated, it is the work of the California method with its frequent back-straining turnings that many gar-deners object to. Modifications have focused on reducing or eliminating the need for turning. Some gardeners are able to substitute bottom aeration for turning, by constructing their bins 1 foot off the ground to make use of con-vection currents. One "corn-poster" claims to have reduced composting time to 6 days using this method, with thorough grinding of materials. We will examine this approach in more detail later in this chapter.

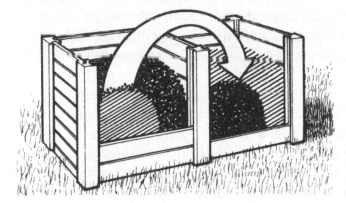

Turning the compost properly is essential to the California method. Transfer the material from one bin to the next, so that the outer layers are moved to the middle of the heap after turning.

THE BIODYNAMIC METHOD

The biodynamic method of farming and gardening was developed by a group of people surrounding or influenced by Rudolf Steiner, an Austrian social philosopher who died in 1925. He, in turn, had been influenced by the German poet and dramatist Johann Wolfgang von Goethe. The biodynamic method is part of a wider philosophical worldview called anthroposophy, a worldview with both scientific and humanistic roots that aims at the creation of a new culture based on the unity of all life processes. An excellent, clearly written reference on the principles of biodynamic gardening is Wolf-Dieter Storl's book *Culture and Horticulture.*

In his book *Bio-dynamic Farming and Gardening*, Dr. Ehrenfried Pfeiffer, who served as the director of the Biochemical Research Laboratory at the Goetheanum in Dornach, Switzerland, and who was a disciple of Rudolf Steiner, explains the biodynamic composting system: "The setting up of the compost heap is carried out as follows: The first step is to dig a pit for the pile from 5 to 10 inches deep. . . . This should be covered, when possible, with a thin layer of manure or compost already rotted. . . . The structure and consistency of the compost should be moist, but not wet."

The biodynamic compost pile is trapezoidal in shape with a base width of 13 to 15 feet and a top width of 6 feet. It is 5 to 6 feet high. Alternate layers of compost material (any organic material) and earth are used with lime or other rock powders sprinkled between layers. When complete, the pile is entirely covered with soil.

When manure is composted, bedding straw, leaves, or sawdust are layered with it. Piles are moistened with sprinkled or pumped liquid manure or rainwater. Brushwood or drainage tiles in the bottom of the shallow pit provide drainage. Only freshly fallen leaves, those that have not dried or "washed out," are used. When garbage is used, it can be covered temporarily with matting or evergreen branches.

So far, the biodynamic method is not much different from the Indore method or any partly anaerobic, slow-acting method of composting. The trademark of the biodynamic method comes with the next step.

When the pile is about a yard high, special biodynamic preparations are added to the pile. These preparations are known by numbers and are obtainable only from specially designated and certified biodynamic farmers of

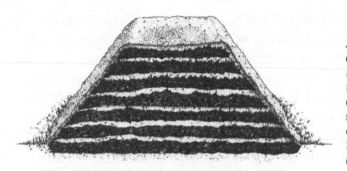

A cross section of a biodynamic heap shows layers of compost materials alternated with layers of soil. Each layer is sprinkled with lime or other rock powders, and the completed pile is covered with soil.

standing who alone know how to make them. These preparations are not to be sold for profit.

The preparations are made from various plants that have traditionally been employed as medicinal herbs. Among them are chamomile, valerian, nettle, yarrow, dandelion, and horsetail. These plants are themselves composted by the farmers and given a long fermentation process. They are buried at certain depths in the earth in contact with certain parts of animal organs. The biodynamic farmers believe that the scientific basis for the changes that occur during the fermentation of compost has to do with hormone influence. They believe they can direct the composting process in the garden through predetermined use of these plant preparations. The humuslike mass resulting from the composting of the special herbs is distributed as a compost activator or inoculant. Each compost pile needs only a tiny amount of these preparations; the prescribed quantities treat 7 to 16 tons of compost.

In 3 to 5 months, the biodynamic pile is turned and mixed. More preparations are added at this time, if necessary. The turning is important for aeration and to expose all weed seeds to the inner part of the pile. Dr. Pfeiffer says that it is the lack of air in the middle of the pile that, coupled with the conditions of fermentation, destroys the seeds.

Biodynamic gardeners believe that everything in nature is there for a purpose. All substances are related dynamically. Weather and the phases of the moon, they say, should be studied so the farmer can work in harmony with them by intention, just as the early peasant once used them through instinct or superstitious tradition.

Through experiment and observation, a biodynamic gardener seeks materials with the qualities most helpful to specific plants. These materials can then be used in custom-blending compost for each plant. This sometimes involves particular minerals known to be needed by that plant. Tomatoes, for example, do well in compost made from their own discarded leaves and vines, while sugar beets need a boron-rich compost made with such substances as seaweed, and potatoes do well in a calcium-rich horseradish compost. Stinging nettles aid in the rapid decomposition of other weeds and organic matter and are an essential ingredient of biodynamic compost.

Evaluation of the biodynamic method is made difficult by its ties to philosophical intangibles and by its adherents' claims of scientific precision. The experiments carried on by Dr. Pfeiffer's laboratory and at other centers show that seeds and plants treated with biodynamic preparations grow faster and are healthier than those grown in control experiments. However, most of the reasons used to explain this phenomenon are still speculative. Other studies have shown higher reproductive vigor among animals fed biodynamically grown hay, as compared with those fed hay fertilized conventionally. One study in Germany demonstrated that vegetables produced biodynamically had superior storage qualities.

Some modern composting experts, such as those who developed the California method, have found that activating preparations in general neither aid nor hinder the properly managed composting operation. It is possible that the biodynamic preparations, all made from plants rich in micronutrients or natural acids, bring anaerobic processes closer to the chemical state of aerobic processes than they would otherwise be, but this has not been proved conclusively. Modern scientific composters cannot, of course, measure the effects of inner attitudes on composting. These remain an article of faith to the followers of the biodynamic method and anthroposophy.

On one point at least, evidence indicates that the early biodynamic theory is in error. It is high temperature, not lack of air, that causes weed seeds to be destroyed in the center of the heap. Turning the pile more often than is called for in the biodynamic method is required for the destruction of weed seeds.

However, gardeners who wish to explore the secrets of the most highly regarded farmers in Europe may learn much from biodynamic methods. Beyond tips for fine-tuning your composting techniques, by studying biodynamics you can gain a greater appreciation of the subtleties of compost and its importance in restoring health to ravaged soils.

THE CITY PEOPLE'S METHOD

Helga Olkowski and Dr. Bill Olkowski, coauthors of *The City People's Book of Raising Food*, produce much of their own vegetable supply on a comparatively small plot of land in a city.

The composting method they practice and recommend to the urban gardener is a "fast" aerobic process. One reason for their recommendation comes from the special need urbanites have to avoid offending neighbors through foul smells and the nuisances, such as stray dogs, rats, and flies, these smells may bring. By maintaining an aerobic pile through frequent turnings, unpleasant odors are avoided.

In a time of increased incidence of often expensive litigation resulting from neighborhood friction, gardeners must be careful to keep composting operations inoffensive. Many modern city dwellers, not understanding the need for or the importance of composting, associate it with offenses to public health like leaving garbage exposed on the street. Public education about composting is needed; so are definitive court rulings on the side of careful composters, and sound municipal ordinances.

The Olkowskis, in outlining their method, suggest putting a sturdy, covered bin in a shady place, such as the north side of a garage, so that the contents will not dry out too rapidly. Three bins are ideal to facilitate turning.

About use and timing, they say the following:

> Usually it takes us about a week or so to use up the compost once it is made, as we don't have much time to devote to gardening generally. Since it takes about three weeks for a batch to be ready for use, this means we end up making one every month or so. However there are times during the summer when both our garden needs and garden wastes demand a more rigorous attention to the system.

During this period, they explain, they make compost every 2 weeks, using a three-bin "assembly line" that has one batch cooking and one being used at all times.

City people, the Olkowskis remind us, have an additional reason to balance high-nitrogen and high-carbon materials in their piles. If high-nitrogen materials like chicken manure are added to the pile "in such quantity that there is more than one part of nitrogen to approximately 30 parts carbon, the excess nitrogen will be respired by the microorganisms as ammonia." Ammonia odor, though less distressing than the odors of putrefaction found in an anaerobic pile that has not heated up, still upsets neighbors.

The Olkowskis recommend human urine as an excellent nitrogen source. Urine, since it is liquid, is easy to apply and can be substituted for some or all of the moisture added to the pile.

Studies at the Rodale Institute have concluded that human urine contains enough nitrogen to be effective as a compost activator. It is relatively disease-free and is less likely to lose potency than some animal manures because it is

🌱 COMPOST IN A BAG

Even if you live in an apartment and have absolutely no space for composting, this recipe for compost in a bag can help you recycle some of your kitchen wastes into fertilizer for your houseplants. It's also a great way to teach children about composting.

Start with a medium-size plastic bag and a twist-tie. Watertight, self-sealing bags also work well.

Place 1 cup of shredded organic matter in the bag. Use your imagination and your available resources here—try coffee grounds, tea leaves, fruit peels, leaves, grass clippings, apple cores without seeds, carrot or potato peels, wood ashes, and so on—any kind of organic material you might normally throw away. The more finely you can chop up or tear these items, the more effective your mini-compost bag will be.

Add ½ cup of garden soil to your bag. This is important for providing the microorganisms that will do the composting "work." Well-decomposed leaf mold or finished compost will work here, too. Don't substitute sterile potting soil; all its microorganisms have been sterilized away.

Add 1 tablespoon of alfalfa meal or alfalfa pellets, available as rabbit or hamster food.

Pour in 1 ounce of water, and seal the bag. Shake the bag to mix all the contents thoroughly. Squeeze the bag daily to mix your compost (the equivalent of turning a compost pile).

Every other day, leave the bag open for the day to let air in. Without air, your organic matter will decompose improperly and will smell bad. If the contents of your bag smell, they may be too wet or in need of more mixing. In 4 to 6 weeks, your compost should be finished and ready to use.

easier to apply soon after it is excreted. As a liquid, it can be stored in a closed container. Perhaps the only drawback to using urine as a compost nitrogen source is that of public perception. Give careful consideration to the advantages and disadvantages of adding urine to your compost pile. The urine of sick people should not be used.

Helga and Bill Olkowski recommend using a layering technique to build the pile. They use sawdust as a bottom layer and then alternately layer green and dry material, sprinkling urine or another easily sprinkled nitrogen source, like dried blood or alfalfa meal, over each layer as they build. Although they abandoned the use of a grinder because of its fuel consumption, they still chop large or tough dry materials with a cleaver. "After the pile is built," they continue, "you may need to water it. If you have been adding urine every other layer or so, it may be wet enough."

They turn the pile after a day or so by forking it into an adjacent bin. The same procedure is followed in subsequent turnings every 3 days. As city dwellers, the Olkowskis particularly wish to avoid the odors of an improperly aerated pile that has gone anaerobic. On the other hand, they advise against using side vents in a bin because, they claim, it will increase the heat loss and encourage fly breeding around the cover edges. Neighbors object to flies as much as they do to offensive odors.

COMPOST TUMBLERS

A number of manufactured composters on the market use a cabinet or barrel form, mounted on a stand to make turning easy. Some are even motorized for turning. Plans for building a barrel composter appear in Chapter 10. Such structures are best suited to urban composters and small gardens where space is at a premium.

Compost tumblers have many advantages if you need only small amounts of compost or want an easy, foolproof method for composting kitchen wastes. Some people who don't even garden use them as waste recycling systems and give the finished compost to friends who can use it. The main drawback is that once the drum has reached capacity, you have to wait 2 weeks until that batch is finished before adding fresh materials. Several plastic buckets with tight-fitting lids can store kitchen wastes during this time, using sawdust or a similarly absorbent material to keep odors at a minimum.

For the compost to be finished as quickly as possible, you should provide adequate moisture and try to balance the carbon/nitrogen ratio as you fill the tumbler. You can compost meat scraps without fear of invasion by vermin, and coarser materials can be screened out and returned to the drum for another go-round. Gardeners who use tumblers report minimal odor problems. This system offers many of the benefits of hot composting while virtually eliminating the effort of turning.

THE JOHNSON-SU BIOREACTOR METHOD

David Johnson, a researcher at New Mexico State University Institute for Sustainable Agriculture Research, developed a method for home-scale or small farm use that produces a superior-quality compost product. According to Johnson's analysis, this system cuts the water required by a factor of six and reduces time needed for finished compost by two-thirds, producing a "high quality, nutrient rich, fungal dominated, high-microbial-biomass and biodiverse compost."

Instructions for building the Johnson-Su Bioreactor and for preparing materials to be composted involve building a wire mesh bin attached to a pallet, into which perforated septic system pipes are inserted while the contents are being loaded. The reactor should be loaded all at once, and the perforated pipes can then be removed and reused. Materials should be shredded and then fully wetted before being loaded into the reactor. The bin should be kept moist, and worms can be introduced once temperatures fall below 80°F (27°C). To produce the highest-quality product, Johnson recommends letting it sit for at least a year.

THE RAISED-BIN METHOD

Turning a compost pile can be a tedious and strenuous job, especially for a retirement-age gardener. Complaints about the hard work of fast composting will be familiar to anyone who has resisted composting for such reasons.

A solution to this problem is the open-hearth-bottom bin sitting on a cement slab. A grill made of three lengths of 1-inch pipe 1 foot long sits 1 foot above the slab. The grill allows air into the center of the heap for complete composting. The bin itself can be made of salvaged wood or other materials.

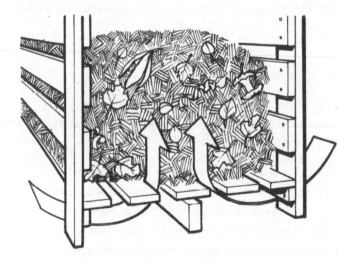

As the compost in a bottom-aerated bin heats up, air is pulled up and through the compost by natural convection, reducing the need to turn the pile.

One gardener has found that hollow concrete blocks lying on their sides, with pipes thrust through the centers of the blocks that are set 10 inches above the ground, also works well.

The first experimental raised bases were made by US Public Health Service researchers who found that 1 ton of rapidly decomposing compost uses up 18,000 to 20,000 cubic feet of air daily.

The theory behind the raised-bin method is that as the pile heats up, it pulls up the cooler air from the ground. This air percolates through the mass, aerating it as it passes upward. It is believed that forced aeration by convection currents (cool air pulled in by heat) is more thorough than aeration through turning.

Dr. Golueke, in *Composting*, states that the major difficulty of aeration such as that achieved in elevated piles is that it is difficult to diffuse the air through the pile so that all parts of the pile are uniformly aerated. Air channels form and airflow is short-circuited through these channels, causing materials near the channels to dry out—a particular problem when this method is used in municipal composting. There is less of a problem in small-scale operations that don't use high-pathogen materials like sewage sludge and night soil. Weed seeds, however, require high temperatures for destruction, and dryness can be a problem in any compost operation.

It is easy enough for curious composters to experiment with raised-bottom bins. As a cautionary measure, avoid potential pathogen sources with this method.

OGDEN'S STEP-BY-STEP METHOD

Sam Ogden, in his book *Step-by-Step to Organic Vegetable Growing*, gives detailed instructions on how to start a compost pile using his cool, partly anaerobic method.

> I started in the spring by laying out on a level piece of well-drained ground a rectangle about 5 feet by 12 feet, marking the corners with stakes. Then I lay up an outside wall of one or two thicknesses of sod or cement blocks. My system requires the maintenance of two compost piles, one of which ages for a year while the other one is being built, so in preparing for current use of the pile which has stood a year, I strip off all outside material, much of which is only partly decomposed, and place it within the borders of my sod strips as the first layer in my new compost pile. From now on, all decomposable garbage from our house, and from our neighbors' as well, if I can get them to sort their waste, is spread on the pile and covered with a thin layer of topsoil before it has a chance to become nasty.

This method allows you to add materials gradually over spring and summer, and it involves no turning. It does, however, require patience, since the compost is not ready to use until a year from the following spring. "By that time," says Ogden, "the pile is 2 years old . . . having taken 6 months to build and 18 months to cure."

The drawbacks of this method, according to Ogden, are the following: (1) It requires at least two piles and space for a third; (2) it takes more than a year to get started; (3) it won't handle materials that are hard to decompose, unless they are chopped up; and (4) it is not foolproof. Sometimes garbage added to such piles in large quantities putrifies without oxygen and turns into a black, slimy mess instead of crumbly compost. Ogden avoids the problem by spreading garbage thinly and covering it with soil.

Sam Ogden is frank about the shortcomings of his method, but he feels its near effortlessness compensates for them. He suggests using a rapid method, like the California method, to supplement his system during the first year, when it is getting started.

Ogden advises his readers against using leaves or grass clippings in the step-by-step method, instead suggesting that these materials be piled separately because of their tendency to create anaerobic conditions. Fresh grass clippings are especially problematic in this type of system, since without plentiful aeration they will form a slimy mass instead of breaking down quickly. They pose less of a problem in hot composting systems where air is plentiful. Leaves, on the other hand, can be used if they are spread thinly or shredded first.

Ogden's sensible step-by-step method is particularly recommended where (1) large quantities of compost are not needed to replenish the land and there is no need for haste; (2) human energy and machines for grinding are lacking; (3) supplemental materials for fertilizing and enriching the soil can be used (that is, animal manures, quick-method compost, or broadcast alfalfa, soybean, or bloodmeal); and (4) winters are severe and compost is needed early in spring.

It is quite easy to have two of Ogden's piles going for early-season use in successive years, while at the same time practicing quick methods for making compost to use during the growing season and for fall enrichment.

PIT COMPOSTING

Ever since some primitive cave dwellers dug a hole to bury their fish bones, garbage pits, in one form or another, have been with us. In most compost literature, the word *pit* is used interchangeably with *bin* to refer to a masonry-enclosed, boxlike structure sitting either on ground level or slightly under it. We will use *pit* only for compost-holding containers that actually go down into the ground at least a foot or so. Most compost made in these structures is partially anaerobic. Bins, pits, and the special methods they require are discussed in Chapter 10.

THE MOVABLE COMPOST PILE FOR RAISED BEDS

Recently there has been much interest in the raised-bed method of intensive gardening, a method commonly used in France and in Japan. In this country, the system has been practiced for many years on the West Coast and is now being adopted by gardeners with small plots all over the United States.

In raised-bed gardening, plants are tightly grouped in small beds. Since more nutrient demand is made on soil by closely grouped plants, beds are dug about 24 inches deep, and the soil in the beds is carefully prepared and contains large quantities of compost and/or manure. Root systems develop vertically instead of horizontally in the beds, which reduces the need for watering and heavy fertilization during the growing season. Mulch is not needed, for the plants themselves shade the soil and form a living mulch.

Beds in the raised system are about a foot higher than ground level. In such enriched and carefully drained beds, crops can be planted at intervals closer than normal, and complete accessibility allows for staggered spacing and interesting and beneficial interplantings. Interplanting not only conserves space but promotes growth and guards against pests. Rock powders are also frequently used in preparing raised beds.

One gardener has devised a special composting system for use with intensive raised beds. He writes:

> My aim was to take the compost pile with its lively earthworm colony out of its isolated site away from the garden, and make it instead a part of the garden where it is most needed–in my raised beds. . . . The beds are 6 feet wide by 50 long and two cement blocks or 16 inches high, while the soil level in the beds is about 8 inches high.

This gardener scooped out the soil at one end of the raised garden bed and built a three-sided structure with cement blocks. Grass clippings, hedge cuttings, and the remains of an old compost heap were placed in the structure. Grass, soil, manure, and ashes were layered until the pile reached 4 feet in height. When the compost was finished, it was shoveled down to the level of the bed, for use in other parts of the garden. The top and left-hand blocks were moved down the line to form another bin alongside the first, hopscotching up the row with a minimum of work.

To anyone who has discovered that no plant or weed grows better than the one accidentally "planted" where an open-bottomed compost pile once stood, this on-site method makes good sense. Its chief advantage is its handiness for use, both as a receptacle for weeds and debris and, later, as a source of finished compost. Even in intensive gardening, where every inch of land counts, enough room for a bin can generally be found, and in fast-method composting you only need spare the space for 14 days. The land repays its use by allowing even more intensive planting of the next crops. If space is not an issue, move the pile up the bed only once or twice in a season, as adjoining crops are harvested. You can then use the compost to prepare the whole bed the following spring.

WINDROWS AND PILES

Piles and windrows are both heaps for open composting. The systems are used in the open, on the ground, with no confining structure like a bin, pit, or pen. Windrows are elongated piles that require periodic turning to expose all

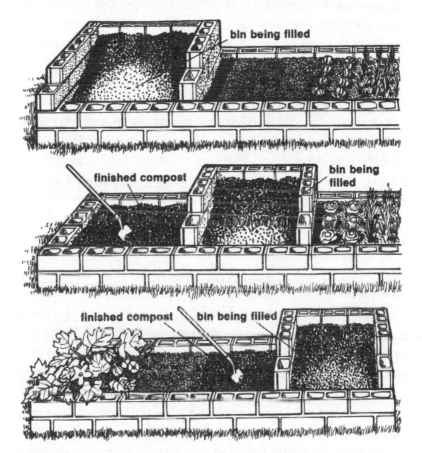

bin being filled

finished compost

bin being filled

finished compost   bin being filled

Combining a compost pile with raised garden beds creates a convenient and efficient way to nourish intensively grown crops. The pile is located nearby for easy disposal of garden wastes; as it "moves" down the bed, it leaves enriched soil where new crops will thrive. As each pile is finished, the rear and left wall of the bin are hopscotched over the remaining wall and rebuilt to form a new bin. When the pile reaches the end of the bed, the process is reversed.

particles of the mass to similar conditions within the windrows. They are often used in large-scale agricultural or municipal composting operations and may be anywhere in the spectrum of hot to cool, depending on how often they are turned.

Even in the far northern parts of the United States, windrowing can be practiced on any drained land. Some people set shed-type roofs over windrows to protect them from heavy rains. In severe weather, shed sides may also be added to protect active piles. Windrows may be of any convenient length. Regarding their height, Dr. Golueke in *Composting* explains, in speaking of municipal composting, that height is critical because too shallow a pile loses heat too rapidly and too high a pile can become compressed by its own weight, with a resulting loss of pore space that can lead to anaerobic conditions.

Dr. Golueke recommends a maximum height of 5 or 6 feet for freshly ground municipal refuse. This will shrink during decomposition and then be re-formed to the recommended size when the pile is turned. The width at the base should be 8 to 10 feet. In dry climates, you should shape the pile so it is flattened on top, like a trapezoid, to trap moisture. In rainy climates or wet weather, mound the top to shed water. A layer of hay or straw will protect the windrow from the weather while preventing moisture loss through evaporation.

MULCH AND SHEET COMPOSTING

Although not ordinarily considered a composting system, simply spreading organic materials in a thin layer directly in the garden to decompose offers many of the benefits of compost with less need to handle and move materials. This approach is referred to as sheet composting. It includes such practices as mulching, which performs several functions in addition to contributing organic matter to the soil. Green manuring is another form of sheet composting, in which certain crops or even weeds are grown and incorporated into the soil to add organic matter that doesn't have to be carried to the garden and spread around. Several variations on this theme follow.

In its simplest form, sheet composting consists of spreading any raw organic wastes, such as manure and weeds, over a piece of land and tilling them in. This method is more often associated with farm-scale applications, using power equipment. It can be done on a smaller scale but generally requires taking the treated area out of production for at least a season.

The danger of sheet composting as a compost-making method is that the carbon-containing residues you use will call upon the nitrogen reserves of the soil for their decomposition. The high-nitrogen materials, on the other hand, may release their nitrogen too quickly or in the wrong form. What can be accomplished in a pile in a matter of weeks, given confined and thermophilic conditions, may take a full season in the soil.

Green manuring—the growing of cover crops to be turned under—is the most practical way to add substantial amounts of organic matter to a large garden or homestead field. A green manure crop, often legumes like clover, indigo, winter peas, cowpeas, soybeans, lespedeza, fenugreek, or vetch, is planted after a food crop is harvested. Even weeds may be used; as you know, they plant themselves. The cover crop is then tilled or plowed under at least 2 weeks before the next crop is to be planted. The type of crop used as a green manure and its stage of growth when tilled under are factors that can moderate possible short-term nitrogen depletion. Legumes such as vetch and clover will contribute more nitrogen than will nonlegumes such as rye or buckwheat. Young, succulent growth provides more nitrogen and decomposes more quickly than does coarser, more mature growth. However, the higher C/N ratio of mature growth gives it greater value for improving overall soil structure.

Green manuring may be combined with sheet composting. In fact, it is a good idea to add natural rock powders when you till under, because the decay of the organic matter will facilitate the release of the nutrients locked up in these relatively insoluble fertilizers. Some farmers spread finished compost when turning under green manure, claiming this accelerates its decomposition.

In the sort of ideal circumstances few of us enjoy, green manuring and sheet composting go on in one garden plot while food crops are rotated onto another plot. Rotation and cover cropping are also effective ways of foiling pests and diseases.

Other variations on sheet composting include the popular approach dubbed a "lasagna garden." This is a no-dig method of starting a new garden plot in a patch of sod by first spreading a layer of cardboard—easily obtained from the local recycling center or an appliance store in large sheets. On top of the cardboard the gardener then spreads manure, leaves, mulch hay, grass clippings, chipped yard waste, food waste, and any other available organic materials in layers. If built in spring, the lasagna then cooks over the course of the season and can be cover-cropped to get it ready to plant the next year. The lasagna can also be prepared later in the season and covered with a good layer of mulch over winter, to be cover-cropped the next spring.

Another approach to sheet composting popularized by Sepp Holzer's permaculture teachings is called *hugelkultur,* from the German word that simply means "mound culture." A great technique for land with poor drainage, it involves piling a mound or windrow of wood scraps, tree stumps, brush, and similar bulky carbonaceous materials, then covering it with a generous amount of soil and compost and allowing it to rot down over several seasons. A tall mound will turn into a raised garden bed rich in nutrients and full of air pockets that settle little by little as the wood rots. "As the years pass, the deep soil of your raised garden bed becomes incredibly rich and loaded with soil life," says permaculture evangelist Paul Wheaton.

"NO-WORK" MULCHING

Ruth Stout popularized her "no-work" deep-mulch gardening system in the 1950s. Her answer to just about every garden chore is a permanent layer of deep mulch covering the entire garden. This requires a relatively fertile soil to begin with. Once established, the mulch eliminates the need to till, hoe, cultivate, weed, and fertilize. You only need to pull back the mulch to plant seeds or pop in seedlings, and it will serve to retain moisture, moderate soil temperatures, and prevent the growth of weed seedlings. Earthworms and other beneficial organisms are encouraged by mulch–however, so are mice and slugs, which are definitely unwelcome garden visitors.

Ruth Stout convinced a whole generation of gardeners to mulch as a way of saving labor through such testimonials as this:

> I am not a particularly vigorous woman, but I do all the work in a garden 40 by 60 feet, raising enough vegetables for my husband, my sister, myself, and many guests. I freeze every variety, from early asparagus to late turnips. We never buy a vegetable. I also do my housework, raise quite a few flowers, rarely do any work after 1:00 p.m. I'm scarcely ever more than just pleasantly tired.

It would be hard to find a more convincing testament to the labor-saving advantages of mulch than Ruth Stout's description of her own good life. If you are an urban or suburban gardener, however, you may find that the time you save in hoeing is spent in traffic jams, as you chase all over the county looking for hay for sale, or spent vacuuming the messy hay residue out of the back seat of your car once the hay has been found. Labor economy is not the only kind of saving, either, and when you add the price of hay or straw to the cost of the gasoline used in looking for it, you may be fully ready to return to the cheap old hoe.

When compared with composting, mulching is a slow method of adding nutrients to the soil. The process is at least partly anaerobic, for air is sealed off from underlying materials by the top layers. High-nitrogen materials, such as partly rotted manure and garbage, decay rapidly when applied in mulch. High-carbon materials like hay and straw serve better to retain water and retard weeds. Since mulch sits on top of the earth and is not mixed with soil, this high-carbon, decay-resistant material will not tie up large quantities of soil nitrogen all at once as it would if plowed under. However, it will add bulk and nutrients to the soil very slowly; it may be that your soil needs only these slow additions. If so, mulching alone may suffice to keep your garden in shape for several years.

Almost all compostable wastes can be used for mulching. However, it is almost impossible to layer and mix correct proportions of ingredients in mulch form. Rapid decomposition of mulch is impossible because of the lack of self-insulating mass, but even if you could put a 5-foot layer of mulch on your garden and aerate it regularly, the temperatures generated would burn or wilt anything growing there and do damage to the soil and its organisms.

If you need to add large quantities of humus to your garden for building the soil's texture and increasing its productivity, or for modifying the pH level, many experts agree that you would do well to combine the labor-saving advantages of mulch with a seasonal composting program.

Some-Work Mulching

Texas gardener Hank Lyle describes a modification of the Ruth Stout method that is more suitable for building up problem soil. The soil he started with was "red clay, baked by the sun. What wasn't clay was a very hard soil that looked lifeless."

Lyle plowed under his first garden, then applied a mulch of weeds and other materials 4 inches deep over his 150- by 50-foot patch. After dampening it with a hose, he broadcast 35 pounds of cottonseed meal by hand (he says a lawn fertilizer spreader would have worked better). The cottonseed meal acted as a high-nitrogen layer in the compost.

The next layer consisted of 3 inches of leaf mold. This layer was dampened, and an additional 40 pounds of cottonseed meal was applied over it. The sheet compost settled to a height of 6 inches. Lyle continues the account:

> What we had now was a giant compost pile which was also a mulch. After three days we used a tiller (with the two inside rows of tines removed) to stir and fluff the mulch and mix in what soil the tines could pick up. . . . We dampened the heap again with the spray nozzle.

By the evening of the 4th day, Lyle reported, the material had begun to heat up under the top layer. More materials (leaves, grass clippings) were added, with 15 pounds of cottonseed meal being sprinkled over each inch of material. Every 4th day, the tiller was used to mix the material. The account continues:

> By the 20th day, the material had shrunk considerably. We noticed that the soil beneath the compost was beginning to soften and turn dark brown. There were earthworms, too. Before we had started the compost, hardly a worm was to be found.

Lyle continued foraging for organic materials to add to his garden wherever he could, topping it off with a layer of cottonseed hulls from an abandoned gin. This he left for the winter, to absorb the rains and continue decomposing. By spring all that remained was a 3-inch layer of cottonseed hulls. This layer was kept for a year-round mulch.

When compared with rapid-bin composting, Hank Lyle's novel type of sheet composting shows much similarity to the conventional method. It provides moisture through hosing, aeration through tiller turning, a C/N balance of materials through the use of premixing layering techniques and thorough sprinklings of high-nitrogen cottonseed meal, and it allows for an aging period (winter) after the initial temperature rise. It would probably be classified as a long-term method, although in its particulars it is most similar to the California method and it is mostly aerobic. Unlike the California method of bin or windrow composting, it involves a maximum "pile" depth of less than 10 inches, so the mass cannot insulate itself enough to achieve thermophilic temperatures long enough to kill weed seeds. No potentially pathogenic raw material was used, so the absence of high temperatures was not a serious drawback to this method.

The important difference between Hank Lyle's and Ruth Stout's methods is that, in his, no crop growing went on during the mulch composting period, so the temporary nitrogen drain caused by rapid decomposition didn't threaten crops. The whole plot was used as an oversize compost pile. The chief aim of the process was soil fertility and soil tilth. Weed reduction and water retention were only secondary. At this point, Lyle probably won't have to repeat the initial fallowing and enriching of his plot for many years. He can now make compost in a bin or pit, using the finished compost in the rows he makes in his replenished year-round mulch of hulls.

TRENCH AND POSTHOLE COMPOSTING

Burying compost in trenches or holes dug in the garden is a less popular composting method that nonetheless has staunch adherents. Although it shares some of the disadvantages of both pit composting and sheet composting, some gardeners swear by it for rapid improvement of unusually poor soils.

Nedra Guinn, a gardener in southeast Tennessee, dug trenches 12 inches deep and 18 inches wide, the length of a garden row. These were filled with compost materials including hay, leaves, weeds, tree trimmings, and grass. The materials were then packed down and covered with manure, watered, and mulched. Guinn planted directly into the mulch and experienced no nitrogen deficiency in crops, but other gardeners who wish to try this method are cautioned either to top the trench with topsoil or to risk nitrogen depletion. The drawbacks of trench composting are the tendency to the formation of pockets of anaerobic activity, the slowness of decomposition, and the possibility of nitrogen borrowing from plants.

Some gardeners have discovered that the traditional posthole digger is a quick and convenient tool for spot composting. The following account describes the method used by organic gardener Michael Timchula:

Making compost in postholes can be done from early spring to the latest fall day. If you plan ahead, you can make enough holes in areas where the snow does not pile up too deeply, or in sheltered places, so that you can continue composting throughout the winter.

When cleaning up the garden and yard in early spring, keep the posthole digger handy. As soon as you get a small pile of debris, twigs, leaves, and so on, dig a posthole about 12 to 18 inches deep and bury the debris, topping it off with a handful or two of manure. Cover the hole with the best of the topsoil that was removed and scatter the rest. Watering is usually not necessary, as the hole tends to collect enough moisture to ensure proper composting.

Keep the posthole digger with you at planting time. After planting and laying out your rows and hills, dig holes near a hill, in the center of a row, or between plants and fill them as described. In this way, feeder roots will seek out the fresh compost as the plants grow, and lush growth will result. The compost holes serve to hold the moisture, and a weak compost tea leaches out to feed the plants.

Cultivating time is when the postholer can be put to good use. In a row that will not need to be disturbed or cultivated for the rest of the summer (next to the carrots or chard or another vegetable that lasts all summer), start digging a row of holes very close together. Pack young weeds, clippings, trimmings, and so on, a handful or two of manure, and the day's garbage and cover lightly with topsoil. Keep one or two holes dug ahead so that you always have a place for making compost. In a large garden, you may need more than one row for the entire season.

ANAEROBIC COMPOSTING

It is possible to make compost without air. In 1968, J. I. Rodale presented this thoughtful and succinct review of the method in the pages of *Organic Gardening and Farming*:

> About 19 years ago, I first discussed a process of making compost by the Selby enclosed method which is for the most part anaerobic. Most readers who wrote in about their reactions were in favor of the new idea. But a few were highly critical. They considered it almost irreligious to abolish the aerobic concept of making compost, and said that anaerobic conditions lead to putrefaction.

Covering a compost heap with heavy black plastic allows composting to proceed under anaerobic or semi-anaerobic conditions.

Those who have criticized the enclosed method of making compost should realize that only in a portion of the period of composting in the Sir Albert Howard (Indore) process are the conditions aerobic. Let me quote from his *Agricultural Testament:* "After the preliminary fungus stage is completed and the vegetable wastes have broken down sufficiently to be dealt with by bacteria, the synthesis of humus proceeds under anaerobic conditions when no special measures for the aeration of the dense mass are either possible or necessary." About half the period is aerobic and the last half anaerobic.

In addition, two distinct drawbacks exist in the usual form of making compost which permits air to come freely into the heap. First, it causes oxidation which destroys much of the organic nitrogen and carbon dioxide, and releases them into the atmosphere. Second, valuable liquids leach downward and out of the mass into the ground underneath where they are wasted.

The purpose for making compost anaerobically is to prevent or reduce oxidation. Oxidation of nitrogenous substances is always accompanied by the production of a great quantity of free nitrogen compounds. Manure kept in efficient conditions in an open pit loses 40 percent of the nitrogen originally contained. Although this loss is relatively small in comparison with the 80 or 90 percent loss as a result of improper storage, it is also relatively large in contrast to the 10 percent or less obtainable by using closed pits. In them, fermentation takes place out of contact with air. Only a small nitrogen loss occurs.

One difficulty has been finding an efficient and simple way to practice anaerobic composting. One technique is to enclose the compost in a polyethylene wrapping, and gardeners and farmers in all parts of the country have reported highly successful results in covering heaps with heavy black plastic.

Composting without air is not the most popular method used by gardeners, but it does claim some adherents, and it is a useful method in certain situations.

🌱 A COMPOST CHECKLIST

Following are several checkpoints to help you gauge the success of your compost. These points will serve as a standard from which you can determine the efficiency of your composting methods.

- ✓ **Structure.** The material should be medium loose, not too tight, not packed, and not lumpy. The more crumbly the structure, the better it is.
- ✓ **Color.** A black-brown color is best; pure black, if soggy and smelly, denotes anaerobic fermentation with too much moisture and lack of air. A grayish, yellowish color indicates waterlogged conditions.
- ✓ **Odor.** The odor should be earthlike, or like good woods' soil or humus. Any bad smell is a sign that the fermentation has not reached its final goal and that bacteriological breakdown processes are still going on. A musty, cellarlike odor indicates the presence of molds, sometimes also a hot fermentation, that has led to losses of nitrogen.
- ✓ **Acidity.** A neutral or slightly acidic reaction is best. Slight alkalinity can be tolerated. Remember that too acidic a condition is the result of lack of air and too much moisture. Nitrogen-fixing bacteria and earthworms prefer a neutral to slightly acidic environment. The pH range for a good compost is, therefore, 6.0 to 7.4. Below 6.0 the reaction is too acidic for the development of nitrogen-fixing bacteria.
- ✓ **Mixture of raw materials.** The proper mixture and proportion of raw materials is most important! Indeed, it determines the final outcome of a compost fermentation and the fertilizer value of the compost. On average, an organic matter content of from 25 to 50 percent should be present in the final product. If mineralized soil and subsoil are to be used, soil that has frozen over winter secures better results. Ditch scrapings, or soil from the bottom of a pond, should be frozen and exposed to air for a season before being incorporated into compost.
- ✓ **Moisture.** Most composting failures result from a failure to maintain the proper moisture conditions. Moisture content should be like that of a wrung-out sponge: No water should drip from a sample squeezed in the hand, yet the compost should never be dry.

SOLVING A HEAP OF PROBLEMS

If you discover problems with your composting process, oftentimes they can be corrected by turning the pile and adjusting one or more of the conditions required by the compost organisms. Following are some commonly encountered compost problems and some alternatives for remedying or preventing them.

PROBLEM	REMEDY
Wet, foul-smelling heap	Turn pile and add high-carbon, absorbent materials. Protect pile from rain.
Dry center and little or no decomposition of materials	Turn pile, thoroughly soaking each layer as it is replaced. Cover with plastic to retain moisture.
Dampness and warmth only in middle	Increase amount of material in pile and moisten.
Damp, sweet-smelling heap but no heat	Add more nitrogenous materials such as bloodmeal, fresh manure, or urine, and turn or aerate.
Matted, undecomposed layers of leaves or grass clippings	Break up layers with garden fork or shred them, then re-layer pile. Avoid adding heavy layers of leaves, grass clippings, hay, or paper unless first shredded.
Large undecomposed items	Screen out undecomposed items and use as starter for next pile.

The small-lot gardener, for instance, might find that composting in a garbage can or plastic leaf bag is the only way to produce compost without offending neighbors' sensitivities. Making anaerobic compost in plastic bags also solves the turning problem. Filled with a mix of organic matter, one of these "compost cases" can be tied shut and placed in any convenient sunny location. The bag can be rolled daily to mix the contents. By keeping a few such bags going at a time, this system provides an ongoing means of composting kitchen garbage and a regular source of small amounts of finished compost.

COMPOSTING WITH EARTHWORMS

If you let them, earthworms will do most of your composting work for you, in the garden, on the farm–or even in your basement.

Earthworms are amazing creatures, capable of consuming their own weight in soil and organic matter each day and leaving behind the richest and most productive compost known. The castings of earthworms contain from 5 to 11 times the amount of available N-P-K as the soil the worms ate to produce those castings. How do earthworms perform this magic? The secretions of their intestinal tracts act chemically to liberate plant nutrients with the aid of soil microorganisms. And what earthworms do for the major plant nutrients, they do for the micronutrients, too. Earthworms literally tunnel through your soil, day and night, liberating plant nutrients wherever they go. Let loose in a compost heap, they will quickly reduce it to the finest of humus. Mulch your garden with organic matter of nearly any kind, and earthworms will never stop working on it until they have reduced the mulch to dark, rich humus. If you encourage earthworms to stay in your soil, or work with them in producing compost, they will virtually ensure that you produce successful compost.

The secret in producing compost with earthworms is in learning a little about earthworms and their needs. If you buy 1,000 red wigglers and thrust them into the middle of your compost pile, you will likely have 1,000 dead red wigglers the next day. Most earthworms, you see, cannot tolerate the heat of an actively working compost heap. You will also want to learn to distinguish among the various major earthworm species, since their needs are quite different, and so are their capabilities in helping you make compost.

Most people see earthworms as a welcome natural addition to their composting efforts and as affirmation that they are doing things right. But gardeners could make better compost if they saw the earthworm as a necessary component of the whole process, just as important as air, water, or organic matter. The earthworms can do much of the work and make composting faster—but in return, the gardener must learn to make compost with the earthworm's needs in mind, and discover which species of worms are suitable for various composting situations.

EARTHWORMS IN THE INDORE METHOD

Earthworms will naturally be attracted to an Indore compost heap, attacking it from the bottom. The base layer of brush will soon become reduced in bulk and filled in with finer debris. Field worms (*Allolobophora caliginosa*) and night crawlers (*Lumbricus terrestris*) will quickly infiltrate this layer, to turn and mix the earth with the organic matter. They will also reproduce quickly, increasing their population many times over. If the heap is maintained for a year or more in one location, the earth below it will become rich, friable, and loaded with earthworms. With each rain, some of the nutrients from the compost will leach deep into the soil, spreading out from the actual edges of the heap. Earthworms will mix these nutrients into the soil and stabilize them for growing plants. This enrichment of the soil beneath the heap is a good reason for changing its location every year or so. Any prized plants grown where an old compost heap was built will flourish beyond reasonable expectations.

As the materials in the heap decompose and turn to humus, field worms will advance farther up into the heap. Still, they will not flood the entire heap, as will the manure-living species. The limiting factor is the high temperature; even an inactive, aboveground heap will not be attractive to field-living species. Night crawlers like even cooler temperatures but will feed at the bottom of the heap. If in autumn and early spring they penetrate a well-advanced heap, you know you can use it for soil improvement.

Although manure-type worms can work at higher temperatures than field-living species, even they will be killed in the intense heat of a working compost heap, where temperatures can reach 150°F (66°C). Do not introduce

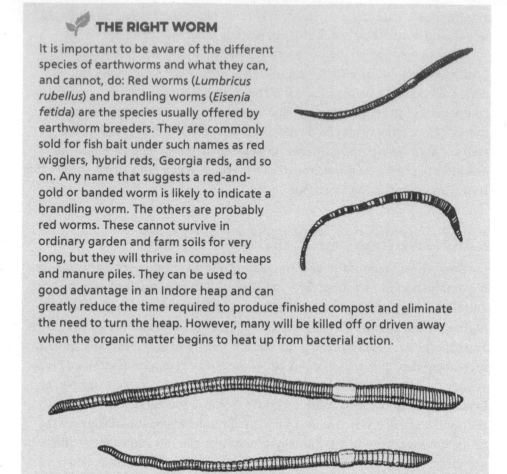

🌱 THE RIGHT WORM

It is important to be aware of the different species of earthworms and what they can, and cannot, do: Red worms (*Lumbricus rubellus*) and brandling worms (*Eisenia fetida*) are the species usually offered by earthworm breeders. They are commonly sold for fish bait under such names as red wigglers, hybrid reds, Georgia reds, and so on. Any name that suggests a red-and-gold or banded worm is likely to indicate a brandling worm. The others are probably red worms. These cannot survive in ordinary garden and farm soils for very long, but they will thrive in compost heaps and manure piles. They can be used to good advantage in an Indore heap and can greatly reduce the time required to produce finished compost and eliminate the need to turn the heap. However, many will be killed off or driven away when the organic matter begins to heat up from bacterial action.

Red worms (top) *and brandling worms* (bottom) *are most often raised and sold by commercial breeders, but the larger, soil-dwelling night crawlers* (above, top) *and field worms* (above, bottom) *are more familiar sights to most gardeners.*

them until the interior of the pile has cooled down to the outside temperature. Normally this will be about 3 weeks after the last materials have been added to a well-constructed heap. At this point, dig holes at various points in the heap and drop 50 to 100 worms in each. About 1,000 worms (a convenient number to order) will serve to inoculate a 4- by 6-foot pile. If manure-type worms and their castings were well supplied in manure that went into the heap and have survived the heat, there will be no need to introduce worms from an outside source.

In a matter of days, the worms will be consuming the organic matter, leaving rich castings wherever they go, and reproducing at a high rate. In a well-tended compost heap, 1,000 reds or brandlers can increase to 1 million in a year or two.

Manure-type worms will do much better in the Indore heap if larger quantities of manure are included in the mixture. Instead of the 2-inch layer usually recommended, add 4 or 6 inches. If no manure at all is used, the worms will still have a good chance to thrive, although their progress will be slower.

On a larger scale, commercial worm composting operations such as Worm Power use a mechanized continuous flow bed that allows finished vermicompost to fall through a mesh screen as fresh material is continuously added to the top layer. When a high level of consistent quality is required, the feedstock must be carefully controlled. Dairy manure is generally prepared for the worms by composting in an aerated static-pile system, ensuring that any pathogens or weed seeds will be killed.

No-Heat Indore Composting

A variation of the Indore method makes it possible to produce compost quickly with very little heating, using earthworms. Construct the heap so that it is longer and wider than a normal heap, but only 12 to 18 inches high. Shred all materials as finely as possible, and introduce manure-type worms immediately. They will go to work right away, and the heap will never heat up greatly because of the large surface area; the center of the heap will be too close to the cooling effects of the outside air. The major disadvantages are that it takes up more ground surface area, and the shredding of materials takes time and requires fossil energy to operate a gasoline-powered shredder or rotary mower. Also, any weed seeds present will remain viable.

Maintaining the Earthworm Population

When removing finished compost for use on garden plots or farm fields, be certain to save a good number of earthworms for future composting operations. There are several ways to do this. The easiest is to remove only half the

When earthworms are released into an Indore heap, night crawlers will penetrate only the bottom layer of brush, field worms will work in the bottom two layers of material, and red worms and brandling worms will be found throughout the heap.

heap at a time, spreading out the remainder to serve as the base for the new heap. If your manure worm population is not as great as you wish it to be, you can save even more by "scalping" the heap in several steps. Earthworms are repelled by light; if exposed, they will quickly dive down beneath the surface. Remove finished compost from the outer parts of the heap, to a depth where worms are exposed. Wait for about 30 minutes, then take another scalping. Continue in this manner until you have removed as much compost as you want. The earthworms will have been driven into a compact area at the bottom of the heap. At this point, spread out the remaining compost containing the earthworms, and cover it immediately with new manure and green matter. If, as so often is the case, the outer scalp of the heap has not composted fully (since it is the newest material), then set aside this first scalp and put it back after you have finished the operation. It will be the first material to be attacked in the new heap.

EARTHWORMS IN BINS AND PITS

Red worms and brandling worms cannot survive northern winters without some kind of protection. Further, earthworms are the favorite food of moles, which can easily penetrate an Indore heap and decimate your earthworm population in an amazingly short time. The answer to both dangers is a compost pit dug beneath the frost line and outfitted with a heavy, coarse screen on the bottom to keep out moles but allow the free passage of soil-dwelling earthworms. Manure-type worms will not migrate deep into the soil.

Often, bins and pits are combined. The earth is dug out to a depth of 16 to 24 inches (deeper in areas such as Minnesota and Maine), and boards are used to extend the pit into an aboveground bin.

For the gardener who seeks to build a compost/earthworm pit for the first time, here are some basic instructions:

1. Stake off an area 3 to 4 feet wide and as long as you wish the pit to be.

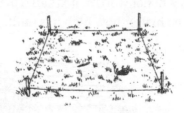

2. Excavate the earth from this area to a depth of 16 to 24 inches. (If you live where winter temperatures get to –10°F [–23°C] or colder, make it 24 inches.) Pile the excavated soil to one side, in as compact a heap as possible, for later addition to the pit.

3. Drive 2x4 stakes into the four corners of the pit, if you will be using boards. (Scrap lumber from old buildings is fine.) A layer of ¼-inch, rustproof wire mesh in the bottom of the pit will protect your earthworms from moles.

4. Nail boards all around the pit. Keep one end open so you can work with the material. Use stakes to hold loose boards in this area. Add boards on top of each other, leaving about ¼ inch between each for aeration. Add boards only as the pile of materials requires them for support. The boards aboveground need never be higher than 16 inches above the ground surface; if the pit is 16 inches deep, this will mean a total of 32 inches of vertical board area. (Remember that these earthworms will not work more than 6 to 8 inches below the surface of the heap, no matter how high it is built.)

5. If you elect to use concrete blocks instead of wood, excavate the soil to a depth of one or two blocks, and add no more than two layers of blocks above the ground. At this low height, the blocks can be set in loosely, without mortar. Allow a little space between them for aeration.

Many gardeners find it helpful to divide the pit into two sections, one for new compost and the other for old. As finished compost is removed from one section, the earthworms are transferred into the newer heap on the other side, and a new heap is begun in the just-emptied side. In this way, there is always a ready supply of compost for garden use, and the earthworms are constantly maintained. An ideal setup would comprise two double pits.

Some gardeners outfit their bins with loose-fitting board lids, hinged on one side so that they swing up and open easily. This device keeps out the sun and protects the surface of the heap from excessive heat during summer, enabling the worms to work nearer to the surface where new material is deposited. It also keeps out predators during the night and conserves moisture during hot and dry periods. When a lid is used, keep a constant check on moisture. Add water as necessary, or—better—open the lid during rainfalls if moisture is needed.

WINTER PROTECTION IN THE NORTH

In the South, where winter temperatures rarely go below 20°F (–7°C), red worms and brandling worms can be maintained easily in outdoor pits with a minimum of protection. A few layers of burlap bags and a mound of straw piles over the beds will offer all the insulation needed, even if they are occasionally covered with snow. In places like Minnesota, Montana, and Vermont, however, where winter temperatures routinely dip to –20°F (–29°C), special protection is a must.

A good winter-protection system is explained fully in Henry Hopp's booklet *Let an Earthworm Be Your Garbage Man*. It is essential reading for any Northern gardener who decides to construct earthworm pits.

For winter protection, the booklet recommends digging a compost pit 16 inches deep and lining it with two layers of concrete blocks belowground, with a third layer aboveground. Pile the removed soil at the edge of the pit and cover it thickly with straw. Line the bottom of the pit with garbage, and cover

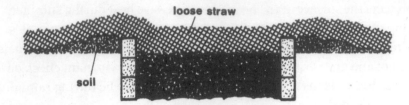

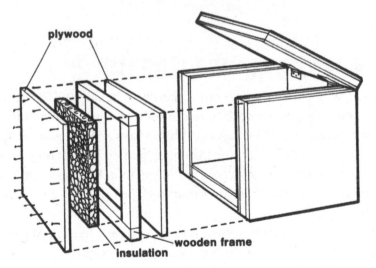

During northern winters, protect earthworm pits with a thick mulch covering. Bins may be insulated by surrounding them with bales of hay and straw and covering the lids with mulch. A year-round insulated bin can be built with walls made by sandwiching rigid insulation between layers of plywood.

it with 2 to 3 inches of soil, then with burlap bags. Water if needed. The pit can be covered with wire mesh weighted down with bricks or concrete blocks.

In winter, cans of garbage are added to the pit under the burlap and covered with a layer of soil.

Even in 20-below weather, the earthworms keep working and the composting process continues. By spring, the kitchen refuse added the previous autumn is ready for use in the garden.

INDOOR COMPOSTING DURING WINTER

Earthworms can be used indoors in winter to produce a small amount of compost from kitchen garbage and even newspapers. Generally, 1 pound of earthworms will eat 1 pound of garbage and produce 1 pound of compost each day, although this varies. There have even been a few commercial earthworm composting units placed on the market, but a simple homemade system is both easy and inexpensive and just as effective. It can be used anywhere, winter or summer, and it can be expanded into as large an operation as you wish.

This method is detailed by Mary Appelhof in her manual *Worms Eat My Garbage*. Her rule of thumb: 1 square foot of surface area is needed to digest each pound of waste material generated per week. It is best to begin on a modest scale. Construct a wooden box 2 feet wide, 2 feet long, and 1 foot deep. Or get a vegetable lug box from your local supermarket, and if it has large spaces between the boards, tack in plastic screening to hold the earthworm bedding. If you construct your own box, provide for drainage and aeration by drilling a half-dozen $1/_8$-inch holes in the bottom and some more around the sides. A box 2 feet square and 1 foot deep will accommodate 1,000 adult worms (or "breeders," as they are called in the trade), or you can order a pound of pit-run worms (all sizes) that will do just as well.

You can prepare a bedding as follows: Wet a third of a bucketful of peat moss thoroughly and mix it with an equal amount of good garden loam and manure; add some dried grass clippings, hay, or crumbled leaves, if you wish. (Don't use oak or other very acidic leaves.) Soak this mixture overnight.

The next day, squeeze out the excess water, and fluff up the material (which we will now call bedding). Line the bottom of the earthworm box with a single layer of pebbles or rocks. Then place 4 inches of the bedding material rather loosely on top of the pebbles, and wait for a day to see if any heating takes place. If initial bacterial action forces the bedding temperature much above 100°F (38°C), all the worms will be killed. Any heating that does occur will subside within 48 hours.

When you are satisfied that the bedding will present no serious heating problems, push aside the bedding material, place the worms and the bedding from their shipping container in the center, and cover them loosely with your bedding. Place a burlap bag, several layers of cheesecloth, or wet newspapers on top of the bedding, and moisten it with a houseplant sprayer or sprinkling can.

Keep the bedding moist but never soggy. If the container begins to drip from the bottom, place some sort of container, such as a plastic dishpan, under the box to catch the drippings. Use the drippings to water your houseplants.

Start out by feeding the earthworms cautiously. If you give them more than they will eat in a 24-hour period, the garbage will sour, creating odors and attracting flies, or it will heat up, killing the worms. Begin with soft foods, such as cooked vegetables, leftover cereal (including the milk), vegetable soup, lettuce, bread scraps, soft leaves of vegetables, even ice cream. A little cornmeal will be appreciated, and coffee grounds can be added at any time. Do not use onions, garlic, or other strongly flavored foods.

Place the food on top of the bedding, and tamp it gently into the bedding. After a week or two, your earthworms should have adjusted to their new home and should be on a regular feeding schedule. You can help them along, and build better compost, if you add a thin layer of partially decayed manure from time to time (being sure that it is past the heating stage but not completely composted).

Every 2 weeks, the bedding in the box should be turned and aerated. Reduce the amount of food after such turnings, since the worms will not come to the surface as readily for a day or two after having been disturbed.

After a month, you can add another 2 inches of bedding material to handle the increased worm population, and after 3 months it will be time to start another box.

When you are ready to divide the box, prepare a second box as you did the first. Then arrange a good-size table under a 100-watt hanging light so that the light comes to within 2 feet of the table surface. Lay a plastic sheet on the

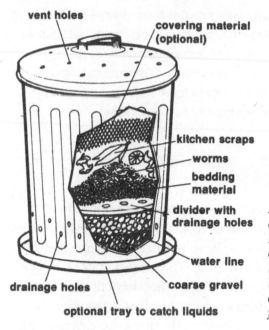

vent holes

covering material
(optional)

kitchen scraps

worms

bedding
material

divider with
drainage holes

water line

drainage holes

coarse gravel

optional tray to catch liquids

A modified plastic garbage cab makes an indoor worm composting bin. Holes allow for ventilation and drainage. Moisture levels are maintained by keeping a few inches of water in a bottom layer of gravel. The worms and bedding materials are separated from the gravel by a round divider.

table. Dump the worms and bedding on the plastic, and heap them into a mound that peaks to within a foot of the lightbulb. Pick off the pebbles and return them to the first box.

Any worms that have been exposed in turning the box will quickly react to the light by digging toward the center of the mound. This will allow you to scrape much of the bedding into a bucket. Wait another 10 minutes, then scrape away another layer of compost. After several such scrapings, all the worms will have dived into a compact ball at the bottom of the mound, where they can easily be divided and put back into fresh bedding in the two boxes.

Boxes can be stacked in tiers by affixing ½-inch-square wood strips, 14 inches high, into the four corners of each box. The strips on one box will support the box on top of it. The boxes can be watered easily with a small houseplant hose or with a portable insecticide sprayer. The drippings from all but the bottom box will fall into the box beneath it.

An even simpler method of indoor worm composting involves a plastic garbage can with some small modifications. A large plastic tote bin will serve as well and can fit into a smaller space. You can make holes for ventilation and drainage with a hot knitting needle, being careful not to breathe the fumes.

Air enters through holes in the lid, and water drains from holes 3 inches above the base. The bottom 6 inches should be filled with a coarse material such as gravel, sitting in 3 inches of water. A wooden barrier between this drainage area and the worms' living quarters prevents you from intermingling the materials when renewing the worms. Be sure to leave some holes to allow water to drain. Proceed to introduce worms and garbage as previously described.

EARTHWORMS ON THE FARM

In the 1940s, US Department of Agriculture scientists Henry Hopp and Clarence Slater found some very poor clay subsoil, containing no earthworms and virtually no organic matter, and by adding lime, fertilizers, and manure, grew a modest stand of barley, bluegrass, and lespedeza on two separate plots. On one, they left the growth untouched, while on the other they cut the topgrowth to form a mulch, and they added some earthworms to the soil.

By the following June, the plot containing earthworms was covered with a rich stand of all three crops, while the section without worms supported almost nothing but weeds. The total vegetation in the wormed plot was five times that of the wormless one. The plot with worms also had far better water-absorbing and water-holding capacity, and twice as many soil aggregates—all the result of earthworm action.

The lesson learned here is one of which every organic farmer should be keenly aware. No soil should be left unprotected over winter. Large-scale mulching and sheet composting will protect earthworm populations, and the earthworms will improve the soil structure and crop-growing capacity.

COMPOST STRUCTURES

Gardeners have designed a host of imaginative structures for composting. Compost can be made in cages, in block or brick bins, in pits and holes, in revolving drums, in garbage cans, and even in plastic trash bags. A compost structure can be designed to be beautiful, to make compost in the shortest possible time, or to be moved from place to place with the least effort. It can be designed to make compost with no turning required or to suit the needs of earthworms. Compost structures, in short, are designed to suit the user's needs and resources.

For most home composters, building a bin that makes use of existing or readily available materials is the most practical course. A composter in California constructed a bin using the aluminum sides of an old aboveground swimming pool. Even using bales of spoiled hay to form a temporary structure is a way to make the most of your resources in creating a composting structure, as well as the compost pile itself.

The choice of compost structure is, then, a personal decision, one that should not be made without some prior research and, perhaps even more important, some experimentation. It is experimentation that leads to new structures.

The first decision to be made is whether a structure is needed at all. The gardener or farmer with plenty of room, ample materials, and sufficient time may need no compost enclosure of any kind. In this case, the traditional Indore heap is quite suitable.

If yours is a city or suburban lot, however, you might find that the open heap takes up too much room or offends neighbors and family. If space is limited, an enclosure can produce more compost in a smaller land area. It can be more attractive and keep out animals and flies. If you cannot devote a permanent spot to compost making, you will want to investigate portable structures that can be broken down and moved in minutes. If your garden is located where winter temperatures are severe, a compost pit dug below the frost line can enable you to compost all winter long. If you want to work with earthworms in composting, then you will need to consider some special outdoor structures, and perhaps others for basement composting. Perhaps a commercially built revolving drum suits your needs because age or infirmity prevents you from turning the heap, or simply because the drum produces quick compost and attracts no pests. Perhaps you even prefer to make compost in plastic bags because of its simplicity.

It is certainly true that one compost structure is not best for everyone. It may even be that everyone needs a structure designed especially for him or her. We hope that by describing different structures, we will give you some insight into matching construction with your individual needs. If you are like most gardeners, you will take one of these suggested forms, adapt it to your needs, use it for a year or two, and then make your own adjustments until you have evolved the perfect structure for you.

PENS AND BINS

By far the most common compost forms are bins and pens. To simplify, let us call a bin any container with concrete, brick, wood, or masonry sides that is fairly substantial and permanent, and a pen any structure with wire or hardware cloth sides that is a less permanent installation. Not that they're that easy to classify—there are many kinds of structures called bins and pens.

In general, pens have the advantage of allowing for free circulation of air. Their disadvantage is that they also allow for free circulation of flies and four-footed pests. Bins are more stable and protecting structures, but they are often insufficiently ventilated. Neither the bin nor the pen has as great a tendency to go anaerobic as the pit, and both are easier to keep tidy than open composting forms.

A shady, sheltered spot not far from either garden or kitchen is an ideal location for either pen or bin. Often, a space between house and garage or garage and shed allows the right amount of room. A three-compartment bin

The Lehigh bin uses alternating 2×4s held together with ⅜-inch rods.

with tight floor and sides and with each compartment measuring a cubic yard in size makes for the neatest and easiest handling for turning. In such a structure, there is at all times one batch working and one being used.

An advocate of bottom aeration claims to have made a free compost bin in 1 hour using available cement blocks and some leftover strong iron piping, plus surplus 1- by 2-inch wire mesh. The 4- by 8- by 16-inch cement blocks were laid horizontally with plenty of air between each block.

The pipes were thrust across the bin from side to side over the third course of blocks, to provide the pile with a strong bed. On top of the pipes, two lengths of wide wire mesh were laid to hold a bottom layer of coarse garden debris and twigs. This layer and the mesh and pipes held back finer material and allowed for bottom aeration. The gardener never turns his compost but mixes materials together.

Lehigh-Type Bins

The Lehigh-style bin is easy to erect and disassemble. It is adjustable in size, attractive, portable, and long lasting, and it provides for proper ventilation and protection.

Construction is of alternating 2x4s with the corners drilled out and held together with $3/8$-inch rods. Five 36-inch 2x4s to a side will make a bin capable of producing approximately 1 cubic yard of compost at a time.

There have been several variations of the Lehigh bin, some using logs or poles instead of 2x4s. However it is designed, the low cost, effectiveness, and portability of this structure has made it one of the most popular in use today.

Cage-Type Bins

Cage-type bins are simple and inexpensive to build, allow good air circulation, are portable, and enable quick turning of the heap because of a removable front panel. The Lehigh bin lacks this last feature.

There are many variations of cage-type bins, all of which require relatively little lumber, since wire screening forms most of the panels.

The wire-and-wood bin shown on page 199 can be built using scrap 2-inch lumber covered with $1/2$-inch chicken wire mesh. The bin is formed by two L-shaped sections held together with screen-door hooks.

To turn the pile, unhook the sides and reassemble the two sections next to the now freestanding pile. Layers can be easily peeled off with a pitchfork and tossed into the empty cage. Keep a hose handy during turning, to add moisture as needed. A properly built and maintained pile in this well-aerated bin can produce 18 to 24 cubic feet of finished compost in 14 days.

The New Zealand Bin

Perhaps the classic among compost bins is the wooden New Zealand box that was originally designed by the Auckland Humic Compost Club to admit as much air as possible from all sides. It can be used to make several batches of compost in different stages of decomposition, ensuring a continuous supply, and it can be a very attractive structure.

There are several variations of this box, but the simplest one is a wooden structure 4 feet square and 3 feet high or higher with neither top nor bottom. The frame is held together by 2x4s. The wooden sides consist of pieces of wood

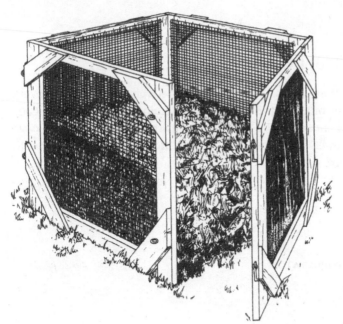

The wire-and-wood cage-type bin is inexpensive and portable.

The variation on the standard New Zealand box is divided to allow production of several successive batches of compost at once.

Project

Building a Rodent-Proof Composter

Before rodents discover that your compost is a steady supply of kitchen leftovers, you may want to consider building this caged compost bin. Lap-joint construction for the 2x4 framing was chosen for its simplicity and strength. A hardware-cloth lining supported by 1- by 3-inch and 1- by 2¼-inch stock keeps the pile neatly contained and animals out.

Tools required

Electric drill

Screwdriver

Saw (circular saw or handsaw)

Hammer

Paintbrush

Wire cutters

Materials

Lumber—cut list

Cut lumber into the following lengths. Use untreated pine painted with a preservative or flat black paint. Measure and cut the pieces as you assemble them, to be sure they fit together correctly.

2 pcs. 36" x 2" x 4" (frame sides)

2 pcs. 33" x 2" x 4" (frame sides)

4 pcs. 16" x 2" x 4" (legs)

4 pcs. 14⅞" x 2" x 4" (support braces)

5 pcs. 32¾" x 2" x 4" (bottom frame)

4 pcs. 16½" x 1" x 3" (corner braces)

11 pcs. 32¾" x 1" x 3" (top and horizontal large frame sides)

4 pcs. 31⅛" x 1" x 3" (horizontal small frame sides)

4 pcs. 32" x 1" x 3" (vertical large frame sides)

4 pcs. 32" x 1" x 2¼" (vertical small frame sides)

Hardware

- **4 medium hasps**
- **2 hinges, 1½" x 2½"**
- **36 wood screws, #10 x 1½"**
- **16 pcs. 16d common nails**
- **1 pound 4d common nails**
- **16' x 36" hardware cloth ½" x ½"**
- **½" staples**

Construction

1. Assemble the base as shown in the illustration using #10 by 1½-inch wood screws at the corners. The 2x4 pieces bearing the load of the compost are cut at 45-degree angles at both ends and nailed across the corners with four 16d common nails in each piece. The leg braces are also cut at 45-degree angles and fastened with #10 by 1½-inch wood screws as shown.

2. To construct the bottom support frame, remove half the thickness of the wood on each end to a length that is equal to the width of the 2x4 (usually 3½ inches) on all

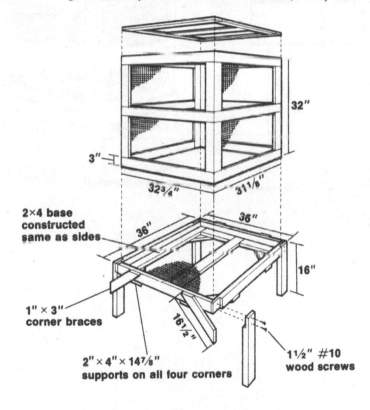

32"

3"

32¾"

31⅛"

2×4 base constructed same as sides

36"

36"

16"

1" × 3" corner braces

16½"

2" × 4" × 14⅞" supports on all four corners

1½" #10 wood screws

five pieces. On two pieces, cut a groove (dado) half the thickness of the stock at the center to accommodate the middle support. Use #10 by 1½-inch wood screws for assembly, two per joint.

3. The remaining side frames and top are cut and assembled the same way as the base with the exception of using 4d common nails instead of screws at each joint and clinching on the reverse side.

4. For easy access to the compost, hasps are fastened to the top corners of the side frames, and two 2½- by 1½-inch hinges are attached to the top. Paint the entire unit with a good grade of enamel paint or a nontoxic wood preserver. After the paint has dried, cut pieces of ½- by ½-inch hardware cloth to fit the interior of all frames, and attach them with ½-inch staples.

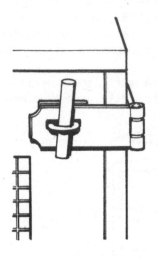

The four side frames are joined at their tops with hasps and easily removed pegs.

The hinged top frame permits easy access to compost.

6 inches wide by 1 inch thick. A $\frac{1}{2}$-inch air space is allowed between every two boards so that air may penetrate into the heap from all sides. The boarding in front slides down between two posts so that boards can be removed one by one when complete access to the contents is needed for turning or loading. The open side may also be built up gradually as the pen is filled. Cover the top of the pen with hardware cloth, rolled canvas, burlap, or screen.

If you are using a single bin like the New Zealand box, be sure to allow for a working space in front of the box equal to two or three times the floor area of the box. This much space is needed for turning the pile. You pile up the material outside the bin and then replace it within the bin, mixing so the outside material is placed toward the inside of the new pile.

One variation on the New Zealand box holds four separate bins for compost in different stages. The dividers between the compartments are removable to permit quick and easy shifting of compost from one bin to another.

🌱 USING YOUR THREE-BIN COMPOSTER

The following week-by-week schedule will help you get the most from your three-bin composter. The schedule is self-perpetuating. Check moisture content when you transfer compost from bin to bin. Add dry material if it seems soggy; water it it's too dry. To boost microbial activity, mix some soil or active compost into the material from the holding bin when you transfer it to the center bin.

Week 1: In the center bin, build a traditional layered compost heap, including high-nitrogen materials such as manure or alfalfa meal. Spread a base layer of dry leaves or straw in the holding bin; toss in kitchen wastes or garden trimmings every day or so.

Weeks 2 and 3: Remove a few front boards from the center bin and stir the compost. Keep adding to the holding bin.

Week 4: Remove all front boards from the center and end bins, and transfer the compost to the end bin to speed the composting process. Then remove the front boards from the holding bin and shovel that material into the center bin. Finally, spread a new layer of dry matter in the holding bin.

Week 5: Check the compost in the end bin. It should be ready to use on your garden.

Block and Brick Bins

Block and brick bins are permanent if mortared, but cement block bins can be constructed without mortar and can then be moved at will.

The block or brick bin is easily constructed. Usually, blocks are laid to permit plenty of open spaces for air circulation. But they can also be closely stacked, set into the ground, and mortared together, or formed into a cylindrical shape with an access gate at the bottom.

Gardeners who insist on a well-groomed compost area may prefer to have a large, rectangular, brick or block, chimneylike structure with several compartments. Use wooden hinged lids to cover the structure. In a three-bin unit, the first two bins are used in turning while the third stores finished compost. The bottom of the bin, if made of concrete, should slant one way so drainage may be caught in a gutter leading to storage cans. A combination of bricks and boards may be used, with boards set into slots along the front opening. Boards can be removed for access to the compost.

Rough stones laid with or without mortar in an open-fronted, three-fourths cylinder shape (like a larger edition of a state park barbecue pit) make an attractive rustic bin.

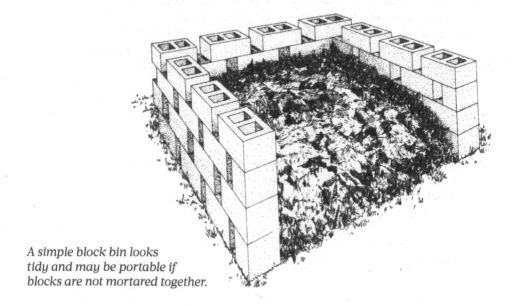

A simple block bin looks tidy and may be portable if blocks are not mortared together.

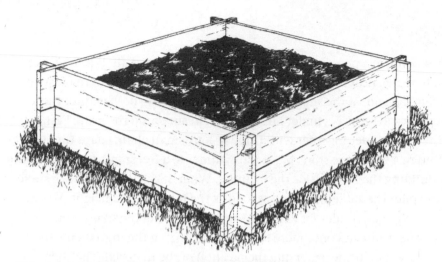

This simple bin is made from slotted boards and can be easily moved.

The Movable Slat Bin

Another type of portable bin can be constructed of wooden slats. This bin needs no hardware for support—no hooks, nails, or screws.

To make it, cut 10-foot-long 1- by 10 inch boards into 60-inch lengths. Slot each board 4 inches in from the end, $4^5/_8$ inches across its width, so the boards can be nested, as shown. The finished bin is $5^1/_4$ inches square and $18^1/_4$ inches high inside—perfect for even the smallest lot.

Winter Bins

Winter composting does not have to be confined to a pit. An existing compost bin, well insulated with bales of straw or hay and covered for protection from the elements, can continue the composting process during cold temperatures, although at a slower rate than during warmer weather. Structures similar to cold frames can also be used for cold-weather composting, using south-slanting glass lids to catch the rays of the sun and protect the heaps from rain, snow, and drying winds. Manure added to such bins helps to keep temperatures high enough for microbial activity.

PENS

The very simplest pen can hardly be called a structure at all. It is, however, quick to make, neat to use, and it costs little. You just buy a length of woven-wire fencing and, at the site of the compost heap, bring both ends of the fencing together to form a cylinder large enough to surround the heap. Fasten the ends of the cylinder together with three or four small chain snaps that you can find in a hardware store. Move the cylinder to a freestanding position and start building the heap inside the cylinder. When it is half full, drive a stake into the pile. The stake should be as long as the total desired height. You can disassemble the cylinder for easy turning by removing the snaps. You set the cylinder up again and once more turn into it, shifting the ingredients from outside layers to inside, reversing the position of the material. The stake not only helps maintain the shape of the pile but also aids in directing water into the heap.

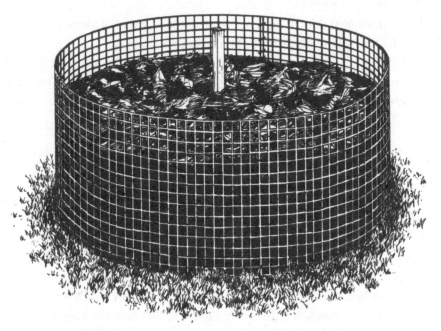

A hardware-cloth cylinder forms a very simple, movable pen.

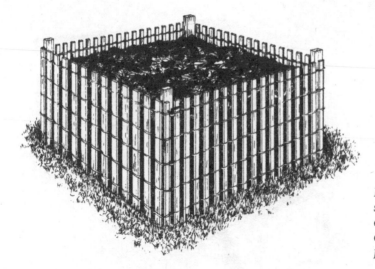

Recycled materials, such as snow fence, can be used to construct a compost pen.

A partly anaerobic version of the woven-wire cylinder is lined with a length of roll roofing that is wired to the fencing. The roofing is durable and prevents small bits and pieces from falling out of the bin.

After the bin is full, it is covered with a layer of 6-mil black plastic and left to decompose. Turning is not necessary with this system, although composting will take longer and high temperatures will not last long enough to kill weed seeds.

A refinement of the all-wire pen is the wire-and-tomato-stake pen in which ½-inch-mesh poultry netting is placed inside an enclosure made by driving 4-foot tomato stakes 1 foot apart in a 10- by 5-foot rectangle and looping baling wire around the top of each stake to weave all stakes together. Small pieces of wire hold the poultry netting to the stakes. Use additional lengths of wire to reinforce the top. These pass from side to side and keep the stakes from spreading apart under the pressure of the compost. These wires are removed when the compost is turned. This type of structure is movable and reusable. However, neither pen will resist large dogs or tunneling rats.

Recycled hardwood pallets make excellent compost bins. They can be quickly assembled by driving in fence posts at the corners. A chicken wire or hardware-cloth liner serves as a rodent barrier.

Other materials that can be used to construct pens include snow fences, lattice fencing, steel posts and chicken wire, furring strips, prefabricated picket fence sections, woven-reed or rattan fence sections, heavy window

Stair-stepped bins make use of a sloped area.

screens, storm windows with hardware cloth replacing glass, and louvered house blinds.

Pens and bins can be made to fit the contours of uneven land. One such structure consists of three bins in stair-step order going up a hill, partially cut into the bank. This can work well if your home sits on a rise above the location of the garden. Composting starts in the highest bin. The pile is turned by dropping the partially decomposed compost down a step, inverting it in the process. The second turning goes into the third box. The finished compost can then be removed from the lowest box.

PITS

Pits for composting are dug into the ground and may be partially–or wholly–underground. The chief advantage of the pit form is its stable, secure, insulated structure. A masonry-lined, covered or coverable pit is secure from dogs, rats, clever raccoons, most flies, and wind and rainstorms. Pit composting is ideal for severe winter weather because subsurface ground warmth and the heat-retaining properties of concrete enable bacteria to go on working longer. Some Northern composters have a pen for summer and a pit for winter.

However, proper composting does not take place in a pit when compost becomes soggy and anaerobic. Provide some drainage to lessen the possibility of anaerobic conditions. Improper aeration and the greater possibility of anaerobic conditions remain, however, the two greatest drawbacks to pit composting. If you have the time to turn frequently and don't mind the extra strain on your back muscles in raising forkfuls of material from a lower-than normal position, you may find ways to avoid these problems. Some pits are large and wide enough so that a person can stand at pit-bottom level while turning.

A compost pit can be built of concrete or masonry. It is not advisable to use pressure-treated wood, which generally contains toxic heavy metals that can leach into the compost, as a pit liner. A pit must have subsurface walls to prevent drainage water from entering the compost from the soil or the ground surface. Such drainage water would leach nutrients from the compost.

A useful combination of a composting method and a compost-containing structure is the earthworm pit. Earthworms aid in aerating and mixing the materials, thus eliminating some of the drawbacks of anaerobic pits. The pit, in turn, helps protect the worms from cold weather. More details on earthworm composting are given in Chapter 9.

One gardener combined the earthworm pit with the movable-box method. He dug a rectangular hole about 18 inches deep in a flowerbed. At earth level over the pit he placed a rectangular, bottomless, and topless wooden box of slightly larger dimensions than the hole. The hole was filled in layer style with kitchen garbage, manure, and green matter. When the frame was filled, too, the composter placed a board over the top and watered well. In 3 weeks, when the heat of the pile had decreased, earthworms were added.

Another successful pit is the one used by a New York State gardener. It is 4 feet wide, 4 feet deep, and 6 feet long with concrete sides and bottom. The bottom has an inset drainage grid similar to those used in basements and showers. Walls are 8 inches thick and project 18 inches above the ground. The top is made of tongue-and-groove boards nailed to 2x4s. A hinged lid provides access. Earthworms do the work of aeration in this pit, and garbage and leaves are the chief materials used.

An inexpensive pit may be made by digging a section of a masonry flue liner into the soil, leaving about 3 inches of it projecting above ground level. A thin layer of concrete poured into the pipe serves as the floor. A small flue liner 2 feet square may not require bottom drainage if earthworms are used, but check frequently for anaerobic conditions. Terra-cotta tiles are also useful for lining pits. These can be used for the sides in combination with a hardware cloth bottom to prevent rats from getting in from underneath. Build twin pits to make the turning job easier.

DRUMS

Where space limitations or offending odors are concerns, composting in drums provides an alternative to bins, pens, and pits. A metal or plastic barrel, with drainage holes in the bottom, can be raised off the ground with bricks or blocks to permit aeration. Layering kitchen wastes with absorbent materials like shredded paper or straw can help control odors; without turning or rolling, this method produces compost slowly but does provide a place for waste disposal.

STRUCTURES FOR CITY COMPOSTING

Is there any perfect form of compost making for a city gardener? Helga and Bill Olkowski, in *The City People's Book of Raising Food*, suggest a well-built two- or three-bin brick structure set between two houses. Runoff is caught in sawdust at the bottom of the bin, and the sawdust is turned with the pile. As garbage accumulates on its way to the bin, the Olkowskis layer it with sawdust in 5-gallon cans with tight-fitting lids. Sawdust is added every time fresh garbage is put into the can. The sawdust controls odor and putrefaction. In loading the bins, however, you should remember to compensate for the high-carbon content of the sawdust by using more high-nitrogen wastes.

Other city gardeners, who lack even a small space between houses, have composted successfully in garbage pails and metal drums. The danger with these methods is that they may quite easily become anaerobic and ferment. If you think it is hard enough dealing with garbage in a city, you should try to take care of a huge drum of fermented garbage. If, however, you really need to try these methods, provide aeration and drainage with holes in the bottom and sides of the drum or can. Set it in the basement or another protected area, preferably outdoors. Elevate the can or drum on bricks or concrete blocks, and set a pan, larger in diameter than the drum, underneath it to catch drainage.

🌱 GARBAGE CAN COMPOSTING

Use this system to compost kitchen scraps during winter, or use it year-round to compost all the waste produced by a small yard and garden.

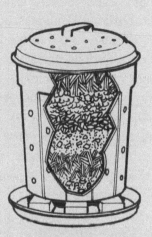

Directions

Use a hammer and a large nail to punch holes in the bottom, sides, and lid of a garbage can. Place the can on a large tray to catch draining liquid if desired.

To start the composting, place a 3-inch layer of finished compost or soil in the bottom of the can. Add finely chopped kitchen scraps followed by an equal amount of shredded newspaper, grass clippings, and/or shredded leaves. Add more material as available until the can is full, then layer new materials into another can and allow the first to finish composting—about 3 to 4 months.

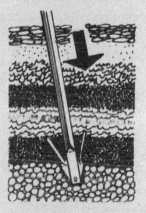

Tips to Make Your Composter Work Its Best

- Protect the composter from freezing temperatures—put it in a garage or cellar.
- Start with soil or finished compost, and add a little more on top of each addition.
- Chop, shred, or even blend all additions as finely as possible.
- Add kitchen scraps before they start to smell.
- Mix the composting material after each addition and every few days. If you don't, it may produce unpleasant odors. Stir with a stick, roll the can back and forth on its side a few times, or use a compost-turning tool.
- Add water sparingly and only if your materials are very dry.

Layer garbage with high-carbon-content materials just as you would in a regular pile. Composting is not really an indoor activity, and turning is especially hard to do in a limited space.

Trash cans can be used more readily for outdoor composting by cutting out the bottoms and setting them firmly into the ground to prevent tipping. California composter Helene Cole suggests using several of them and simply waiting 6 to 12 months for the finished product. Chopping your wastes first will speed up the process. A few air holes drilled in the lid will keep the earthworms that do most of the work in this system happy.

Another much more sensible indoor method is the earthworm box discussed in Chapter 9. Worms are easily raised in basements where fairly stable temperature conditions can be maintained. Worms do the turning in worm boxes, and the results of their labors are rich worm castings for compost and perhaps a little extra income for you during fishing season. If you live in an apartment, discuss composting or worm-raising plans with your landlord before launching your career. In mild climates, a worm box can work happily on a balcony or terrace.

Refer to the Appendix for sources of nifty urban-appropriate barrel composters and fully enclosed bins that are vermin-proof and may also include odor-control structures.

COMMERCIAL COMPOSTERS

A number of very good commercially produced composting units are now on the market. Generally built on the revolving-drum or upright-cylinder principle, these structures are designed to produce high-quality compost quickly and with a minimal effort on the part of the user. Articles in the *Wall Street Journal* have noted that commercial composting units represent overkill for most people, since similar composting conditions can be created without a commercial bin. Constraints on space, time, and physical ability, however, will continue to make such products appealing to many home composters.

The Green Cone is a smaller, cone-shaped composter designed to decompose kitchen wastes. This closed, sun-heated composter features a below-ground basket for contact with the soil and a double-walled plastic cone to collect heat from the sun. Relatively small and innocuous looking, the Green Cone can be located close to the kitchen for easy waste disposal, but it is not

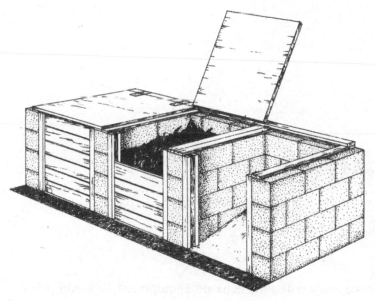

A covered, multi-bin structure works well for urban and suburban composting.

meant to handle yard wastes and produces very little compost. These Green Cones are sometimes distributed by local waste management offices to help reduce the amount of organic materials heading to the landfill.

A list of online retailers of composting units and supplies is included in "Equipment and Tool Sources" starting on page 283. In general, these composters are designed for small-lot gardeners who want to make compost quickly and without offending the neighbors or attracting animals. Although such conditions can be met with a homemade bin, commercial composters offer valid alternatives for an efficient, attractive composting unit.

11

SHREDDERS AND OTHER EQUIPMENT

Compost can easily be made without mechanical equipment. However, more compost can be made–in a shorter time–when the materials are first shredded or ground. For this reason, the compost shredder has become a standard fixture in many gardens and small farms. Shredder design has been improved over the years, and modern shredders bear little resemblance to those primitive, bulky, and often dangerous models of the past. (See the Appendix for a list of companies and websites offering garden and composting equipment.)

There are many advantages to using a shredder as part of a home composting program. The benefits of shredding compostable materials include the following:

- **Speed.** Your compost piles really will heat up and break down within 2 weeks because the shredder chews the compostable materials into small bits, making the job of the decomposers much easier.
- **Quantity.** You'll have plenty of compost when you need it, provided you keep working at the shredder.
- **Quality.** You'll have better, more uniform compost because the shredder breaks up the materials more thoroughly.
- **Mixtures.** You can "mix your own" right at the machine, to ensure a balance of nutrients or to make a compost specially designed to meet the needs of your soil.

- **Variety.** You can readily set up a program using different kinds of mulches and composts for various parts of the garden.

There is another factor about the compost shredder that will appeal to the hardworking gardener—it's a tool you can bring to the work. This is a real boon to the compost maker who wants to have several heaps piled up in the garden where they are needed. The movable shredder makes this easy because it can go to work wherever the ground is reasonably level.

Shredders are designed to do big garden jobs for you. First, they can speed and ease your task of preparing mulches. Cut-up and macerated leaves, weeds, and other similar materials make much better mulch than the rough raw product because they hold moisture better and form a thicker blanket that chokes off the weeds.

The shredder is especially useful when you are getting ready to build your compost heap. Again, it will take the raw stock and chew it into the kind of shape that eases the job of the decomposers in your pile.

A third use that contributes to shredder popularity is the grinding and pulverizing job it can do with finished compost. The fine compost that can be achieved is ideal for potting soil and for use on lawns, in flowerbeds, in greenhouses, and in other "high-quality" jobs.

If you buy a shredder, you may find that you no longer have to travel far and wide in search of compostable materials. One gardener describes having changed his whole view of his trees, shrubs, and hedges after acquiring a shredder—now they are sources of trimmings that can be readily made into compost.

Interest in shredding equipment has grown in recent years, spurred by legislative restrictions on yard waste disposal, and equipment manufacturers have responded with a wide variety of machines. Shredders currently on the market range from small electric units designed to shred leaves and kitchen wastes, to units combining a chipper/shredder with a leaf vacuum/blower, to heavy-duty chipper/shredders capable of reducing 3-inch-thick limbs to a fine mulch. Prices are equally variable; chipper/shredders range in cost from about $150 for a small electric leaf shredder to more than $1,500 for a heavy-duty, 15-horsepower model.

Options and accessories have expanded the applications of home shredding equipment. As with many types of power machinery, operators are no longer forced to struggle with pull starters; electric models are available, and many gas-powered machines come equipped with electric starters. The majority of shredders are actually chipper/shredders—with a chute for feeding hard-to-shred materials like branches and cornstalks to a knifelike chipping blade.

Large-size hoppers for feeding in leaves are offered as accessories on many machines, as well as screens and grates of varying sizes to allow a variety of materials to be shredded. Other options include collection bags for catching shredded material and tow bars that allow some units to be pulled behind garden tractors.

FEATURES TO CONSIDER

Like any major purchase, selecting a chipper/shredder requires evaluation of several factors before buying. When choosing a machine that will be a valuable asset to your composting efforts, compare the type of materials you expect to shred and the ease of moving the shredder to your composting area with the durability of both the whole unit and its cutting mechanisms. Consider power sources: Is electricity available, or do you want a gas-powered unit? Are you satisfied with the safety features and the warranty? Finally, do the level of use you plan for your machine and the quality of the resulting shredded material justify the cost of the purchase?

Some heavy-duty chipper/shredders are capable of chopping up branches as thick as 3 inches in diameter and can shred large volumes of organic materials.

Materials

Anything that is organic and compostable, and can be reduced to a workable aggregate or mass in your shredder, is grist to your grinding mill. Large-scale gardeners find that there is plenty of material on the home grounds to keep the shredder busy for a series of weekends, particularly in the late summer and fall. There are the weeds, the grass clippings, the crop residues, and the leaves. Add to these the contents of your garbage pail and other household wastes, and you will have no trouble finding material to shred.

Next, you might be able to get wood chips from the municipal road department, sawdust from a local lumberyard, and corncobs from the nearest feed mill. All of these varieties of cellulose are fine for mixing with the garbage (so long as the cobs are ground up). If the cobs have not been ground, then you should go slowly. Experimentation is called for here, since tough cobs have a habit of flying back up out of the hopper, right at your head. Some gardeners have reported that thoroughly soaking the cobs—up to a week under water—softens them and makes shredding easier and less dangerous. Some of the larger machines can handle cobs with no difficulty at all.

No garden chore is easier or more pleasant than shredding dry autumn leaves. But if your leaves have wintered over and are tough, wet, and rubbery, feed them into the shredder in very small handfuls followed by dry sawdust, and be prepared to stop occasionally to clear the screen.

The Cutting Mechanisms

There are three or four basic systems for reducing and mixing your organic wastes. In one system, hammermill tempered-steel flails revolve freely on a rotating shaft and so have the ability to absorb shocks from hitting stones. There also seems to be a minimum of blockage in the mixing chamber caused by wet materials.

Another system uses sets of hardened-steel teeth or knives, fixed rigidly on a revolving shaft, working in combination with interior baffle plates and the bottom screen that together tend to keep the material in contact with the knives.

The smaller shredder/bagger machines work with a series of two or three rotary blades similar to those of a lawn mower. In some models, these

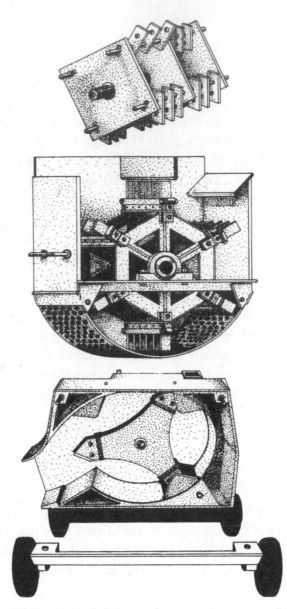

There are three types of cutting mechanisms used in most shredders: (top) *steel flails that revolve freely on a rotating shaft;* (middle) *fixed steel knives on a revolving shaft, working in combination with baffle plates and a bottom screen;* and (bottom) *rotary blades similar to those on a lawn mower.*

whirling knives pass between stationary cutters that are part of the frame or chassis to achieve more complete cutting. The turbulence created by the rotary blades also whirls the aggregate out through the vent that permits you to deposit it right where it is needed—either in the compost pile or in the planting row.

At least one shredder now on the market uses nylon line, like that used in string trimmers, as a cutting mechanism for shredding leaves and other relatively "soft" materials.

Shredder Design

The design of a shredder has much to do with its efficiency in shredding wet or dry materials. In general, shredders can be divided into two types. Indirect-feed shredders work well on dry or damp refuse, but they may perform poorly on wet, sticky compost, soils, and manures. Direct-feed shredders handle both dry and wet materials, although some designs within this group work better on wet materials than others.

The main difference between the two types lies in the design of the rotor assembly and its relationship to the feed-hopper throat. The illustration below shows the generalized construction and refuse flow of indirect-feed shredders. The feed hopper is mounted on the side of the shredding chamber, and the rotor assembly (the rotating hardware that does the shredding) passes in front of the hopper throat at 90 degrees to the movement of refuse in the hopper. When the refuse enters the shredding chamber, the rotor assembly blades

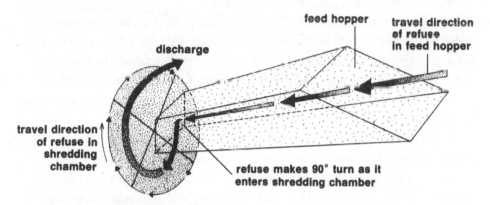

An indirect-feed shredder design.

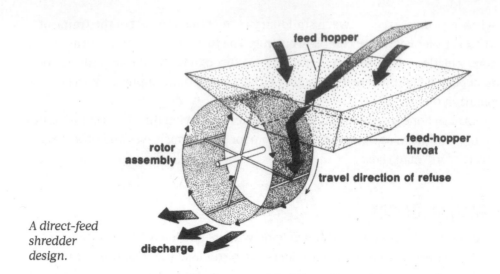

feed hopper

rotor assembly

feed-hopper throat

travel direction of refuse

discharge

A direct-feed shredder design.

smash into it. Because the rotor assembly spins rapidly, the time interval between blades striking the refuse is very short. Therefore, the rotor blades smash the material into very small pieces. The spinning rotor assembly sucks the fragments around the circular shredding chamber before they're blown from the discharge chute.

The illustration above shows a typical direct-feed shredder with rigid tines on the periphery of the rotor assembly. The tines are short, narrow pieces of steel that tear refuse apart. For fragment size control, most rigid-tine shredders use some combination of (1) adjustable discharge door, (2) semipermanent screen or bar grate, and (3) baffle plate.

The baffle plate forces the refuse in the shredding chamber against the tines. A powerful spring holds the baffle closed while the rotor assembly tries to push refuse past the baffle. The greater the spring tension, the more the baffle will slow the travel of refuse through the shredder. Once shredded refuse moves past the baffle, the tines carry the fragments over a curved piece of perforated metal.

If the piece of metal has round holes, it's called perforated metal. If it has slots, it's called a bar grate. The screens and bar grates in this style of shredder are securely bolted to the lower front of the shredding chamber. Fragments smaller than the holes or slots are driven through, while larger pieces are swept around the shredding chamber and further reduced in size. Screens and bar grates perform well for sizing dry leaves, stems, and vines. The fragments pass easily through the screen and pile up near the front of the shredder.

But if you try shredding wet, sticky material, the screens and bar grates will soon plug. Therefore, most rigid-tine shredders have an adjustable discharge door located at the top front of the shredding chamber. The rotor assembly twirls any soggy refuse around the shredding chamber, across the plugged screen, and to the open discharge door, where it is kicked from the shredder. Since this refuse is only partly shredded, when your pile is drier, you'll probably want to reshred it with the discharge door partly closed. This second shredding will give you smaller fragments that will decompose quicker in your compost pile.

However, if you want to aerate wet, half-finished compost, you may run into problems. Since wet refuse tends to plug screens, you may have to remove the screen before feeding the refuse. Shredding without a screen won't give you much size reduction but will aerate your compost, thus speeding it toward complete decomposition.

Jamming and Clogging

Overloading the machine—any machine—will result in jamming and stalling. This is especially true when you are shredding fibrous, damp, or wet materials. Work with as large a screen as possible—1³/₄ inches is ideal. Some manufacturers offer a grating of rods or square roller bars that seem to be nearly jam-proof. Another solution to the problem is a rack that encloses only half the shredding chamber, available on some models.

If possible, shred leaves when they are dry. Allow green, leafy trimmings to wilt in the sun for a day before shredding. Mixing wet and dry materials together can also reduce clogging running a handful or two of dry wood chips through the shredder will carry out much of the softer, clinging material that can jam the machine. If you are shredding very wet, soggy, and rubbery leaves, work slowly, alternating drier materials with the leaves, and plan to stop occasionally to clear the screen, grate, or collection bag opening.

In the best case, your shredder will have a screen or grate size appropriate for the material being shredded. Operating a shredder without a screen or grate should be done only if it is in keeping with the manufacturer's safety recommendations.

A clutch–either a centrifugal clutch, which depends upon the speed of the motor to activate it, or one that is manually operated–helps to avoid jams. This calls for alert operation of the machine, but it can save a lot of time spent in clearing out the shredding chamber. Some models also offer a king-size, spring-held, stone-ejection plate that is a real time-saver. A quick tug on its handle opens up the mixing chamber and spills the damp mass out to save you still another jam. By all means, ask about these plates when shopping around for a shredder.

Machine Mobility

Wheels are important. In the spring and autumn, you will want to wheel your shredder right down the garden rows, shredding leaves and crop residues right where the next crop will be planted. Check the wheels on the shredders you are considering. They should have at least a pair, rugged and rubber tired and placed so that they will support the machine with ease, comfort, and safety when you move it. Some of the larger models come with three wheels, and others have four. Make sure the machine you are thinking of buying handles easily over rough ground.

SAFETY FIRST

It is a good idea to get into the habit of wearing both safety shoes and safety glasses when operating the shredder. Shredders, especially gas-powered models, can be very noisy when running; use earplugs or some other type of hearing protection when operating your machine. If yours is an electric model, be certain that it is properly grounded, and do not operate it under wet or damp conditions. To avoid danger in feeding materials into the hopper, make use of a flexible stick as a pusher. A large sunflower stalk works well and later can be fed to the machine as "dessert." A rigid stick may jam the machine or even bounce back to injure the operator. Many shredders include a feeding stick or pushing device to help you direct materials into the hopper. Stand clear of the exhaust chute while the machine is in operation; flying shreds and pellets of cellulose can feel like buckshot. Some shredder or mulcher models come with pivoting metal rods with which the operator maneuvers the material into place and directs it downward. The temptation is to use your hands instead.

When operating a shredder, tie back long hair and wear gloves, close-fitting long pants and long sleeves, goggles, and hearing protectors.

Resist this temptation. Shredders have no way of discriminating between sticks and fingers, and they will shred either quite easily. For maximum safety, always follow the usage guidelines provided by the manufacturer and wear appropriate clothing and safety equipment.

RENT OR BUY?

Gardeners on a small scale might find that the most economical way to gain the advantages of a shredder without making the investment is to rent a machine in spring and fall and to prepare enough material for several compost piles at one time. Material to be shredded can be stored in heaps, located strategically around the garden, until the shredder is rented. Materials, once shredded, can again be stored until garbage or partially rotted manure becomes available to use with it. It is less important to grind soft garbage than to reduce the size of fibrous material; and since garbage is often the slowest material to accumulate and the hardest to store, stockpiles of fibrous material already shredded are handy to have around.

Rental fees for shredder use are high, but then so are the costs of purchasing shredders. Part of the high rental rates reflects the fact that shredders are in great demand during certain weeks of the year, while they stand idle for most of the rest of the year. Nevertheless, if you can manage your operations so that you can get by with shredding facilities for only a few days of the year, then you will save money by renting one.

A shredder lends itself well to group ownership. A garden club, a group of friends, or a neighborhood might well consider making a joint investment, sharing the responsibilities for its care and fueling.

SUBSTITUTES FOR THE SHREDDER

Not ready to make a purchase or spring for a rental? You can create similar results with other garden and household tools.

The Rotary Mower

If you have no access to a shredder or a grinder, you can use a rotary mower to grind up straw, weeds, and leaves. Sometimes a mower works even better than a shredder on dry leaves.

For mowers with side exit ports, use a carton or fence, or the side of your compost bin, as a backstop. If your mower can be adjusted, set it for cutting high. Pile up the material in low piles. Then depress the handle of your mower and push the machine forward until the blades are positioned directly above the pile. Lower the machine gradually into the pile, lifting it and dropping it again several times. If the mower seems to be on the point of stalling, depress the handle again to lift the cutting blades. For really fine grinding, repeat the process. Mulching mowers are ideal for this use, since they cut the materials more than once on a single pass.

The Meat Cleaver

Helga and Bill Olkowski, in *The City People's Book of Raising Food*, report that they discovered that coarse materials like melon rinds, dry weed stalks, or straw decompose more rapidly when cut into short lengths of 3 to 8 inches. Convinced of the need to reduce the size of their materials, the Olkowskis bought a shredder. The noise, the danger, the tendency to jam, and the fuel consumption of their machine soon persuaded them that they had made an unwise investment. Finally, they went back to their old method of using a cleaver to shred and chop material.

The Olkowskis' experience points out once more that the choice of grinding or chopping method, like many other choices in composting, is up to you. No one should tell you that you must have a shredder to make good compost. Composters agree that shredders and grinders save time, especially in large gardens. Shredded material composts more rapidly, and machine shredding is quicker than hand shredding. Time saving, then, is on one side of the ledger. Fuel consumption, machine cost, and noise are on the other side. Only you can place a value on your time in relationship to these other factors.

The Food Processor

Some composters use electric blenders, food processors, or meat grinders to reduce household garbage to particles. Meat grinders are painfully slow. Blenders are quicker but can reduce garbage to a pulp that tends to cake when dried out. Food processors are perfect—highly efficient, miniature shredders that will quickly and easily shred materials to your specifications.

Kitchen garbage, of course, doesn't have to be shredded or ground in order to break down sufficiently, since it is the first thing to be attacked by bacteria in the compost heap. Nevertheless, shredding does speed up the process.

Blender Compost

For reducing kitchen scraps to small, readily composted pieces, a blender can be every bit as effective as a shredder. As kitchen scraps accumulate, put them in the blender, add enough water to cover them, and blend until finely chopped. Then pour the "liquid compost" into a bucket with a lid to keep it until you can take it out to the garden. Pour it into a shallow hole dug in your pile, and cover it with a shovelful of compost. Or if your gardening space is limited and you don't have room to make conventional compost, dump your liquid gold directly into trenches dug in the garden, and cover it with a shovelful of dirt. Some people will freeze their compostable refuse until it can be brought to a local composting site or added to a new compost pile.

TILLERS AND TRACTORS

Rotary tillers and garden tractors with tiller attachments are valuable tools in the composting process–particularly in sheet composting and green manuring.

Green manure plants, which can add tremendous amounts of organic matter to the soil, are easily handled with the proper garden power equipment. Fertility-building crops such as rye, clover, and buckwheat can be fitted into the garden rotation schedule. The practice is especially worthwhile in large gardens, where at little cost, time, or effort, a great amount of organic matter is returned to the soil.

Green manuring is an idea and a method that has long been used by farmers to build soil but has largely been overlooked by gardeners. By taking full advantage of tillers and garden tractors, however, you can do as good a green-manuring job as any farmer. You can work into the soil a green manure crop that soon will decay into fertile humus.

Sheet composting is accomplished by spreading extra organic material on the bare ground, or over a green manure crop. Then both the crop and the extra material are worked into the soil, where they will quickly decompose.

Green manuring and sheet composting are often more efficient methods than heap composting, since the decay occurs right in the soil and there is no turning and far less hauling of materials.

The secret behind fast sheet composting is rotary tilling. For example, suppose that at the end of the summer you have several good stands of flowers or other plant debris that you ordinarily gather up and take to the compost heap. Unless shredded, they can take anywhere from 3 to 6 months to decompose. But with a rotary tiller, you can till them in to a depth of 3 or 4 inches, and–at the end of only a few weeks–you will find scarcely a trace of the plants left. Instead there will be only a more fertile soil.

A note of caution: Your soil will thank you for avoiding use of the rotary tiller whenever possible. While it is extremely useful for incorporating green manures and garden refuse, it should not be used to cultivate between rows and similar tasks. By disturbing the soil structure–that is, pulverizing all those aggregates–the soil loses its porosity that allows good circulation of water and air. This inevitably suppresses the all-important microbial community that is responsible for creating soil health. Best practice is to leave a good layer of trash or mulch on the surface, and try to get some kind of plant roots growing in it as quickly as possible. Organic farmers, including Jeff Moyer of the Rodale Institute, have pioneered methods of killing green manure crops without tilling them in, and then planting directly into the brown layer of vegetation, either using vegetable transplants or special tiller-seeders that cut a narrow slice into which the desired seeds, such as corn or beans, can be inserted.

12

USING COMPOST

Your compost is finished. After carefully following the recommended steps for turning the year's bounty of organic materials into rich, mellow humus, you want to be certain that it's used to best advantage—that it benefits your soil most and helps ensure a natural abundance and health in your coming crops.

It is not possible to stress too heavily the "soil bank account" theory of fertilizing. The real purpose of the organic method is to build permanent fertility into the soil by adding to its natural rock mineral reserves and to its humus content. Practically all the natural fertilizers are carriers of insoluble plant food. They start working quickly, but they don't drop their load of food all at once, as does a soluble fertilizer. An insoluble fertilizer will work for you for months and years.

Beyond building nutrient reserves for plants, your soil improvement program should, most importantly, feed the "micro-herd" that is the real source of fertility and health for your crops. This is the essence of the organic gardener's maxim: "Feed the soil, not the plant."

So, you can see that, as an organic gardener or farmer, you are adding fertilizer not only to supply immediate plant food needs but also to build up the soil microbiome that will nourish future crops.

WHEN TO APPLY COMPOST

The principal factor in determining when to apply compost is its condition. If it is half finished, or noticeably fibrous, it could well be applied in October or November. By spring, it will have completed its decomposition in the soil itself and be ready to supply growth nutrients to the earliest plantings made. Otherwise, for general soil enrichment, the ideal time for applying compost is a month or so before planting. The closer to planting time it is incorporated, the more it should be ground up or worked over thoroughly with a hoe to finely shred it. The special tools and equipment we discussed in Chapter 11 will come in handy when you wish to add compost to your soil close to planting time.

If your compost is ready in fall and is not intended to be used until spring, keep it in a protected place. If it is kept for a long period during summer, water the finished compost from time to time.

For organic farmers and gardeners, it's not a bad idea to make applications of compost either in fall or winter or in early spring. The big advantage here is that application at such a time helps equalize the workload. Usually this time of year is the least crowded with busy schedules, and the farmer or gardener can devote more time to doing a good job without interfering with the rest of the crop program. The best practice is to seed a hardy winter or early-spring cover crop at the same time you apply the compost, which ensures that its nutrients will stay put as the growing plants put down roots.

Side-dressing plants with compost is a good way to add nutrients during the growing season.

Just before you first work the soil in spring is a particularly good time to apply compost. Then when the soil preparation is done, the fresh organic matter can be worked down into the soil to supply food for the organisms that give life to spring soil. They become active and start to grow at about freezing temperatures. However, soil temperatures must rise to 50°F (10°C) before they really take on the dynamic action that characterizes a living organic soil. In early spring, the temperature is just about to rise to the level where the vital soil organisms can make use of it.

In summer, plants pull more nutrients from the soil than they do in any other season. But perhaps you didn't realize that in summer the soil has more nutrients available to give to plants than at any other time of the year. During summer, the increased activity of bacteria, fungi, and other soil microorganisms is primarily responsible for the abundance of plant food. These same microorganisms are one of the primary forces that act on organic matter and natural rock fertilizers to make them available to plants. The beauty of this system is that microbes are releasing nutrients to plants most quickly at just the time when plants are growing most rapidly.

Summer can be a fine time to apply compost and the natural mined minerals—rock and colloidal phosphate, greensand, granite dust, and lime. Compost and mined mineral soil amendments of all types are needed even more in summer, because they hold moisture in the soil and stimulate the microbial activity that takes place during warm months. However, don't count on these slow-release materials to help growing crops that suffer from deficiencies. They will not become available until the microbes have had a chance to work on them for a while. The nutrients you add in summer will greatly benefit your plants next year and the year after.

GENERAL RULES FOR APPLYING COMPOST

Apply at least $1/2$ inch to 3 inches of well-finished compost over your garden each year. There is little if any danger of burning due to overuse, as is the case with chemical fertilizers. You can apply compost either once or twice a year. The amount would depend, of course, on the fertility of your soil and on what and how much has been grown in it.

For most applications, it is important that compost be well finished—that is, aged long enough so that the decomposition process has stabilized.

Unfinished compost has been found to retard germination and growth of certain plants. Some plants, such as corn and squash, seem to thrive on partly finished compost, however. In general, be most careful when applying compost shortly before planting or in seeding mixes. Fall soil preparation and mulching applications are less critical.

If you want to be certain that your compost is aged well enough, you can perform a germination test. Soak a few seeds, such as lettuce or radish, in a tea made with your compost, and soak an equal number from the same packet in distilled water. Lay each batch on a paper towel and keep them warm and moist for a few days, until they start to sprout. If the distilled-water-treated seeds germinate better, you know you must let your compost age longer.

🌱 MATURITY TESTING

It is possible to test the maturity of compost by measuring the carbon dioxide and ammonia concentration of the air in a sealed sample. As microbes respire, they release carbon dioxide, just as animals and humans do. If microbes are actively growing, the resulting high level of carbon dioxide serves to indicate that the sample is not fully finished. Excess ammonia is an indication that a high nitrogen source in the compost mix is not fully decomposed and is releasing some of its nitrogen as ammonia. These tests are commonly used by commercial compost companies, but serious garden composters may find them useful. You can purchase compost-maturity test kits online, if interested.

Compost can be added to the soil at any time, and can either be incorporated into the top 4 inches as you prepare your garden beds for planting or added to transplant holes or furrows. A broadfork or similar tool that loosens the soil but keeps its structure intact is a better choice than a rotary tiller. Larger areas can be rotary-tilled before spreading a thin layer of compost, then quickly sown to a cover crop. A light sprinkling of mulch–hay, straw, leaves, or similar dry material–will conserve moisture for the cover crop to germinate and meanwhile protect soil from the weather. Crops such as corn can be seeded directly into a newly seeded cover crop such as clover, which will then form a "living mulch" between the crop rows.

To improve the structure and fertility of poor soil quickly, spread a thick layer of compost followed by a fast-growing cover crop, preferably one with fibrous roots. Living roots are the best hosts for your microbial workforce, secreting sugars that will jump-start your soil's fertility as the soil food web springs into action.

The Forge Garden is a half-acre training site for students and interns at Santa Clara University. Garden manager Katharine Rondthaler describes their minimal till cultivation method, using hand tools between plantings to promote good soil structure and tilth:

> After removing plants from the soil, 3 to 6 inches of compost is added to the top of the soil. Using a digging fork or a broadfork, the compost is lightly incorporated into the top layer of soil. The soil is then raked with a tilthing rake to create a fine seedbed. When annual cover crops are added back to the soil, the cover crop is cut, leaving the roots in the soil, and then plant material is chopped into 3- to 6-inch pieces. It is immediately added back and forked into the soil to allow it to break down. In addition to promoting good soil structure, this process improves permeability, drainage, and water-holding capacity.

THE VEGETABLE GARDEN

Your vegetable garden will thrive if you give it liberal amounts of compost. (See the table "Compost Application Guide for Vegetables" on page 233.) Dig it in during fall, bury it in trenches, put it in the furrows when you plant and in the holes when transplanting seedlings. When the plants begin to grow rapidly, mix compost with equal amounts of soil and use it as a top-dressing; or mulch the plants heavily with partially rotted compost or with such raw compost materials as hay, straw, sawdust, grass clippings, or shredded leaves.

There is one rule to remember when mulching: The finer the material, the thinner the layer you will need. Remember that compost used at planting time should be well finished, especially for potatoes, which are prone to become scabby when in contact with incompletely decomposed manure. You may safely use partially finished compost only on heavy feeders like corn and squash.

For sowing seeds indoors or in a cold frame, put your compost through a sieve made of hardware cloth mounted on a wooden frame, then shred it with a hoe or even roll it with a rolling pin to make it very fine. See recipes for compost-based potting mix starting on page 236. The ideal seeding mixture is fine textured and crumbly and tends to fall apart after being squeezed in your hand.

COMPOST APPLICATION GUIDE FOR VEGETABLES

Nutrient Requirements
EH = Extra heavy
M = Moderate
H = Heavy
L = Light

VEGETABLE	NITROGEN	PHOSPHORUS	POTASSIUM	pH FACTOR
Asparagus	EH	H	EH	6.0–7.0
Beans, bush	L	M	M	6.0–7.5
lima	L	M	M	5.5–6.5
Beets, early	EH	EH	EH	5.8–7.0
late	H	EH	H	same
Broccoli	H	H	H	6.0–7.0
Cabbage, early	EH	EH	EH	6.0–7.0
late	H	H	H	same
Carrots, early	H	H	H	5.5–6.5
late	M	M	M	same
Cauliflower, early	EH	EH	EH	6.0–7.0
late	H	H	EH	same
Corn, early	H	H	H	6.0–7.0
late	M	M	M	same
Cucumbers	H	H	H	6.0–8.0
Eggplant	H	H	H	6.0–7.0
Lettuce, head	EH	EH	EH	6.0–7.0
leaf	H	EH	EH	same
Muskmelons	H	H	H	6.0–7.0
Onions	H	H	H	6.0–7.0
Parsley	H	H	H	5.0–7.0
Parsnips	M	M	M	6.0–8.0
Peas	M	H	H	6.0–8.0
Potatoes, white	EH	EH	EH	4.8–6.5
sweet	L	M	H	5.0–6.0
Radishes	H	EH	EH	6.0–8.0
Rutabaga	M	H	M	6.0–8.0
Soybeans	L	M	M	6.0–7.0
Spinach	EH	EH	EH	6.5–7.0
Squash, summer	H	H	H	6.0–8.0
winter	M	M	M	same
Tomatoes	M	H	H	6.0–7.0
Turnips	L	H	M	6.0–8.0

THE FLOWER GARDEN

Finely screened compost is excellent to put around all growing flowers. Apply it alone as an inch-thick mulch to control weeds and conserve moisture, or top-dress it mixed with soil. In spring, you can loosen the top few inches of soil in your annual and perennial beds and work into it an equal quantity of compost. And use compost generously when sowing flower seeds.

Compost tea is an excellent way to give your flowers supplementary feeding during their growing season. Put a generous amount of compost in a burlap sack or other permeable container, place it in a watering can, add water, and sprinkle liberally around the plants. The can may be refilled with water several times before the compost loses its potency. (You'll find more tips for using compost tea later in this chapter.)

Another advantage for flower growers is that plenty of compost has been found to keep the moisture level of the flowerbed too high for ants.

YOUR LAWN

To build a lawn that stays green all summer, has no crabgrass, and rarely needs watering, use compost liberally when making and maintaining it. Your goal is to produce a thick sod with roots that go down 6 inches, not a thin, weed-infested mat lying on a layer of infertile subsoil.

In building a new lawn, work in copious amounts of compost as deeply as possible. If your soil is either sandy or clayey (rather than a good loam), you'll need at least a 2-inch depth of compost, mixed in thoroughly, to build it up. For Northern gardeners, the best time to install a new lawn is in fall. But if you want to get started in spring, dig in your compost and plant annual or perennial ryegrass, which will look quite neat all summer. Then dig this green manure in at the end of summer and make your permanent lawn when cool weather comes. Southern gardeners might be better off starting in spring with a ryegrass cover and then overseeding with a lawn mixture the following spring.

To renovate an old, patchy lawn, dig up the bare spots about 2 inches deep, work in plenty of finished compost, tamp and rake well, and sow your seed after soaking the patches well.

Feed your lawn regularly every spring. An excellent practice is to use a spike-toothed aerator, then spread a mixture of fine finished compost and bonemeal. Rake this into the holes made by the aerator.

You can use a fairly thick covering of compost—just not so thick that it covers the grass. This will feed your lawn efficiently and keep it sending down a dense mass of roots that laugh at drought.

TREES AND SHRUBS

Despite the attention that has been given to backfilling mixtures for the planting holes of trees and shrubs, this is one place where compost should not, as a rule, be used. Evaluations of trees planted in holes backfilled with amended materials show that this practice encourages root growth only in the original planting hole—roots don't extend out into the surrounding soil—and such plants are susceptible to waterlogging, wind throw, disease, and insect problems.

A better use of your compost for feeding newly planted trees and shrubs is top-dressing the soil area surrounding the plant and watering the compost in. Small "plugs" of compost may also be augered in around the drip line; manure tea feedings are beneficial, too.

Established shrubs should be fed yearly by having a half bushel of compost worked into the surface soil, then mulched.

The "ring" method is best for feeding trees: Starting about 2 feet from the trunk, cultivate the soil shallowly to 1 foot beyond the drip line of the branches. Rake 1 or 2 inches of compost into the top 2 inches of soil. Another way to feed established trees is to apply compost tea, beginning around the base of the trunk and working out toward the drip line.

When hilling up the soil around your rosebushes for winter protection, mix plenty of compost with it—they'll get a better start next spring.

FRUIT TREES

The ring method is ideal for fruit trees, too. You can work in as much as 3 or 4 inches of compost, then apply a heavy mulch that will continue to feed the trees as it rots. Some gardeners merely pile organic materials as deep as 2 feet around their fruit trees, adding more material as the covering decomposes. You can even add earthworms to speed the transformation to humus. Berry

The ring method of feeding established trees and shrubs calls for compost to be raked into the soil from about 2 feet from the trunk to 1 foot beyond the drip line of the branches.

plants may be treated the same way, with lower mulches, of course, for low-growing varieties.

Another good trick for pepping up old fruit trees is to auger holes a foot apart in the soil all around the tree and pack these with compost.

HOUSEPLANTS

Lots of humus means extra-good moisture retention and air circulation in houseplant soil. A good potting mixture is composed of equal parts of loam, sand, and compost, the last put through a ¼-inch mesh. Leaf mold compost makes a fine, loose soil, while for acid-loving plants like azaleas, compost made from pine needles or oak leaves is best. Feed your houseplants every 2 weeks during their growing season with compost tea, made by suspending a cheesecloth bag of compost in water and using the liquid when it is a weak tea color. In general, compost can be added to potting mixtures as one-fourth of the total.

To rejuvenate the soil in window boxes, tubs, and indoor plant boxes, scratch an inch or so of compost into the surface twice a year. Occasional light top-dressings of compost are also excellent for the soil in greenhouse benches. Vermicompost is even more nutrient packed for container growing and is widely available commercially if you do not maintain your own worm bed. Plants in containers also benefit from regular feeding with compost tea.

SOIL-COMPOST MIXTURE FOR STARTING SEEDLINGS

You can help ensure good germination by adding compost to seed-starting flats and beds. Make a mixture of two parts good garden loam; one part fine, sharp sand; and one part compost. Mix well and put 8 inches of the mixture into the hotbed, cold frame, or flat. It's a good idea to let this growing medium age for several months before seeding, especially if you are not sure that your compost has fully stabilized. Sift the soil mixture through a $\frac{1}{4}$-inch mesh screen to provide a fine-textured bed for planting. When screening the mixture, place coarse screenings in the bottom of the flats to provide better drainage.

This mixture provides adequate nourishment for young plants; you don't need to add manure or other organic fertilizers high in nitrogen. Used too soon, these fertilizers can cause the young plants to grow too rapidly, unbalancing their natural growth.

A general-use potting mix for seeding vegetables or ornamentals can be made by combining compost and soil in a ratio of two parts compost to one part soil. Another part of peat moss or coconut coir will ensure good aeration. Nutrient amendments such as lime, bonemeal, colloidal phosphate, greensand, and high-nitrogen materials like bloodmeal, crab meal, or alfalfa meal can then be mixed in. A 5-gallon bucket of soil-compost-peat mix would only need about a cup or a cup and a half of these amendments to provide an excellent initial home for new seedlings. Compost-based potting mixes are commonly available on the market but can vary widely in quality.

STARTER SOLUTION FOR PLANTS

Starter solutions made from compost or manure can be a big help in the growing of vegetable plants. The home gardener as well as the commercial grower can benefit from the rapid and unchecked growth of young plants if the plants have reached a sufficiently advanced stage of growth and if the solution is used before they are moved to the field from the greenhouse, hotbed, or cold frame. Greenhouse operators have long made use of this method to bring their crops to a rapid and profitable production. Earlier yields have also been reported in the field.

The main benefit received from these solutions is that of providing the plant with immediately available plant food. This stimulates leaf and root growth, giving the plant a quick pickup after transplanting. These solutions are used especially on young lettuce, tomatoes, celery, peppers, melons, eggplant, cabbage, cauliflower, and all kinds of transplanted plants.

🌱 A GOOD START

Here is a recommended starter solution you can make from compost.

Fill a barrel or other container one-quarter full of compost. Continue to fill the container with water, stirring several times during the next 24 to 48 hours. To use the liquid, dilute it with water to a light amber color. Pour 1 pint around each plant when setting it out, or later as necessary to speed growth. Liquid compost can be used at 10-day to 2-week intervals, especially when soils are not high in fertility.

Tests have shown that seeds sprout more than twice as well when soaked in a solution of this kind, as long as the compost is sufficiently finished. In the wild, practically all seeds depend upon the moisture that seeps into them through a layer of nature's compost. In soaking the seed flat, place it in a large container holding an inch or two of starter solution. Allow the flat to soak until its sandy surface shows signs of dampness.

As an additional bonus, seed flats containing mature compost and handled in this way seldom suffer loss from the damping-off of seedlings.

HOW TO USE COMPOST TEA

The juices of compost can be the best part. Often, some of the valuable nutrients in compost are dissolved in water quite readily, and in solution these nutrients can be quickly distributed to needy plant roots.

Since plants take up nutrients along with water, the use of compost tea makes quite a bit of sense, particularly during dry periods when plants are starved for both food and water.

A 5-gallon plastic bucket with a lid may be turned into a simple compost tea system with the addition of hose connections at the top and bottom of the bucket. Water enters through the bottom connection, circulates through the compost, and exits at the top as compost tea.

Many problem plants and trees can be nursed back to health by treating them with compost tea. You can use it on bare spots on your lawn, on trees that have just been transplanted, and on indoor plants that need perking up. You can even use it on vegetables in spring to encourage them to mature earlier. Compost tea is especially effective in greenhouses, where the finest soil conditions are needed for the best results.

It is really no trouble to make compost tea on a small scale. For treating houseplants or small outdoor areas, all you have to do is place a burlap or cloth bag filled with finished compost in your watering can and add water. Agitate it for a couple of minutes, or let it sit for a while, then pour. Nothing could be easier. The compost can be used several times, as one watering will not wash out all its soluble nutrients.

The remaining compost is almost as good as new and should be dug into the soil or used as mulch. It takes the action of soil bacteria and plant roots to extract the major value from compost.

Developing a continuous system for making compost tea for the home grounds requires a little more ingenuity and mechanical skill. One method is to attach a hose connection and an outlet pipe to a plastic bucket with a lid that will stand up under normal water pressure. The type of 5-gallon plastic pail in which primer paint, drywall joint compound, and a variety of commercial food products are sold can be used for this project. Create a water intake near the bottom of the bucket by drilling a hole just large enough to insert a garden hose replacement coupling. Use epoxy to attach the coupling to the bucket and to seal the edges of the hole. Make an exit for your compost tea near the top of the bucket, opposite the water intake. The water has to circulate up and through the compost before it can get out of the bucket. Epoxy a piece of PVC pipe into the exit hole to create a spout to which a sprinkler head may be attached. A second hose connection can also be used in the exit hole, allowing the bucket to remain stationary while compost tea is sprayed through a hose coming from the exit.

The operation of this compost watering can is simple. You attach the water supply to the intake connection, and the hose or sprinkling device to the exit connection. The bucket may be carried to different parts of your garden, and one charging of compost lasts for about 15 minutes of watering. A screen placed over the exit hole on the inside of the bucket prevents solids from escaping and clogging the sprinkling heads.

Compost tea has taken its place as a valuable addition to the gardener's toolkit. When applied to foliage with a sprayer or used to drench roots during transplanting, it offers a rich brew of diverse beneficial microorganisms as well as a small amount of readily available plant nutrients. Compost tea also suppresses plant diseases by colonizing plant leaves and roots, thus preventing pathogens from gaining entry. Special equipment used to make a fermented brew of true compost tea has gained popularity among organic farmers. Beyond the simple compost in a burlap bag approach–which professional brewers refer to as a watery compost extract–tea brewers first extract the beneficial compost organisms and then culture them in a water solution. The water is kept well aerated, and a food source for the microbes, such as small amounts of sugars and proteins, is added. According to Dr. Elaine Ingham, who is considered the guru of compost tea, this process promotes the growth of fungi and discourages the pathogens and anaerobes that can cause problems such as mildew and blight.

Organic farmers wishing to use compost tea in a foliar application will need to make sure they start with compost that complies with the National Organic Program requirements (see Chapters 8 and 13). Orchardists have also found compost tea applications to be helpful in preventing scab in apples, a treatment typically applied at least 120 days before harvest of an edible crop, in keeping with NOP requirements. Alternatively, a plant-based brew that is based on a recipe for effective microorganisms (see page 164) offers similar benefits without requiring documentation of proper composting.

LARGE-SCALE COMPOSTING

Despite the enormous growth in awareness of recycling and the value of composting, the vast majority of Americans, both urban and rural, rely on public or private solid-waste companies to dispose of household garbage. In 2014, according to the EPA, about 258 million tons of municipal solid waste was generated. Of this, compostable wastes such as paper, cardboard, yard trimmings, and food scraps are the majority. About a fifth of this waste stream consists of food scraps alone. While about 70 percent of yard trimmings now find their way to composting facilities, less than 5 percent of food scraps are diverted from landfills or incinerators.

A comprehensive study titled *The State of Composting in the US* was published in 2014 by the Institute for Local Self-Reliance (ILSR) and the *BioCycle* magazine staff. The report illuminates the scope and scale of municipal and commercial composting in this country, collecting information about the extent and scope of composting operations from 44 states. A few significant facts from this study include:

- Almost 5,000 composting facilities were identified, of which 71 percent compost only yard trimmings.
- Institutions and farms or other agricultural sites make up 15 percent of the number of composting facilities.
- The average reported tonnage of organic waste diverted per composting facility was only 5,155 tons.

- More than 180 communities have now implemented residential food-scrap collection programs.

While increasing numbers of schools, supermarkets, restaurants, and other businesses and institutions are separating their organic wastes for composting, the infrastructure available is clearly inadequate to support the need.

Not long ago, farm manure was considered a waste problem, and composting was practiced only by a few dedicated "fanatics." Following the implementation of the USDA National Organic Program in 2002 and the dramatic expansion of the organic market that it stimulated, increasing numbers of farmers are converting to organic methods. The USDA organic standards require careful management of livestock manure and recycling other plant and animal materials as the first choice for supplying nutrients to crops and to "improve or maintain" soil health.

Likewise, many food-processing industries, facing stiffer environmental regulations, are being pressed to find ways to recycle organic wastes—and many are turning to composting for solutions. Since the 1990s, concentrated animal feeding operations (CAFOs) have proliferated, coupled with a decline in the number of medium-size mixed livestock and crop operations. The enormous water pollution problems created by this trend have forced such industrial livestock operations to find alternatives that allow the nutrients in their huge manure streams to be returned to the soil without endangering precious marine and freshwater ecosystems.

The legal climate has changed, too, although the regulatory hurdles can still be daunting. States and municipalities, including New York City, have instituted aggressive restrictions on food and other organic wastes that can be sent to landfills. Curbside pickup programs and local organic waste drop-off points have become commonplace in urban centers across the country. Even as many states and municipalities actively encourage composting to meet recycling goals and to ease the strain on landfills, they also face problems in regulating composting facilities under rules designed for other solid-waste disposal systems. As composting projects proliferate, site selection issues arise; environmental consciousness can backfire when people think of these facilities as waste disposal sites.

Private companies have entered the market to recycle organic wastes of all kinds through a host of methods—some of which confer more soil-building benefits than others. USDA restrictions on what organic farmers can apply to their land and crops have complicated the waste recycling scenario, as some organic wastes, most notably municipal sewage sludge, are definitely off-limits for organic farmers. An entire industry has developed to produce and approve a host of manufactured fertility inputs according to the National Organic Program regulations.

Along with increased demand for certified organic foods, demand has also been burgeoning for "natural" garden fertilizers, as increasing numbers of urban and suburban gardeners learn to produce the freshest, healthiest foods for their families. Home gardeners now have a bewildering array of composted and compost-based products from which to choose. We'll take a look at how you can evaluate composted products, what to be wary of, and what benefits they offer.

Although composting is an age-old technology, it is a new industry, with many issues in need of clarification and new business models needed as it enters the mainstream. As anyone who has gone from backyard to market gardening knows, the complexities of doing anything multiply when it goes large-scale. The US Composting Council, formed in 1990, is a national organization dedicated to the development, promotion, and expansion of the composting industry. It espouses a vision declaring that "compost manufacturing and compost utilization are central to creating healthy soils, clean air and water, a stable climate, and a sustainable society." Incorporated as a trade association, the council also encompasses a nonprofit fund to administer research and education activities. *BioCycle* is its official publication.

In the pages that follow, we'll explore the methods being used and the challenges faced by those working to recycle the mountains of farm, industrial, and municipal organic wastes produced daily. You can use this information to aid their efforts, whether by encouraging your community to implement a composting program, testifying in favor of siting a composting facility in your neighborhood, or purchasing compost from the farmer down the road.

COMPOSTING ON THE FARM

The post–World War II agricultural trend toward mechanization, specialization, and consolidation of farmland into the hands of fewer and larger owners has resulted in a curious situation: Today, many large farms produce no manure at all. The tendency to specialize, to produce large quantities of one crop for market in what is called monoculture, plus the substitution of machines for horses and mules, has led to this imbalance and removed the primary ingredient for compost–manure–from the farm.

By the same token, livestock and dairy production, through the same process of mechanization and specialization, has become concentrated on large farms and feedlots. Most Americans purchase their beef, pork, and chicken, including eggs and dairy products, from huge confinement operations that are concentrated in a few regions of the country. There, manure accumulates in enormous quantities where there is insufficient plant matter with which to compost it and not enough land on which to distribute it in a balanced fashion.

The decade of the 1980s saw tumultuous changes in the picture of family farms in the United States. Thousands of small farmers lost their land, which was consolidated into bigger, heavily mechanized, more specialized–and more debt-ridden–"production units." This trend has continued unabated in the 21st-century, despite the upsurge of young farmers seeking to relocalize the food system and produce food in an ecologically and socially harmonious way. Many farmers now work land owned by banks, insurance companies, and large agribusiness firms. The livestock industry, starting with poultry and more recently including pork, beef, and even fish, has become more vertically integrated. This means that farmers and farm managers have little leeway for making decisions that may affect short-term profits and, more important, have less direct incentive to care for the land so that it maintains its long-term productivity.

On the Right Track

There are hopeful signs, though. Skyrocketing consumer demand led to quantum leaps in the number and seriousness of farmers who are converting to organic methods. The US organic foods industry was valued at close to $50 billion in 2016 and has continued double-digit growth since before the implementation of the USDA's National Organic Program–except during the recession years of 2008 and 2009, when a modest 8 percent growth was well above the conventional grocery industry. Composting and the recycling of plant and animal materials, along with cover cropping, are enshrined in the

USDA standards as the primary means of providing for soil health and crop nutrition.

Increasing concerns about rural groundwater contamination and farm-worker health have inspired farmers and their advisors to search for alternatives to agrichemicals. Water quality concerns have escalated in regions where agricultural runoff and contamination from CAFOs threaten freshwater bodies such as the Great Lakes. Toxic algae blooms caused by agricultural runoff–primarily from raw manure and highly soluble synthetic fertilizers–have become a fact of life in lakes and ponds nationwide. These severe public health and environmental problems have led to stringent new regulations aimed at farm practices that are a prime contributing factor.

According to the Sustainable Table food program, animal feeding operations produce about 100 times more manure each year than the amount of sewage sludge processed in US municipal wastewater plants. A 2,500-cow confinement dairy farm produces as much "waste" as a city with about 411,000 residents. Unlike human wastes, there is almost no requirement that livestock waste be treated.

Federal law now requires all CAFOs that discharge any wastes into surface water to apply for a permit, including a nutrient management plan, which must be open for public review. However, when there is that much manure being stored in one place, generally in liquid form in giant lagoons, accidents are guaranteed to happen. For example, when Hurricane Floyd swept through North Carolina in 1999, almost all the state's manure lagoons spilled over into waterways.

Many state agriculture departments are jumping on the bandwagon, and *sustainable* has become the adjective of choice for new programs. Couple this with the solid-waste crisis, which has made the recycling of organic wastes a potential source of income, and you can see that information and incentives to try composting on a farm and industrial scale have never been higher.

ARGUMENTS FOR COMPOSTING ON FARMS

Modern farms operate like businesses, with tight budgets and tighter schedules; unlike most businesses, farms often function with only one or a few employees doing the myriad tasks needed to bring livestock and crops to full production. Composting livestock manure, then, must be viewed as an added step in the production schedule–the benefit must equal or exceed the cost in time, effort, and energy. Since spreading uncomposted manure is a fairly common practice on most farms, the extra steps required to compost it include mixing it with appropriate carbonaceous materials, allowing time for decomposition, providing space for storage during composting, and allowing for any transportation of materials to and from the composting area. Yet studies of compost applications to farmlands repeatedly demonstrate that the benefits of composting can more than repay the additional effort it entails.

When manure is composted before it is spread, the farmer realizes four advantages: First, composting stabilizes the nutrients in manure, reducing concerns about runoff into surface waters. This also creates greater flexibility about when it can be spread, since there is no danger of harming crops. Second, by reducing the volume of the original material by 50 percent or more, composting reduces the number of loads the farmer must haul out to the field. Because compost is so dry compared with fresh manure, some farmers actually use it as bedding for their livestock. Third, as we noted in Chapter 3, composting kills weed seeds and pathogens that may be present in raw manure as well as conferring increased disease resistance on crops. Finally, compost improves soil structure and biological activity to a greater extent than does uncomposted manure.

Composting Considerations

Even if compostable materials are freely available from local organic waste generators, farm-scale composting requires both time and some expense. Businesses that separate organic wastes, increasingly required by local and state regulations, will pay tipping fees to haul it away, but this system has to be a reliable service that entails specialized equipment and a well-managed composting site. Farmers who take up composting must be prepared to make a lot of adjustments in how they manage their labor and capital resources. Says Robert Rynk, the former Cooperative Extension agricultural engineer at the University of Massachusetts, "Modern composting requires money and attention. It involves a commitment of land, labor, and equipment. If you plan to sell compost, expect to spend time marketing it. In short, a successful composting operation deserves the same commitment given to other farm operations like milking, egg handling, or pest control."

If a farmer is already managing manure as effectively as possible, composting can result in reduced nitrogen levels applied to crops. This is because some nitrogen loss, through leaching and ammonia release, is inevitable with any composting process, whereas the full nitrogen value of manure can be retained if it is stored properly and incorporated into the soil immediately after spreading. Slower composting at lower temperatures better conserves nitrogen, but this approach runs afoul of the USDA's compost requirements. Organic farmers must hot-compost or use a vermicompost system or else follow requirements for use of raw manure that essentially eliminate its use during the growing season.

Despite the brisk activity in improving farm composting methods, there are still relatively few farmers who carry out any kind of composting practice. Of the roughly 7,000 composting operations identified in the ILSR and *Bio-Cycle* study, only 400 represent on-farm or agricultural sites. In addition to the management time and expense involved, obstacles to on-farm composting include regulations and licensing requirements that commonly treat on-farm composters who receive organic wastes from off the farm as waste management facilities.

Farmers who do carry out a systematic composting program report significant improvement in their soil structure, crop quality, and animal health. In addition, there are other practices closely related to composting, and sharing its principles, that a larger number of farmers have found feasible. We will look first at some additional agricultural composting methods and then, briefly, at some related practices.

AGRICULTURAL COMPOSTING METHODS

Manure, as we have discussed, is the most readily available and valuable compost ingredient for farmers. Manure may come in many forms, depending on the type of livestock, how the animals are housed and bedded, and what kind of storage system is used. Ideally, bedding will be some carbonaceous material like straw, sawdust, dried leaves, or shredded newspaper, used in the right proportions to balance the manure's nitrogen and create the perfect moisture level. When this isn't the case, the farmer must adjust the mixture to compensate, usually by mixing in more high-carbon materials.

In *Biological Reclamation of Solid Wastes,* Dr. Clarence Golueke states that the most serious problem in composting manures is that they must be either dried or liquefied to slurry before they can be handled efficiently. If liquefied, they can be digested anaerobically for methane production or used in spray irrigation. Composting, however, demands that manure be dried. Once the drying and mixing have been done, the material can be composted in windrows. The trick is to get the manure wet enough so that the composting process goes on, yet dry enough that it will not pack or form balls.

Many food-processing wastes are similarly wet, sloppy, and high in nitrogen content. The secret to making best use of these sources of fertility is in knowing how to combine them effectively to provide the best conditions for compost organisms. The same considerations discussed in connection with backyard composting apply. Moisture control is probably the trickiest aspect of farm-scale composting. Adding more dry, high-carbon materials, shaping the windrow to either shed or absorb water, covering the pile, turning more or less frequently, and wetting down the piles are all techniques farmers can use to adjust the moisture levels in their compost.

A small farm or homestead seldom accumulates enough manure and litter in a week or less to permit the building of a compost stack or windrow that is large enough to heat up properly. Instead, small-scale farmers must use stacks that permit the addition of material as it becomes available. On homesteads and small diversified farms, manure and litter are usually stacked and handled by hand with a pitchfork. Machinery can, however, be used to convey material to the stack and to load the final humus into carts, trucks, or spreaders. Assess your needs carefully: If the time you spend forking litter every week could be more wisely spent, a loading machine can be a good investment.

Some small growers use wire cages or pallet bins like those discussed in Chapter 10, arranging them at convenient locations alongside their fields. These bins are filled as plant debris, manure, weeds, and off-farm organic wastes are collected. This ensures a steady supply of finished compost, available right where it's needed.

Farmers needn't be too concerned about the quality of the finished product when the compost is strictly for on-farm use. If some of the materials are incompletely decomposed, or it is coarse and lumpy, it can still offer the same benefits as uniform, finely textured, finished compost. Farmers can also screen their compost for special applications like potting mix and fine seedbed preparation, or for use as a midseason side-dressing. If compost is only partially finished, however, it should be worked into the soil at least a week or two before planting or spread when a cover crop is incorporated. When off-farm sales of finished compost are considered, more care must be taken to produce a consistent, uniform, thoroughly decomposed product.

In some respects, equipment for composting on the farm differs from that used in the home garden only in size. Shredding equipment, for example, is available in large tractor-driven models equipped with conveyer belts. Mowing equipment, though much larger, is basically similar in design to what a gardener uses.

The farmer needs special spreading equipment for applying compost. Manure loaders and spreaders can be used to mechanize the handling not only of manures but also of sawdust, corncobs, and other organic materials. A 30-inch-wide loader scoop on a hydraulic or mechanical lift can pick up several hundred pounds of manure or other material at one time.

There are essentially three methods used for large-scale composting: windrows, static aerated piles, and in-vessel (contained) systems. The static aerated-pile method requires some means of circulating air through the pile. Enclosed digesters and fully mechanized systems are generally costly and so are seldom found on farms. Some more innovative farmers are using aerated-slurry and methane systems, and experimenting with aerated static piles and heat recovery using the Jean Pain approach (refer to Chapter 5). However, the most common farm composting method by far is the windrow system.

The Windrow Method

The basic requirements for composting don't change with the scale of operations. In large systems, however, small problems that may be inconsequential to the home composter tend to become magnified. One conclusion to be drawn from this is that forethought is critical to the success of a large-scale composting project. Before any material is trucked in or piles made, ask yourself where they will be put. Does the site drain properly? If your climate is humid, can you provide for collection of leachate so that precious nutrients won't be lost?

Every windrow is constructed according to the same basic design: 4 to 5 feet high, 2 feet or so wide at the top, 8 to 12 feet wide at the base, with length limited only by available space and materials. Windrows can be formed using a

Windrows are commonly used for both farm and municipal composting. Even in-vessel composting operations use windrows to finish their compost. A variety of special equipment is available for aerating windrows, including machines that travel alongside or over the piles, turning the material as they go.

variety of materials and equipment, turned more or less often depending on desired speed of decomposition or time available, and sheltered or left open to the elements. As long as the needs of the microbes are met, success is ensured.

The simplest way for a farmer to begin composting is with equipment already on hand or readily available from neighbors. This method, described in the book *The Soul of Soil: A Guide to Ecological Soil Management,* can be used by almost any farmer who has access to manure and a manure spreader.

Farm-scale composting requires a small tractor with a power take-off (PTO), a PTO manure spreader, and a second tractor with a front-end loader. Most manure spreaders make good compost machines, although side-delivery types and those with unconventional beaters are not appropriate.

The procedure is straightforward, but takes practice to master. Piles of material are arranged parallel to the projected length of the windrow. The full manure spreader begins unloading, while the front-end loader alternates between the raw materials piles, dumping the proper proportion of each into the spreader. Once the pile is about four feet high and six to eight feet wide (with

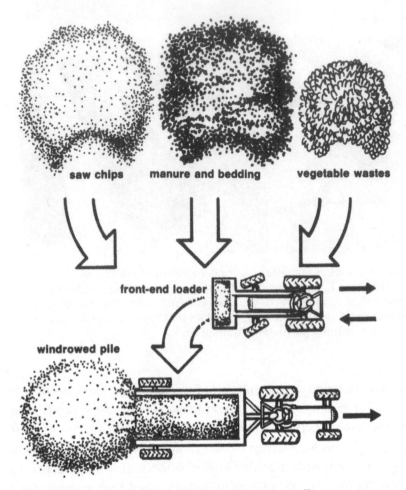

saw chips | manure and bedding | vegetable wastes

front-end loader

windrowed pile

On-farm windrows can be formed using a tractor pulling a manure spreader and a second tractor with a front-end loader. Raw materials are placed in the spreader, using the front-end loader; the windrow forms as the manure spreader is pulled forward. (Stewart Hoyt, The Soul of Soil: A Guide to Ecological Soil Management*)*

some hand-shaping in the early stages), the spreader is inched forward to let the raw materials hit against the new pile and fall into place. As the manure spreader slowly pulls forward, the pile is formed.

Most larger-scale on-farm composting operations that rely on turned windrows use either specialized compost-turning equipment that straddles the windrow and aerates it with beaters attached to a rotating shaft, or they have developed windrow-turning techniques that use basic tractors and bucket so as to keep the pile sufficiently aerated. The book *Compost, Vermicompost, and Compost Tea* describes several techniques used by northeastern farmer-composters.

Rhode Island composter Mike Merner has developed what he calls a "double aerated" block system in which he uses a large payloader with a 5-yard bucket to form and turn the piles. Elevating the bucket to its highest point, he gently dribbles out the materials onto the pile–then repeats. In this manner, he is able to build higher piles than the normal 5- to 6-foot windrow and thus put more compost in his limited space without sacrificing quality.

At the Highfields Center for Composting, Tom Gilbert developed what he calls the "rolling method," using a standard tractor and bucket loader. Piles are built to be 6 to 8 feet tall and 12 to 14 feet wide. Careful recipe development aims at a true 30:1 carbon/nitrogen ratio, appropriate moisture, and bulk-density levels as the pile is built. Tom says it is critical to get the bulk density right in this method. The piles are monitored for temperature, moisture, and odors and turned when the temperature drops. The pile is rolled by using the bucket to scoop up a layer two bucket-depths in from the wide part of the windrow, which is lifted and folded over the top to push it to the other side. In this manner, the pile is slowly rolled sideways across the site as it is turned. This system saves 50 percent of equipment and operator time, compared with a complete turn, Tom says. Besides aerating the areas that need it most, it offers the advantage of avoiding unnecessary agitation. Just as in the soil, avoiding excessive disturbance promotes fungal development and minimizes loss of nitrogen and organic matter. While decomposition is slower, it saves time and energy and makes a higher-quality product.

The late Arnie Voehringer, farm manager at White Oak Farm in Belchertown, Massachusetts, on the other hand, was trained in the Lubke method of composting, which calls for close control and monitoring of compost conditions, with piles no higher than 4 feet and no wider than 8 feet. Carbon dioxide levels in the core are measured regularly, and if they get too high, the pile must be turned. Product quality is also evaluated, through both chemical analysis and germination testing, with the goal of producing the highest possible quality compost.

Many farmers as well as larger-scale commercial compost operators use special fabric covers to protect windrows from the elements, control odors, and prevent access by vermin. Fleece or spun polypropylene covers allow air circulation and repel water, which in turn reduce leaching and nutrient loss as well as protecting ultraviolet-sensitive microbes from sunlight. Compost covers can also provide some insulation in colder climates, allowing composting to proceed through the winter months. Some farms may build large pole structures as compost shelters, and commercial composters will often cure the final product in such storage facilities, where each batch may be tested, screened, and bagged for final distribution.

Methane Digesters

The methane digester is a chamber or unit (often a mechanized drum) in which anaerobic digestion is carried on within a controlled environment. Anaerobic digestion differs drastically from composting in its oxygen requirements. The presence of oxygen or any highly oxidized material can inhibit methane-producing anaerobic bacteria.

In his *Biological Reclamation of Solid Wastes*, Dr. Golueke defines anaerobic digestion as a process in which "wastes are 'stabilized' through biological activity in the absence of atmospheric oxygen with the concomitant production of methane (CH_4) and carbon dioxide (CO_2)."

According to Dr. Golueke, the anaerobic digestion of farm wastes was practiced on a small scale on a few farms in France and Germany during World Wars I and II. The gas produced was used for cooking.

Methane production on farms has been practiced in rural India, where both human and animal wastes were being used in more than 1,500 digester installations by the late 1960s, and in mainland China, where low-technology digestion has been advanced to a high level. Interest in methane production in the United States is increasing as natural gas prices rise.

A methane digester operates in two stages. In the first stage, organic matter—manure, crop residues, bedding, sawdust, and other dry and wet material—is liquefied into volatile solids of an acid nature by anaerobic bacteria and chemical processes. In the second phase, methane-forming bacteria consume the volatile acid to produce the biogas that is captured in the digester. Biogas contains about 55 to 70 percent methane. Methane is the major ingredient of natural gas, and it burns virtually pollution-free.

In the methane-forming process, nitrogen from the raw manure is transformed into organic ammonia and bacterial protoplasm. The digested slurry, therefore, has a higher available nitrogen content than raw manure.

Several different materials can be used in anaerobic digesters. Manure sludges or slurries generally have a higher nitrogen content than sludges or slurries made with nitrogen-poor wastes. Digested swine manure, for example, contains from 6.1 to 9.1 percent nitrogen, while digested municipal refuse is only 0.6 to 2.5 percent nitrogen. Sludges from refuse, however, tend to have larger particles and may do more for soil structure.

Methane production alone will not make a small-scale digester pay for itself. Energy is spent collecting and hauling materials for the digester, and this energy must be balanced against the energy produced. If compost for soil improvement is sought, however, the added bonus of fuel production may give the edge to a methane digester when you compare it with a medium- to large-scale windrow composting system for dealing with dairy and feedlot wastes.

Increased interest in renewable energy and organics recycling have led some utilities to invest in methane fueled electricity generators. This story was aired on Minnesota Public Radio in 2008:

> The 200 cows on Jerry Jennisson's central Minnesota dairy farm make 1,100 gallons of milk every day, and they make even more manure, as much as 3,000 gallons daily.
>
> In the past Jennisson stored the manure in lagoons and used it as fertilizer. But now he's also using it to make electricity.
>
> It's a fairly simple process. The manure is piped from the barn to a 40-foot silo. It's heated to 100 degrees. That's when bacteria naturally present in the manure gets to work and makes methane.
>
> "The gas bubbles to the top," Jennisson said, pointing to a system of pipes. "And then flows through that pipe and down over there and is plumbed directly into the engine."
>
> The methane powers a specially rebuilt Chevy 330 engine. The engine turns a 37-kilowatt generator. Half the electricity created actually goes back into the process of making methane. A local power company will pay Jennisson to put the other half on the grid.

Methane resulting from decomposing organic wastes that have been dumped in landfills is also now being widely captured. Landfill gas, as it is known, is collected and directed to a central point where it can be processed and treated, depending on its intended use, used to generate electricity, replace fossil fuels in industrial and manufacturing operations, or upgraded to pipeline-quality gas.

INDUSTRIAL AND MUNICIPAL COMPOSTING

A few years ago, the world smirked as a ship laden with municipal incinerator ash was forced to sail from port to port, finding that nobody was willing to accept delivery of its toxic cargo. According to the US Environmental Protection Agency, the ash contained aluminum, arsenic, chromium, copper, lead, mercury, nickel, zinc, and dioxins. The ship's 2-year search for a place to unload the ash was symbolic of the new political sensitivity about any one region's becoming the dumping ground for another's trash, as well as the dawning public consciousness that we were running out of places to put it all. The relatively recent rise in popularity of composting as an option for dealing with municipal and industrial organic wastes has been precipitated largely by the escalating costs–both economic and environmental–of various other solid-waste disposal options.

Although most wastes are still sent to landfills, that option is narrowing and becoming more costly. More stringent environmental requirements to prevent toxic leachate from reaching groundwater have forced the closing of landfills in many states. Others have simply gotten filled up.

MUNICIPAL SOLID WASTES (MSW)

As mentioned previously, the vast majority of municipal wastes now being composted consists of leaves and yard wastes. These materials are easy for families to separate from other trash, they present few difficulties in handling or possible hazardous contaminants, and they constitute a large enough percentage of the municipal solid-waste stream to significantly increase the lifetime of a landfill. Also, when placed in landfills rather than composted, such wastes often become a source of environmental pollutants.

However, yard wastes constitute only part of the organic materials that could be composted but are still choking the nation's landfills. What about the mountain of food wastes and compostable paper disposed of by households and businesses in every community each year? Garbage—meaning the readily decomposable organic wastes derived mainly from food—comprises up to 30 percent of municipal refuse streams. Refuse refers to the whole range of stuff that people now throw away, including yard wastes, packaging materials, unwanted furniture, construction materials, and broken glass, as well as some items that should really be considered toxic waste, such as spent batteries and used motor oil. As is readily apparent, unless garbage and other nontoxic organic materials such as natural fiber rags and paper are kept out of the refuse stream to begin with, composting them presents some thorny—but not insurmountable—logistical obstacles.

Fortunately, a few municipalities have become serious enough about composting their wastes to invest in the technologies necessary to cope with these obstacles. The technologies employed involve either separation of garbage from the rest of the refuse stream or pulverizing the refuse until it is so fine that it is theoretically undetectable in the finished compost.

Mixed municipal solid waste, if little or none of the paper and yard waste are recycled separately, tends to have a high carbon/nitrogen ratio. Composted alone, it will break down very slowly, increasing costs. This is one reason that municipalities often combine solid waste with sewage sludge, animal manure, or some other high-nitrogen industrial waste, an arrangement known as co-composting. There is some controversy about the wisdom of composting paper that is more valuable when recycled into "new" paper products. However, there is usually enough nonrecyclable paper remaining to meet municipal compost needs, and when paper markets are glutted, it is handy to have composting as a backup disposal option. (For more on food-scrap collection and community composting, refer to Chapter 5.)

Sewage Sludge

Composting has been widely promoted as a means of treating another kind of municipal waste product—sewage sludge. This is partly due to the stricter environmental and health regulations placed on sludge disposal in the 1970s and 1980s, such as the EPA's directive calling for elimination of the ocean disposal of sludge. As noted by Gene Logsdon and many other commentators, a truly sustainable society would ensure that the valuable nutrients contained in human manure be returned to the land rather than becoming a serious water pollution hazard. Composting municipal sewage sludge is thus seen by many as an important route to greater sustainability.

Sewage sludge is mostly water, so it is generally dewatered or dried before being composted using a dry, high-carbon material such as sawdust, wood chips, or shredded paper as a bulking agent. Leaves, yard waste, and mixed municipal solid waste are also becoming increasingly popular. Bulking agents that do not rot or that rot very slowly are sometimes used, since they can be screened out of finished compost and reused again and again, saving the cost of continually bringing in fresh supplies.

It has been well established that disease organisms of most types are killed by the composting process, and in fact very few can survive in digested or activated sludge. Composting has been shown to be the only process that both destroys pathogens and creates a stabilized, easy-to-handle product. However, concerns exist about the possibility that some viruses, such as those causing hepatitis, may be able to tolerate even the prolonged high temperatures of composting.

Some sewage sludges, especially those receiving industrial effluent, have high levels of heavy metals–in some cases, content is so high that they will actually retard plant growth. Once the metals are mixed with the sludge, it is almost impossible to remove them, although some interesting work has been done using bioaccumulator plants such as sunflowers to remediate contaminated sludge.

The metals of greatest concern are zinc, copper, cadmium, lead, and nickel. Although the first two are necessary micronutrients, all can be accumulated by plants to an extent that may be either phytotoxic (harmful to the plant) or dangerous for human consumption. The actual uptake of these metals by plants depends on many factors other than their concentration in the soil, among them soil pH and nutrient-holding capacity, organic matter content, type of plant grown, and the presence of other nutrients that may immobilize the metals. In general, keeping soil pH above 6.2 will hold these metals in a form that is unavailable to plants. However, since they are cumulative and persistent in soil, such sludges must be treated as hazardous wastes and not as fertilizers.

The possible presence of other toxic contaminants such as polychlorinated biphenyls (PCBs) and polybrominated biphenyls (PBBs) is another question that often arises regarding the safety of sludge as a fertilizer. The chlorinated hydrocarbons are more of a concern where they may be directly ingested by grazing livestock or inquisitive toddlers, since they are not commonly taken up by plants. Other forms of bioremediation of toxic persistent hydrocarbons, including mycoremediation using mushrooms, offer promising avenues to explore for cleaning up these dangerous residues (see Chapter 5).

The federal government has supported sludge composting. The USDA developed the static-pile forced-aeration composting system at its Beltsville, Maryland, research center for this purpose. The EPA has attempted to rebrand sewage sludge–composted or not–as the beneficent-sounding product called biosolids. This marketing campaign was rightly lambasted in the 2002 book by John Stauber, *Toxic Sludge Is Good for You*. While the book is an exposé of the public relations industry, Stauber does a good job of explaining why *biosolids* is a deceptive term and why sewage sludge is hardly the beneficent fertility aid advertised.

The problem with virtually all municipal sewage sludge in the United States, as detailed by Stauber, is that sewage treatment plants do not separate streams of household sewage from stormwater that washes toxic contaminants from city streets or industrial wastes from a wide array of manufacturing operations. It thus "collects, mixes, and concentrates a wide range of noxious and toxic materials which are then very difficult, if not impossible, to separate and detoxify," asserts Stauber. Add to this the medical waste flushed down drains in hospitals and the household hazardous waste dumped down toilets, and the result is a toxic stew that the most bioactive composting process has yet to render "beneficent."

EPA's campaign to designate biosolids as benign was much in evidence in the drafting of the first regulatory proposal for USDA's National Organic Program. Although EPA staff lobbied hard for inclusion of this material in a list of fertilizers permitted for use by organic farmers, their requests were not accepted by USDA staff in the course of drafting the regulations. Following a request for comment about the compatibility of biosolids with organic principles, public opposition to this practice forced the USDA to explicitly prohibit the use of sewage sludge to produce any organic product when it issued the final standards for organic production, as related by Grace Gershuny in *Organic Revolutionary: A Memoir of the Movement for Real Food, Planetary Healing, and Human Liberation*.

Industrial Wastes

Industrial wastes that can be composted are generated by food processors, clothing and textile industries, and paper and wood industries. In addition, certain inorganic industrial wastes, such as cement kiln dust, basic slag from steel producers, and cellophane and glass by-products, can be valuable additions to compost. Chapter 6 provides more information about specific industrial waste products that may be available to home composters, including cautions about some that may contain toxic contaminants.

Although they aren't as acutely hazardous as some industrial wastes, organic wastes can create big disposal headaches for industries. Wastes that are liquid or highly soluble generally contain high nitrogen levels and so are unsafe to landfill because of groundwater pollution hazards. They can also be potential sources of disease, cause odors, and attract pests. Although there is a market for some high-protein wastes as livestock feed, many nitrogenous wastes are unsuitable for this purpose.

Carbonaceous wastes are expensive to transport and bulky to store, although they pose little environmental threat. There is a demand for high-carbon by-products for such uses as livestock bedding and fuel—many wood-processing plants now use their wastes for on-site power and/or heat. For this reason, industries have looked more closely at co-composting their wastes with municipal yard waste or mixed solid-waste programs.

Demand is escalating for the services of consulting organizations such as Woods End Research Laboratories in Maine, who have helped processors of potatoes, wool, fish and shellfish, fruit, poultry, and paper, among others, to successfully compost their wastes. The key to their success is in careful analysis of the wastes to be composted and creative investigation of other local resources masquerading as waste problems. As composting becomes more attractive to industrial managers, state and county solid-waste districts are often able to serve as clearinghouses for information about the various wastes generated locally. Most states impose some restrictions on industrial wastes in landfills and, increasingly, prohibit them from entering landfills. As noted in Chapter 5, biological filtration systems such as those pioneered by Dr. John Todd and associates are being used not only to treat municipal sewage but increasingly for industrial facilities such as Maryland-based Tyson Foods, whose waste lagoons posed serious water-quality problems. Working with

John Todd & Associates, Tyson Foods turned its sludge-filled lagoon into a thriving ecosystem and compliant wastewater treatment site.

In recent years, many industrial-waste generators have begun assessing their sustainability practices and have instituted composting programs as an alternative to landfilling or land application, sometimes incorporating other locally available organic wastes to help balance the carbon/nitrogen ratio of their own wastes. One example cited by the Institute for Local Self-Reliance is the Novozymes North America enzyme manufacturing facility in Franklinton, North Carolina. In addition to the enzyme-processing sludge from its own facility, the facility accepts clean wood wastes and yard trimmings. Gypsum wallboard from construction debris as well as food waste from its on-site cafeteria and spoiled produce from a local food bank may be included, too.

LARGE-SCALE COMPOSTING TECHNOLOGIES

As mentioned earlier, large-scale composting methods fall into one of three categories: windrows, static aerated piles, and contained or in-vessel systems. Windrow composting is described in our discussion of farm-scale composting methods. Many municipal and industrial composting operations rely on this method, the only differences being the types of materials used and the scale of the equipment employed for turning the windrows. It is the most economical method for smaller municipal yard waste and leaf-composting projects. Depending on how carefully moisture, turning frequency, and materials mix are controlled, windrowing can compare favorably with more expensive in-vessel and static-pile technologies for larger mixed solid-waste systems.

Challenges for Scaling Up

Several issues must be addressed when scaling up.

Sorting it out. Before most mixed municipal solid waste can be composted, it must be sorted. The best time to remove noncompostable or hazardous materials from the refuse stream is before they get there. Now that local recycling programs abound and many municipalities offer curbside pickup of recyclables, less trash is getting mixed in with organic recyclables. The problem is still a major obstacle to food-scrap composting, particularly for institutions such as schools and hospitals, where students and patrons are accustomed to tossing disposable utensils and plates along with food waste.

Mixed solid-waste composting systems thus rely on sorting out the trash from waste streams, sometimes by hand-sorting from a conveyer belt. This method is widely used in countries where labor costs are low. Larger municipal composting operations in North America rely on some kind of mechanical process. These systems can be wet or dry, and they work by taking advantage of the different physical properties of organic and inorganic materials to separate them. Both systems take out heavier, denser inorganic materials through either a centrifuge or some other screening technology that drops heavier particles in a different place than the lighter organic refuse.

ARE BIODEGRADABLE PLASTICS THE SOLUTION?

A contaminant in sewage sludge of which author John Stauber was unaware is plastic. Not the big pieces that may come from discarded plastic bags or packing materials, but microparticles that form when all kinds of plastic materials—including those fleece garments made from recycled plastic bottles—disintegrate but do not biodegrade. Wastewater treatment plants receive large amounts of microplastics that come from households, industry, and surface runoff in urban areas. Most of these microplastics accumulate in the sewage sludge. The effects of these tiny plastic bits on soil life has not been studied, though the problem of plastic pollution in the ocean, and its impact on marine life, is increasingly recognized.

Improvements in the development of so-called bioplastics have brought the possibility of having the benefits of plastic without its damaging impacts on soil and water. If plastic made from plants can be composted and break down into fertilizer rather than hazardous microparticles, wouldn't that solve the problem?

The answer is a firm "maybe." Compostable disposable plates and utensils would certainly solve the problem of source separation in institutional food-scrap composting, but most of these products, including compostable liners for compost buckets that ease the problem of household curbside pickup, only fully decompose under carefully managed conditions. Even the most well-designed and conscientiously managed municipal compost operation may not always maintain the perfect conditions.

The National Organic Program has thus ruled that compost that contains such bioplastic utensils—which are generally not strictly plant based—is not permissible for use by organic farmers.

None is perfect, and the separated compostable material will inevitably still contain light and fluffy but nonbiodegradable plastic, among other things. The problem of bits of plastic and other "visual contaminants" turning up in municipal composts is one of the major stumbling blocks to effective marketing of the end product. Even "biodegradable" plastics do not always break down as completely as advertised.

Shredding. Among the more controversial systems are those that, rather than trying to remove any but the most obvious hazardous and metallic wastes, depend on grinding everything so finely that the undecomposable materials can't be detected in the finished compost. This was the approach used at the Agripost plant in Dade County, Florida, which was to handle up to 500 tons per day of municipal solid waste. This operation had its operating license revoked before it got very far, after the claim that residuals—meaning nonbiodegradable contaminants—total only 2 percent by weight of the finished product was found to be unrealistic.

Most municipal and industrial composting systems use some kind of technology for reducing the size of particles, if only a simple shredder for leaves. The reasons for doing so are the same as those for shredding or cutting up coarse materials for your home compost pile: The smaller the particle size, the faster composting will proceed and the more certain the outcome will be. Shredding and grinding equipment can vary a great deal in sophistication and mechanical complexity, depending on the volume of material being processed and its share of the traits that cause breakdowns or clogging of equipment. Sometimes finished compost is shredded once again, depending on the intended use of the product, to increase its uniformity and ensure more complete stabilization as the product ages. Once fully decomposed, most commercial composted products are screened to eliminate chunks of undecomposed bulking agents or wood chips, with the fineness of the screens used depending on the ultimate use of the product. For example, compost used in seed-starting mixes must be as fine as possible, while landscape-grade compost can contain larger bits of debris.

In-Vessel Systems or Bioreactors

Although windrows are almost always used at some point in the process, some large-scale composters use high-technology, fully enclosed, in-vessel systems that are often referred to as bioreactors. A bioreactor is an enclosed, rigid structure or vessel used to contain the material being composted. Such systems are usually equipped with automated process controls that monitor the performance of the composting process, generally moisture, temperature, and oxygen or carbon dioxide content. Aeration is accomplished by turning, if the system is horizontal, or by dropping, if it is vertical. Some are continuous, in which fresh materials are added regularly at one end and the end product simultaneously removed at the other, while others operate one batch at a time. Materials may enter a building in their raw state, where they undergo mechanical sorting, screening, and shredding, then proceed exactly like an industrial assembly line for aerating, mixing, moistening, and other manipulations. Compost emerges within a few days to a few weeks from when the original materials went in.

The Institute for Local Self-Reliance identifies four types of bioreactors and provides case studies of how each is used in practice.

- **Horizontal bioreactors** generally involve forced aeration and agitation or internal turning and operate in continuous rather than batch mode. Generally well suited to smaller community, on-farm, or institutional applications, they are best suited to capacities of less than 20,000 pounds per day of source-separated materials. Several companies produce such units that can be installed on a site with little additional equipment needed.
- **Tunnel bioreactors** also use active aeration but are better suited to larger-scale applications, with up to 100,000 tons per year in capacity. They generally involve construction of a long, narrow, cast-concrete structure with a positive aeration system built into the floor. They are designed to be filled using heavy equipment and include airtight door systems that are sealed after each filling.
- **Agitated-channel bioreactors** are similar to turned-windrow systems, but within parallel concrete walls. The raw ingredients are loaded into one end and moved down the length of the channel with a turning machine that moves on stationary rails, aerating the mixture as it moves slowly down the bed. Forced-aeration pipes may also be enclosed in a gravel floor, and the whole system will be housed within

a large industrial building. The number and length of beds determines the capacity of the system.

- **Rotary-drum bioreactors** are giant turning drums that move material through the system quickly and generate high temperatures necessary to kill pathogens. They are used primarily for municipal, industrial, and commercial applications such as animal mortalities, meatpacking and rendering wastes, and institutional food wastes. Air is pulled through the system from the discharge end and warmed as it flows through to the intake end. The short cycle of a few days to a week generally requires additional static-pile composting or curing before it can be used. This is one of the oldest municipal composting technologies, and drum units of a range of sizes are available on the market.

Mechanized digesters, obviously, cost more to buy and operate than windrows cost to build and turn. Capital investment and energy costs are high compared to windrow systems of any scale. A typical in-vessel compost system, for example, uses 12 to 15 kilowatt-hours to process 1 ton of refuse. These figures can be compared with the 4 kilowatt-hours per ton for compost windrows. While mechanical digesters require more highly skilled operators, the labor required to tend and maintain them in relation to the amount of material handled is significantly lower than for windrow systems.

Static-Pile Systems

The aerated static-pile system was originally developed by USDA at its Beltsville, Maryland, Agricultural Research Center for the purpose of safely and efficiently composting sewage sludge. The Beltsville process involves mixing sewage sludge with a bulking material such as wood chips and then building a windrow over a series of 4-inch perforated plastic pipes. The pipes are laid out in a series of parallel loops connected to a fan that is used to force air through the pile. This base is covered with peat, wood chips, or mature compost on which the windrow is built, and then air is drawn through the mass intermittently for 21 days. Such an active aeration system eliminates the need for turning and is able to achieve consistently high temperatures needed to ensure elimination of most pathogens.

The passively aerated windrow system (PAWS) was developed in Canada in the mid-1980s as a waste management technique that saves fuel and reduces odor and insects. This system relies on natural air convection created by temperature differences within and outside the pile to draw air through it, much as a chimney draws hot air from a woodstove. The windrow is generally covered with a "blanket" of peat or finished compost that acts as an integrated biofilter to reduce odors, conserve water, provide a barrier to nuisance insects, and insulate the pile. This system is less capital intensive but more demanding of properly balanced raw material mixes to ensure adequate heating. It can also take much longer to achieve full maturity than an actively aerated pile, and moving the pile without mangling the aeration pipes can be tricky.

THE ECONOMICS OF LARGE-SCALE COMPOSTING

The costs of large-scale composting systems can vary considerably, depending on which technology is used and what is being composted. Even if the finished product is given away or actually dumped into a landfill, composting of municipal and industrial wastes is starting to make economic sense. If nothing else, it reduces the volume of the wastes by 50 percent or more and turns them into a stable, nonpolluting material–this is the rationale for composting wastes containing high concentrations of heavy metals. Happily, the demand for compost is increasing at the same time that composting facilities are proliferating, and the economic landscape is shifting rapidly.

The days when advocates claimed that compost sales would completely pay for the costs of disposing of municipal wastes are gone; today tipping fees are the primary major revenue stream for any composting operation, be it municipal, commercial, or industrial. As in any other business venture, it is always best to evaluate the goals and resources available to the operation before investing time, labor, and money in a composting facility. Following are a few factors to consider when planning any new composting operation.

Startup and Operating Costs

The ILSR recommends budgeting at least $25,000 for planning, engineering, and business-plan development, depending on scale and the level of commercial production intended. While a municipal or institutional organics recycling facility may only need to recover direct costs, a commercial compost manufacturer needs to produce a return on investment. Questions that should be evaluated before initiating a project include:

- Sources and volume of feedstock available within a reasonable geographic area, collection costs, and tipping fees that can be anticipated
- Space and siting needs, including cost of compliance with environmental regulations and permitting costs
- Equipment and technology needs, specialized equipment, structures, other fixed assets
- Operating costs, including labor, utilities, insurance, and supplies such as totes or storage containers

Some preliminary number crunching can help you approximate the cost per unit (generally measured in cubic yards) of finished compost. Cornell University did some exhaustive analyses of on-farm composting costs for several New York State farms in the mid-1990s, which showed that a basic tractor and a tractor-driven windrow-turner combination were the most cost-effective methods for windrow composting. Professional composters interviewed for NOFA's handbook series estimated a cost for producing high-quality marketable compost of anywhere from $18 to $25 per yard in the mid-2000s. Institutional composting operations may factor in the savings in tipping fees they avoid, combined with eliminating the need for purchased fertility inputs for grounds maintenance.

Marketing Considerations

Although sales of compost can help offset the costs of waste disposal, marketing the product entails added costs and expertise that may not warrant the effort. While institutional composters may distribute in bulk or for a nominal fee, commercial operations must consider the volume of sales; ingredients needed for specialized blends or boosted nutrient content; the cost of retail packaging versus bulk sales, delivery, and promotion; and, of course, prices that can be charged for the finished product.

Municipal compost, whether derived from sludge, mixed solid waste, or yard waste, often goes directly to public works such as roadside landscaping, parks, and groundskeeping–which, of course, saves on another town expense.

Many leaf and yard waste composting programs give away their compost to local residents and usually have no problem selling what's left to nurseries and landscapers in bulk. In some cases, nominal fees are charged, which still represent considerable savings over the cost of purchasing commercial products like peat moss, topsoil, and fertilizer.

When marketing compost to the general public is considered, it is important to ensure quality and consistency in the product. This means that "visual contaminants"–such as bits of plastic, paper, or glass that may show up in municipal compost–should be eliminated. Moisture levels should be reduced as much as possible before bagging. And every effort must be made to allow the finished compost to age as long as necessary to fully stabilize–ideally at least 6 months.

Since compost is generally marketed as a soil conditioner rather than a fertilizer, it is less critical to make sure that the N-P-K analysis is consistent–however, regular monitoring of nutrients, as well as toxins, is a good idea. Most yard waste composting operations shred the finished product to improve its consistency.

With the rise in municipal and private composting initiatives, however, it is wise to research the market demand and competition before counting on sales of compost to support a new facility. Some areas, such as the Northeast, that are both highly urbanized and already centers of composting activity might generate more compost than the local market could absorb. The Portland, Oregon, Metropolitan Service District commissioned an extensive market survey before adding a mixed municipal solid-waste composting facility to its existing yard waste and sludge composting projects. The results showed that, for the foreseeable future, their market area had plenty of room for more compost.

The best assurance of a market for compost from any source is attention to quality, but there are, at this point, few generally recognized guidelines for the quality of commercial composts. William F. Brinton, founder and president of Woods End Research Laboratories in Maine, has been working on this issue for 30 years. He says that "the ultimate value of a finished compost is its effect on plant life . . . how well a compost nourishes plants and does not harm them, and enriches soil while possibly also suppressing soil-borne plant diseases." The most promising measurements Brinton has developed include the following:

- An oxidation-reduction test to indicate the stability of the compost, and thus its potential for emitting undesirable odors
- A microbial respiration test that, in combination with the first test, gives a more complete picture of a compost's stability
- A measurement of organic acids (acetic, butyric, and propionic acids), whose presence can be harmful to plants
- A measurement of disease-suppression capability, based on research conducted by Dr. Harry Hoitink in Ohio (see Chapter 4)
- A more precise measurement of human and plant pathogens in compost

With this level of attention to detail, large-scale composters can gain the confidence of their markets. Establishing and enforcing minimum industry standards for composted products must be the next step in promoting their wider public acceptance and use. We will conclude this chapter by looking at how, despite the lack of industry guidelines, consumers of commercial composted products might evaluate their choices.

LEGAL ISSUES

Mulching compost on a garden or farm scale violates, of itself, no law that we know of. While individual states vary somewhat in regulations related to composting, no state legally prohibits the practice as such.

It would, of course, contradict the basic principle of soil conservation for any government to restrain or prevent the return of needed organic matter to the land. However, when actual danger to health results from improperly made compost, the responsibility of government is clear. Regulations relative to compost making relate to potential health hazards, environmental protection (particularly water quality concerns), and business licensing related to commercial production and sale of compost.

In many states, laws banning yard wastes and leaves from overcrowded landfills have included legal encouragement for developing municipal composting facilities. Bans on disposal of yard trimmings in landfills have been in effect in 20 states for many years, and a few now have food-waste disposal bans in place. While it doesn't impose a ban, California's waste diversion law, passed in 1999, required municipalities to divert half of their waste stream or face fines. This approach has inspired numerous local organic waste diversion programs. While yard waste composting is a relatively straightforward process that has been widely adopted, ramping up to dealing with food scraps would require more intensive training and facilities upgrades to deal with higher-moisture, more potentially dangerous waste streams. Several states have included some kind of incentive for local communities to institute municipal composting, often in the form of grant programs for pilot projects combined with technical assistance. The State of Illinois, for example, gave out over $4.2 million to 57 local projects in 1990. There is also frequently a built-in market incentive for the finished compost, such as a requirement that state and local agencies give preference to purchasing composted products for all public works needs.

However, the *BioCycle*/ILSR report notes that this enthusiasm by state governments has waned in the years following EPA's push to close substandard landfills. "Trash began flowing long distances by rail and truck," as regional EPA-compliant landfills replaced local ones. A survey conducted for this report indicates that while most of the 39 states that responded offer some kind of education or technical assistance programs for composting, only 14 have grant programs and only 7 have loan programs to help establish composting facilities.

Other government agencies have worked to encourage compost use on farms. The USDA's Natural Resource Conservation Service (NRCS) provides technical assistance as well as some subsidies through its Environmental Quality Improvement Program (EQIP). EQIP is a voluntary program that helps farmers plan and implement conservation practices that improve soil, water, plant, animal, air, and related natural resources on agricultural land and nonindustrial private forestland. This program offers cost sharing of technical assistance services for farmers who want to transition to organic management, including on-farm composting systems.

Virtually all composting limitations or restrictions fall into one of three categories: commercial manufacture and distribution, public health danger, and environmental regulation. Current information on legal requirements and permits needed for siting of commercial composting operations and sale of compost products for all US states that have regulations can be found on the US Composting Council website. The Institute for Local Self-Reliance also offers examples of model rules and policies from states and communities throughout the United States and Canada that serve to both encourage and regulate the production and sale of compost.

Composted biosolids are commonly used to reclaim strip-mined land, and a recent project in Appalachia is attempting to reclaim a former mountaintop coal-mining site as a farm enterprise by composting in place. Livestock such as pigs and goats provide manure, and chipping equipment turns scrubby brush that grows there into a carbon source to create fertile soil.

Finally, the potential for composting to mitigate climate change by reducing greenhouse gas emissions and sequestering carbon in the soil has gained formal recognition through the work of California's Marin Carbon Project. Thanks in part to a grant from the NRCS, the Environmental Defense Fund (EDF) helped create standards that reward ranchers for land management practices that put more carbon in the soil, thereby improving soil health and reducing greenhouse gas emissions. The project developed research-based measurements of carbon sequestration in rangeland to which compost was applied. In 2014, EDF announced the approval of a protocol that allows ranchers to model the increase in carbon sequestration on their land, have it independently verified, and generate tradable offset credits that can generate revenue when sold on voluntary carbon markets.

Compost for Sale

Nearly every state has what is generally termed a "commercial fertilizer law." In part, these laws stipulate requirements for registering, grading, labeling, and selling all products intended "to supply food for plants or to increase crops produced by land." For such products to meet the law and be sold in most states, they must be registered with the agriculture department, show that they maintain various minimums of plant nutrients (N-P-K), and be labeled in accordance with the particular state's code, usually to include a guaranteed analysis of these major fertilizer values. Other provisions in most states limit the percentage of inert matter permitted and instruct that any toxic or "injurious" ingredients included be identified, their quantities listed, and adequate directions for use and warnings against misuse given.

Regulations such as these apply, of course, only where a product is manufactured or processed to be sold. If you plan to distribute a compost product commercially, your wisest first step is to check with the agriculture department in your own state to determine its requirements. Some states do not consider compost—along with various other materials such as limestone, gypsum, and manure—as a "commercial fertilizer" at all. A number of them direct that these be called "soil amendments," "soil-improvement mixtures," "manipulated manures," or some similar designation and insist that they be tagged as "not a plant food product." Again, it is important to emphasize that any state's fertilizer law provisions control only products actually marketed. None of them affects preparation and use of compost or other fertilizer material for yourself. If you plan to sell compost to farmers and gardeners, make sure to check with your state's tax department. Some states exempt fertilizers used to produce food from sales tax, but they may not apply that exemption to compost if it is not considered a fertilizer.

For the compost industry to develop, it is widely agreed that some kind of regulation of product quality assurance will be needed soon. There is, for example, no legal definition of compost to be found in federal or state statutes. At a meeting of northeastern state recycling programs in 1989, representatives concluded that region-wide standards for compost would be difficult but that at least they could "examine the possibility of developing a uniform label that would identify contents of the compost and describe its uses."

As of the year 2000, 12 states had enacted some form of rules or guidelines for compost quality, primarily for products purchased by transportation departments. New Mexico's requirements apply to compost used by the Bureau of Mines for land reclamation, while regulations in Illinois, Maine, Minnesota, and New Jersey apply to compost for general use. The Compost Council of Canada has a more well-developed program called the Compost Quality Alliance, which promulgates a set of voluntary national guidelines. That program includes standardized product sampling, uniform laboratory testing, and appropriate product attributes and usage guidelines for different types of compost products.

Protecting Public Health

The second legal aspect to composting concerns avoiding any "health hazards" that may be involved. This can be significant to the home gardener or farmer making compost, as well as to the municipal or commercial composter. The one important thing to keep in mind is that properly made compost breaks no rules, endangers no one's health, and legally offends nobody.

Almost all states have sections within their sanitation or health codes dealing with waste disposal and public welfare as it may be affected by waste disposal. Most often, the health law is called a "nuisance" regulation. It is essential to understand that by a *nuisance* these laws do not mean something that is simply "annoying" or an arbitrary "bother" to anyone. In this instance, the legal terminology specifically designates a *nuisance* as a condition dangerous to health or a likely hazard to personal or public well-being.

Under the provisions of most nuisance statutes, the state may restrict a composting project or prosecute a violator if unhealthy conditions exist. Conditions considered unhealthy may include the following:

- Allowing wastes to become a potential agent in the transmission of disease
- Allowing wastes to contaminate a water supply or surrounding land
- Allowing wastes to attract vermin or breed disease-carrying insects such as mosquitoes
- Keeping wastes (especially human wastes and dead animals) within a specified distance (usually 300 to 500 feet) of a public thoroughfare

Your home garden or farm composting will not create any of these conditions if it is handled with even a moderate amount of care and consideration for your neighbors' aesthetic sensibilities. Although there have been instances of complaints filed against home composters in years past, properly maintained home compost piles are now more widely viewed as a community asset than as a potential public nuisance.

Municipal compost operations, especially those using sewage sludge, have been scrutinized quite heavily for potential public health hazards. Worker health concerns and odor problems have also been investigated. The sheer volume of materials handled warrants some legal oversight of these facilities, since an improperly managed or sloppy operation can create definite health hazards. For example, if sewage sludge is not scrupulously monitored to maintain high enough temperatures, numerous disease organisms can remain in the finished product. Dust, which may carry fungi and other allergens, must be kept to a minimum. And good ventilation design can drastically reduce the likelihood that objectionable odors will waft about the neighborhood. Recognizing that these concerns all hinge on adequate operator training, some states have begun to institute training programs in proper composting procedures for solid-waste employees.

It should be noted that uncomposted sewage sludge must be regulated more carefully than must composted sludge. Because it could introduce disease organisms into the food chain, restrictions on how and where it may be spread are necessary. Concerns about heavy metals, as is the case with composted sludges, must also be addressed. This is why most states prohibit distribution of sewage sludge to the general public and require those using it for landscaping, greenhouses, and the like to obtain permits.

Environmental Regulation

The third aspect of legal regulation of composting has become the most troublesome for municipal and commercial composters. Most states still regulate composting according to the same environmental restrictions applied to waste disposal methods such as landfills and incinerators. By lumping them together like this, environmental regulations often unnecessarily increase the costs of composting and work at cross-purposes to laws requiring emphasis on recycling in solid-waste plans.

Ironically, greater public environmental awareness about the pollution hazards of waste disposal sites has, in some communities, worked to block the development of compost operations. This is often referred to as the NIMBY or "not in my backyard" phenomenon. In New Milford, Connecticut, many citizens who worked to oppose the siting of an incinerator in that town for environmental reasons also opposed plans to build a municipal solid-waste composting plant–with the alternative being to ship the town's garbage to an incinerator 50 miles away on Long Island Sound.

Says George Kirkpatrick, the state senator in Florida who led the fight for a comprehensive recycling law in that state, "I love to talk to environmentalists who say composting and recycling are going to save us from ourselves. Well, talk to those same environmentalists on the night you try to site the facility. What you hear is, 'We don't want it in our neighborhood.'" There is still a lot of public relations work needed to let citizens know that composting facilities make good neighbors.

Several states are attempting to address the problem of regulating composting facilities independently of other solid-waste disposal sites. Yard waste composting in particular is generally considered benign, and one regulator noted that "many states are relying more on education and guidance than regulations" to see that such facilities are problem-free.

Connecticut is the least restrictive, requiring only that a leaf-composting project register with its environmental agency. Other states require that permits be obtained before starting a composting project, with varying degrees of red tape involved in the permitting process. Sometimes permits are required only if the volume of materials handled exceeds some limit, such as 6,000 cubic yards per year in Maine. In some cases, yard wastes are treated very leniently, but more rigorous requirements apply if other kinds of organic wastes, such as garbage or sludge, are used.

Requirements are typically placed on siting, facility design, and operating standards. Setbacks from adjoining property, bodies of water, or public thoroughfares guard against odor problems and water pollution from leachate. Site-grading and drainage regulations similarly ensure that nutrient-laden runoff won't pollute waterways. Only a few states, including New Jersey, Maine, and Pennsylvania, have rules about frequency of turning or maximum windrow size. So far, only Maine says anything about proper handling of grass clippings, requiring a facility to have enough leaves on hand before it can accept grass. The required ratio of leaves to grass clippings is 3:1. Other states do not accept grass clippings because their high nitrogen content and moisture create putrefaction and objectionable odors.

As composting is increasingly embraced as a solution to solid-waste problems, more states will enact regulations specifically governing composting operations. These regulations are most commonly supervised by state environmental agencies, although departments of public health may also be involved. As more research is conducted into product quality monitoring, you can expect more legal safeguards governing labeling and sale of composted products.

COMPOST REGULATIONS FOR ORGANIC FARMERS

Once the USDA's National Organic Program was implemented in 2002, farmers wishing to market their products as organic had to comply with the myriad requirements of this program. The rules were developed based on long-standing organic principles and practices, including standards created by a host of grassroots farmers' groups. Among the requirements that apply to any organic farm (wherever it is and whatever types of products are grown or raised) are rules that require that any practices used must "maintain or improve the natural resources of the operation, including soil and water quality."

Only natural (nonsynthetic) fertilizers can be used, including minerals such as lime and materials derived from plant and animal matter. Organic farmers are thus encouraged to use manure as a source of crop nutrients and soil fertility. However, food safety concerns have dictated that raw manure must be composted if it is used to produce a crop for human consumption, unless at least 120 days have elapsed before harvest, or 90 days if the crop is unlikely to come into contact with soil (e.g., most grain crops). Specific practice standards for composting were then adopted that are intended to ensure that any human pathogens present will not survive; the standards are not concerned with the quality of the compost. The practice standards for compost are based on rules established by the NRCS for commercial or municipal composting operations.

NOP Compost Requirements

The organic regulations require that composted plant and animal materials be produced though a process that (1) established an initial C/N ratio of between 25:1 and 40:1; and (2) maintained a temperature of between 131° and 170°F (55° and 77°C) for 3 days using an in-vessel or static-aerated pile system; or (3) maintained a temperature of between 131° and 170°F for 15 days using a windrow composting system, during which period the materials must be turned a minimum of five times.

Additional guidance has been issued to permit vermicompost produced at lower temperatures, inasmuch as scientific evidence shows that vermicomposting is as effective as hot composting for reducing the presence of human pathogens. Compost tea can only be used for foliar feeding if it is made in accordance with these rules.

The feedstock for compost, according to these rules, cannot include any substance deemed synthetic unless it has first been specifically approved for use as a farm input. It also cannot have been deliberately combined with a prohibited substance, although conventional crops, manure from CAFOs, and municipal yard waste are not considered to be prohibited feedstocks. If there is cause to suspect contamination, however, the material has to be tested before it can be used. Persistent herbicides, as noted earlier, have caused problems even for careful composters. This is also the basis for disallowing the inclusion of "compostable" bio-based plastic utensils in food-scrap composting. Finally, whether the compost is farm produced or not, the composter must be able to document that these conditions have been met. That is, a log must be kept to show that appropriate turning and temperature requirements have been recorded, and records of where raw ingredients came from must be available for inspection.

Farmers who want to sell compost to other organic farmers, or who want assurance that the compost they buy from a local composting operation meets USDA requirements, should contact their organic certifying agent. Many regional certifiers, such as Vermont Organic Farmers or California Certified Organic Farmers, will evaluate local or regional composting operations as to whether they are meeting NOP requirements and can be used by organic farmers.

SELECTING AND USING COMMERCIAL COMPOSTED PRODUCTS

Although the purpose of this book is to enable you to make your own compost, the increasing availability of commercial composted products offers some options to those who either don't yet have their own compost or don't have enough. The obvious advantage of these products is convenience. There's no need to collect materials, build a bin, turn a pile, or wait longer than it takes to travel to the garden supply store and back. It comes in easy-to-handle packages in which any excess can be stored until you need it. Many compost products are available in specialized blends with other natural ingredients to make them suitable for applications such as lawns, potting mixes, and other special needs. They tend to be uniform and flowable, so they can be used in fertilizer spreaders. And if properly made, they offer all the same soil-improving benefits as homemade compost.

There's one catch to all this, though. The products all cost money—enough to make purchasing compost a significant expense for all but the smallest gardens. Once you've paid $15 or more for a 50-pound bag of commercial compost, you will immediately begin to appreciate the value of all those organic wastes that other people throw away. Before you shell out hard cash for compost, make every effort to be sure you're getting a quality product. A few guidelines will help you evaluate the myriad products out there.

In many places, compost can be purchased in bulk direct from farms and municipal composting facilities. Garden supply stores also increasingly make compost and bark mulches available for bulk purchase. A minimum purchase of one yard of compost is common, and it represents a significant saving over the cost of the equivalent amount bagged. In many cases, delivery is available at additional cost, but even if you don't have a pickup truck available, a mid-size hatchback car or an SUV can accommodate about half a yard when the material is shoveled into recycled bags.

Purchasing Guidelines

First of all, you should find out what raw materials were used to make the product, as well as what other materials were added later to "boost" its nutrient content. Most reputable natural fertilizer companies will provide the information you need, and some include it in their labels or customer information brochures. Oddly enough, fertilizer labels are not always legally required to list ingredients—only N-P-K analysis. Composts usually don't even qualify as fertilizers and are labeled as "soil amendments," with still fewer requirements on guaranteed nutrient contents.

If any of the compost ingredients contained toxic contaminants, it is possible that they have been broken down or rendered unavailable by being tightly held in insoluble organic molecules. In some cases, however, raw materials are so contaminated that the finished product cannot be considered safe to use in your home garden. If a company is composting paper mill sludge, for example, are they checking carefully for possible dioxin residues? Municipal sludge compost, in particular, sometimes contains concentrated amounts of toxic heavy metals—maybe not such a big problem for landscaping or restoring strip-mined soil, but unwise to use for edible crops. State regulations usually prohibit sale of sludge composts with excessive heavy-metal content to the public.

Uniformity is a big problem for composted products—it's difficult to get two batches of compost to come out exactly alike in terms of guaranteed analysis. There are many companies that have worked this problem out, either by carefully controlling the compost recipes or by amending the finished products with other organic materials to comply with their labels. Some will sell composts with specific batch labels, showing how that lot tested out on nutrients and toxins as well. Compost purchased in bulk from your local farmer or municipal recycling facility may not be consistent from batch to batch, but this is usually a minor consideration.

In many ways, the worst problem that arises with purchased compost is incomplete decomposition—the manufacturer did not wait long enough before bagging and shipping it off. This means that your bag may emit rather unpleasant smells when opened, and its contents may harm plants if applied directly. You can remedy this by putting it into your own compost pile to finish or simply letting it sit a while before using it—but it's better not to buy unfinished compost to begin with. Of course, detecting this problem may be difficult. One sign to watch for is a plastic fertilizer bag that looks inflated; this is a result of continued emission of carbon dioxide and other gases by compost organisms. The material inside should look, feel, and smell like good finished compost—if it is too wet, smells weird, or has recognizable raw materials in it, you would be wise to reject it. Mushrooms growing in it are also indicators that compost is unfinished.

Most companies put out a line of compost-based blends with different "boosters" for different needs. Refer to Chapter 6 for information about the various materials that may be added to compost to fortify its nutrient content. The source of these added nutrients can be important, especially if you are an organic producer.

Commercial compost-based products that are approved for use by organic producers are widely available. The Organic Materials Review Institute (OMRI) as well as the Washington State Department of Agriculture (WSDA) organic program, among others, publish lists of farm and processing inputs that have been fully reviewed and determined to be compliant with the National Organic Program requirements. Compost-based products that are on such approved lists are documented to comply with the compost requirements, and any additives, boosters, or "secret formulas" have been reviewed and determined to be allowed for organic production.

Buying Locally

The best compromise, if you find that you must purchase some compost, is to get it from a local farmer or municipal facility. Not only is this the cheapest source you are likely to find, but it is the most conserving of natural resources and provides economic and environmental benefits to your own community. You are also more likely to be sure of the source of materials that went into the compost, as well as the adequacy of the composting methods, when you can visit the facility in person.

Of course, the only way to be sure of what you're getting is to make your own compost. It also happens to be the most economical source of high-quality soil food. If you have a use for compost, there is no reason you can't make your own. Even if you invest in a purchased compost tumbler or bin, you will save a great deal over the price of buying compost in bags. And you can be certain that you aren't spreading toxic substances or harsh chemicals in your garden. With this book, you now have all the information you need to do it right.

APPENDIX: RESOURCES AND INFORMATION

INFORMATION SOURCES

BOOKS

Gershuny, Grace. *Compost, Vermicompost, & Compost Tea: Feeding the Soil on the Organic Farm.* White River Junction, VT: Chelsea Green, 2011. Information on farm-scale composting techniques, with extended appendices, including a recipe calculator, potting mix recipes, and a sample compost production budget sheet.

Gershuny, Grace, and Joseph Smillie. *The Soul of Soil.* White River Junction, VT: Chelsea Green, 1999. A concise presentation of soil ecology and chemistry, with tables listing specific compost materials, green manures, and other resources that allow farmers and gardeners to translate into action the more general information provided by the book.

Holzer, Sepp. *Sepp Holzer's Permaculture.* White River Junction, VT: Chelsea Green, 2011. Sepp Holzer farms steep mountainsides in Austria with an intricate network of terraces, raised beds, ponds, waterways, and tracks, well covered with productive fruit trees and other vegetation. Among the techniques described is his system of *hugulkultur,* or mound culture.

Howard, Sir Albert. *An Agricultural Testament.* Emmaus, PA: Rodale Press, 1972 (special edition). Howard contended that the loss of soil fertility he observed can be repaired by manufacturing humus from vegetable and animal wastes through the composting process. It was this book that led the late J. I. Rodale to begin publishing *Organic Farming and Gardening.*

Jenkins, Joseph. *The Humanure Handbook,* 3rd ed. Grove City, PA: Joseph Jenkins, Inc., 2005. The most comprehensive, up-to-date, and thoroughly researched book available on the topic of composting human manure.

King, F. H. *Farmers of Forty Centuries: Organic Farming in China, Korea, and Japan.* Mineola, NY: Dover Publications, 2004. Reprint of the Mrs. F. H. King, Madison, Wisconsin, 1911 edition. Franklin Hiram King, a former official of the US Department of Agriculture, traveled to Asia in the early 1900s to learn how farmers in China, Korea, and Japan were able to achieve successful harvests century after century without exhausting the soil.

Logsdon, Gene. *Holy Shit: Managing Manure to Save Mankind*. White River Junction, VT: Chelsea Green, 2010. Logsdon artfully describes how to manage farm manure, pet manure, and human manure to make fertilizer and humus.

PUBLICATIONS AND WEBSITES

BioCycle: The Organics Recycling Authority
https://www.biocycle.net/
Published since 1960, *BioCycle* is the go-to magazine and website on composting, organics recycling, anaerobic digestion, and renewable energy.

Growing Local Fertility: A Guide to Community Composting
Brenda Platt, Institute for Local Self-Reliance, and James McSweeney and Jenn Davis, Highfields Center for Composting, 2014.
https://ilsr.org/size-matters-report-shows-small-scale-community-based
-composting/
Illustrated using case studies, offers information on technical, regulatory, and organizing methods to help you develop a local food-scrap composting program in your community.

State of Composting in US: What, Where, Why and How
Brenda Platt, Institute for Local Self-Reliance, Nora Goldstein, *BioCycle*, Craig Coker, Coker Composting & Consulting, July 2014.
Data on how much organic recycling is being done, where, and by whom, with case studies and analysis. Revised every few years with updated information.

PALS Publishing (formerly NRAES)
http://palspublishing.cals.cornell.edu/nra_order.taf?_function=view&ct_id=47
Various in-depth publications about on-farm and municipal composting.

ORGANIZATIONS

ATTRA: The National Assistance Sustainable Agriculture Program
Information on all aspects of sustainable agriculture. Publications related to soil and compost at https://attra.ncat.org/publication.html#soils

Cornell Composting
http://compost.css.cornell.edu/
Cornell Waste Management Institute's website provides access to a variety of composting educational materials and programs developed at Cornell University.

Institute for Local Self-Reliance (ILSR)

https://ilsr.org/

Since 1974, ILSR has championed local self-reliance, a strategy that underscores the need for humanly scaled institutions and economies and the widest possible distribution of ownership. The Waste to Wealth program works with activists, policy makers, and businesses to reduce waste generation and maximize the reuse, recovery, and remanufacturing of these materials and their associated products.

Master Composter Programs

Various states, universities, municipalities, and nonprofit organizations offer Master Composter programs. Often affiliated with a more common Master Gardener Program, they offer classroom, online, and hands-on curriculum designed to train and recruit local volunteers who will promote backyard composting and yard waste reduction in their own neighborhoods. Inquire at your local cooperative extension office.

Rodale Institute

http://rodaleinstitute.org/our-work/compost/compost-current-projects/

The Rodale Institute in Kutztown, PA, offers a Master Composter training program as well as conducting research aimed at perfecting a method of composting that reliably supports the growth of a healthy soil food web and improving the composting guidelines for certified organic farmers and composters.

US Composting Council

https://compostingcouncil.org/

A trade association for the composting industry, with an affiliated research and education arm. It provides resources, educational materials, training, networking, and career advancement opportunities for professionals and all those affiliated with the compost manufacturing and organics recycling industry. *BioCycle* is its official publication, and it hosts an annual conference and trade show.

Woods End Laboratories

https://woodsend.org/

Soil and compost testing, articles, and research reports by Dr. William Brinton.

EQUIPMENT AND TOOL SOURCES

BioCycle Equipment and Systems Directory

https://www.biocycle.net/buyers-guide/
biocycle-equipment-and-systems-directory/

Current listings of sources for any and all equipment and supplies to help establish and maintain larger-scale municipal or farm composting operations. Tools needed for home or small local composting are readily available at local garden and hardware stores, including chains such as Home Depot, Lowe's, and Tractor Supply.

Several good sources of composting tools and supplies, including bins, tumblers, totes, aerators, and thermometers, can be found online, along with helpful advice on how to use them. These are some websites that offer a full range of home composting tools and supplies as well as more ideas for innovative home- and community-scale technologies:

Compost Junkie

http://www.compostjunkie.com

Gardeners Supply Company

https://www.gardeners.com/

Hayneedle, Inc.

https://www.hayneedle.com/stylists/green-living_22/styleboards/composting-containers-accessories_833

Johnson-Su Bioreactor Instructions

http://regenerationinternational.org/bioreactor/

Information on the advantage of this simple technology for producing high-fungal compost and detailed instructions on how to build one yourself

Planet Natural

https://www.planetnatural.com/product-category/organic-gardening/composting/

COMPOST SOURCES

BioCycle's Find-a-Composter Site

http://www.findacomposter.com/#s=1

BioCycle's FindAComposter.com® is a publicly searchable database of composting sites in the United States and Canada. Whether you are looking for a local source of bulk compost or a place to bring your food scraps or yard trimmings, you can enter your location and the type of service you need, then browse the results.

US Composting Council Compost Locator Map

https://compostingcouncil.org/compostmap/

An interactive map that allows you to find a source of quality compost, and access a list of participants in the USCC's Seal of Testing Assurance program.

Compost Junkie

http://www.compostjunkie.com/buy-compost.html

Enter information on where you are and what you need, which allows you to search this database for a supplier near you. The database lists a variety of compost suppliers, including farmers, garden centers, compost manufacturers, landscape supply depots, municipalities, and mushroom compost suppliers.

INDEX

Boldface page numbers indicate photographs or illustrations. Underscored references indicate boxed text, charts, and graphs.

actinomycetes, 28, 33, 35, **38**

activators, 88–90, 164–65

aeration, 17–18, 47, 143–45, **144**, 166–68, **167**

aggregates, 13, 14–16

agricultural composting, 5, 136–37, 160–62, **161**, 171–72, 194, 243, 244–56, **251**, **252**, 268

air, **12**, 17–18, 47, 48, **48**, 143–45, **144**. *See also* aeration

alfalfa, 90

anaerobic composting, 30, 164, 178–80, **179**, 181, 207, 254–56

ants, 33, 36, **39**, 40

apple pomace, 90–91

ashes, 65, 87, 105, 120, 122

bacteria, 27–28, 32, 33, 34–35, **39**, 59–60, 134, 147, 148–49

bagasse, 91, 117

bag composting, 164

banana residues, 91

Bangalore variation of Indore method, 155

barrel composters, 144, 165–66

basic slag, 91–92, 92

beetles, 33, 36, **38**, **39**, 40

beet wastes, 92

Beltsville system, 259, 265–66

bins, **156**, 196

   block and brick, 204, **204**

   bottom aerated, 159, 166–68, **167**, 197

   cage-type, 198, **199**, 200–202, **201**, **202**

   California method, 157–59, **156**, **159**

   for earthworms, 186–91, **187**, **188**, **189**, **190**, 209

   Lehigh-style, 197–98, **197**

   movable slat, 205, **205**

   multi-bin composter, 163, 203, 204, **208**, **213**

   New Zealand, 198, **199**, 203

   raised, 166–68, **167**

   rodent-proof, 200–202, **201**, **202**

   for slopes (stair-stepped), 208, **208**

   three-bin composter, 163, 203, 204, **208**, **213**

   winter (*See* winter composting)

biochar, 2, 88–89

biodynamic method, 5, 160–62, **161**

bioremediation, 74

biothermal energy, 75–77

bird droppings, 85, 86

blood, dried, 97

bokashi, 149

"bone black," 93, 117

bonemeal, 87, 93

boron, 58

boxes, composting in, 191–93

brandling worms, 184, **184**, 186, **186**

   protecting in winter, 189–91, **190**

brewers' grains, 105

buckwheat hulls, 93

calcium, 55, 107, 118

California method, 156–59, **156**, **159**

carbohydrates, 28, 53

carbon, 30, 53, _127–32_, 146
carbon cycle, in composting, _29_, **29**
carbon dioxide, 76
carbon/nitrogen ratio, 30, _122–23_,
    146–47, 157
castor pomace, 93–94
cat manure, 85–86, 140
cattle manure, 139. _See also_ manure
centipedes, 33, 36, 37, **38**
chelation, _57_, **57**
city composting, 210–12, _211_, **211**, **213**
city people's method, 163–65, _164_
cocoa bean shells, 94–95
coffee waste, 95
colloids, 20–22, **21**
compost
    applying, 228–37, **229**, _233_, **236**,
        240–41
    benefits of, 8–25, 11, 12
    buying, 277–80
    checklist for, _180_
    _vs._ chemical fertilizers, 24–25
    earthworms and (_See_ earthworms)
    extract spray from, _62_
    as heart of organic farming and
        gardening method, 11
    as heat source (biothermal energy),
        75–77
    heavy metals and (_See_ heavy metals)
    herbicide-damaged soil and, 22–23
    herbicides in, 61–62, 68, 101–2
    plant diseases and, 23, 59–61, _62_, _238_,
        240
    public health and, 258, 272–74
    in seed-starting soil mixture, 237
    selling, 267–69, 271–72
    soil pH and, 23
    specialized for greenhouses, 60
    as starter solution, 237–38, _238_
    using, 185–86, 240–41
composting, 1
    compared to mulching, 172
    green manures in, 30, 101–2, 172–73

history of, 1–7
materials to exclude, 62, 85–86, 105,
    111, 115–16, 147
materials to include, 81–88, **83**,
    90–121, _102_, _107_, _122–32_ (_See also_
    specific material)
    balancing of, 85
    for enrichment, 86–87
    region specific, 84–85
    sources for, 81–85
NOP regulations for (_See_ National
    Organic Program (NOP))
problem solving, 181, _181_
process of, 1, 26, 27–32, _29_, **29**, 31, **31**,
    33, 53
    activators, 88–90, 164–65
    aeration and, 143–45, **144**, 166–68
    bacteria in (_See_ bacteria)
    basic requirements for, 143–49,
        144
    carbon balance in (_See_ carbon)
    carbon cycle in, _29_, **29**
    carbon/nitrogen ratio and, _122_,
        127–32, 146–47
    as cycle of life, 8–9, **9**
    decomposers in, 28, 32–41, **33**,
        38–39, 42
    enrichment of, 86–87
    food web in, **38–39**
    growth stimulators and, 24
    inoculation during, 59–60, 148–49
    insects and, 36–37, **38–39**, 40–41,
        44, 63
    judging progress of, 33, **33**, 230–31,
        _231_
    microorganisms in, 27–30, 32–36,
        38–39, 46–47
    moisture in, 30, 31, 145–46, _180_
    nitrogen cycle in, _31_, **31** (_See also_
        nitrogen)
    oxidation in, 138, 179
    pH and, 32
    temperature in (_See_ temperature)

programs for
  community-based, 66–73, 70–73
  individual initiatives, 80
  municipal (*See* municipal
    composting)
as recycling method, 10–11, **10–11**
site selection for, 145, 274
of solid waste (*See* municipal
  composting)
turning, 144, 147
composting methods and systems
  anaerobic, 178–81, **179**, 207, 254–56
  biodynamic method, 5, 160–62, **161**
  California method, 156–59, **156, 159**
  choosing, 149–53, 151, 153
    cool, 151, 152, 153
    hot, 147, 150–52, 151, 153
  city people's method, 163–65, 164
  "double-aerated" block system, 253
  hugelkultur ("mound culture"), 174
  Indore (*See* Indore composting
    method)
  Johnson-Su Bioreactor method, 166
  "lasagna garden," 173–74
  movable compost piles, 169–71, **171**
  "no-work" mulching, 174–75
  pits (*See* pits)
  in plastic bags, 164
  posthole composting, 177–78
  raised-bin method, 166–68, **167**
  "rolling method," 253
  sheet composting, 172–77, 226–27
  some-work mulching, 175–77
  static-pile system, 77, 259, 265–66
  step-by-step method, 168–69
  trench composting, 177–78
  "wandering compost pile," 147–48, **148**
  windrows (*See* windrows)
composting structures. *See also*
    compost pile
  barrels, 144, 165–66
  bins (*See* bins)
  boxes, 191–93

choosing suitable, 195–96
for city composting, 210–12, 211, **211,
  213**
commercially made, 212–13
compost/greenhouse combinations,
  76, **79**
drums, 210
garbage cans as, 193–94, **193**, 210–12,
  211, **211**
pens, 196, 206–8, **206, 207, 208**
pits (*See* pits)
trash cans, 210–12, 211, **211**
tumblers, 144, 165–66
compost piles. *See also* compost;
    composting
  hugelkultur ("mound culture"), 174
  movable for raised beds, 169–71, **171**
  "Pain mound" technique, 75, 76
  "wandering," 147–48, **148**
  windrows (*See* windrows)
compost tea, 238–41, **239**
concentrated animal feeding operations
    (CAFOs), 136, 243, 245–46
contaminants, 73–75, 86, 258–59,
  278–79
cool composting, 151, 152, 153
copper, 58
corncobs, 96, 217
cottonseed, cottonseed meal, 4, 96, 99

damping off, 62, 238
decomposers, 28, 32–41, **33, 38–39,**
  40–42
diseases, human, 79, 258
diseases, plant, 47, 59–61, 240
dog manure, 85, 140
"double-aerated" block system, 253
drums, 210

earthworms, 15, 23–24, 33, 36, **39**, 41, 44,
  182–94, 184, **184**, 186, **186**, 189–91,
  190
  boxes for, 191–93

earthworms (*cont'd*)
  composting with, 182–94, <u>184</u>, **184**,
    186, **187**, **188**, **189**, **190**, **193**
  indoor winter composting, 191–94,
    193
  pits and bins for, 140, 186–89, **187**, **188**,
    189, 209
    winter protection in, 189–91, **190**
  plastic garbage cans for, 193–94, **193**
eelworms (nematodes), 33, 36, **39**,
    41, 60
environmental regulations, 65, 243–44,
    274–75
equipment
  for farm composting, 250, 251–53, **251**,
    252
  mowers, <u>102</u>, **102**, 106, 224
  shredders, 214–24, **216**, **218**, **219**, **220**,
    223
erosion, 16–17, **18**, **19**

farms, 244–45
  composting on (*See* agricultural
    composting)
  organic
    NOP regulations for, 240–41, 276–77
    (*See also* National Organic
    Program)
felt wastes, 97
fertilizers
  chemical, 6, 7, 12, 19, 24–25
  commercial fertilizer laws, 271–72
  compost as, 18–20
field worms, 183–84, **184**, **186**
"fire-fanging," 138
fish scraps, 3, 97–98
flatworms, 33, 36, **39**, 41
flies, 33, 36, **39**, 40–41
flower gardens, applying compost to,
    234
food wastes, <u>10</u>, 65–68, 98, 249, 260–61
fruit trees, 235–36, **236**
fungi, 14
  beneficial, 16, 59–60, 148–49

compost solutions and sprays for, <u>62</u>,
    238
  as decomposers, 28, 32, 33, 35–36, **38**

garbage, 10, **10–11**, 98, 256–57
garbage cans, composting in, 193–94,
    193, 210–12, <u>211</u>, **211**
Georgia reds. *See* redworms
gin trash (cotton gin), 99–100
GMOs, wastes from, 99
government regulations, 243, 270–75.
    See also National Organic
    Program
granite dust, 87, 100
grape waste, 100
grass clippings, **83**, 101–2, <u>102</u>, 275
grease and oil, 86
greenhouse/composting combination,
    76, **79**
greenhouse gases, 7, 12, 24, 46, 271
green manure, 30, 101–2, 172–73
greensand, 87, 103

hair, 103
hardware cloth pen, 144, 206–7, **206**
hay, 103–4
hazardous wastes, 68, 73–75, 258–59,
    278–79
heat. *See* temperature
heavy metals, 22, 68, 105, 109, 115, 258
herbicides, 22–23, 61–62, 68, 86, 101–2
hops, 104–5
hot composting, 147, 150–52, <u>151</u>, <u>153</u>
houseplants, applying compost to,
    236–37
hugelkultur ("mound culture"), 174
humanure (human feces), 77–79, 85
humic acids, 15, 24, 50–53
humus, 23, 26–27, 49–52
  colloids and, 20–22, **21**
  minerals and, 20–22, **21**
  plant nutrition and, 20, 23, 49–52
  soil moisture and, 13
hybrid reds. *See* redworms

incinerator ash, 65, 105
indoor composting, 191–94, **193**
Indore composting method, 5, 116, 143,
    153–56, **154**
  earthworms in, 183–86, <u>184</u>, **184**,
    186
industrial wastes, 256, 260–61
inoculation, 59–60, 148–49
insects, 36–37, **38–39**, 40–41, 63
intensive gardening, 169–71, **171**
in-vessel systems (bioreactors), 263–65
iron, 57–58

Johnson-Su Bioreactor method, 166

kelp (seaweed), 87, 114

landfill gas (methane), 75, 255–56
large-scale composting, 242–44, 259,
    261–66
  buying products from, 277–80
  on farms (*See* agricultural
    composting)
  government encouragement of,
    269–71
  in-vessel (bioreactor) system,
    263–65
  marketing compost from, 267–69,
    271–72
  municipal (*See* municipal
    composting)
  public health and, 258, 272–74
  regulation of, 243, 270–75 (*See also*
    National Organic Program)
  scaling up challenges, 261–63, 266–67
  static-pile systems, 259, 265–66
  windrows (*See* windrows)
"lasagna garden," 173–74
lawns, applying compost to, 234–35
leaf mold, 106–8
leaves, 67, 87, 105–8, <u>107</u>
legal issues, 243, 269–72. *See also*
    National Organic Program
limestone, 87, 108

macronutrients, 53–56. *See also* specific
    nutrient
magnesium, 56, <u>107</u>, <u>118</u>
manganese, 58
manure, 19–20, 81–82, 85–86, 109,
    138–39, 140
  composting, 135–36, 248–49
  contribution of to soil, 134–36, <u>137</u>
  from farm animals, 77, 134–42, <u>137</u>,
    246, 255
  finding sources of, 140–41
  fresh *vs.* rotted, 135
  methane digesters and, 254–55
  moisture content of, <u>137</u>
  as nitrogen source, <u>123</u>, <u>137</u>
  NOP composting requirements and,
    276
  organic matter in, <u>137</u>
  from pets, 85–86, 111, 140
  as phosphorus source, <u>137</u>
  as potash source, <u>137</u>
  substitutes for, 142
  using, 133–42, <u>137</u>
manure tea, 141–42, **141**
manure-type worms, 183–85, **184**,
    186
mesophilic organisms, 32, 34, 152
methane digesters, 254–56
methane (landfill gas), 75, 255–56
micronutrients, 20, 28, 56–58
microorganisms, 27–30, 32–36, **38–39**,
    46–47
microplastics, <u>262</u>
millipedes, 33, 37, **39**
minerals, 20–22, **21**. *See also* specific
    mineral
mites, 33, 36–37, **38**, **39**
moisture, 16, 30, 31, <u>137</u>, 145–46,
    <u>180</u>
molds, 14, 35–36. *See also* fungi
"mound culture" (*hugelkultur*),
    174
movable compost pile, 169–71,
    171

mulching
  as composting method, 172, 174–78
  materials for
    buckwheat hulls, 93
    cocoa bean shells, 94–95
    coffee waste, 95
    corncobs, 96
    grass clippings, 101
    leaf mold, 106–7
    leaves, 105–8
    paper, 109–10
    peat moss, 110
    spent hops, 104–5
    straw, 117
    tanbark, 117–18
    tea grounds, 118–19
    tobacco wastes, 119
    wood chips, 120–21
  "no-work" mulching, 174–75
  some-work mulching, 175–77
mulching mowers, 102, **102**
municipal composting, 242–43, 256–59.
        See also large-scale composting
  California method in, 156–57, **156**,
        159
  concerns about, 68–69
  disposal of compost, 267–69, 271–72
  early growth and missteps of, 64–69
  food waste in, 10, 65–66, 98, 249,
        260–61
  hazardous waste and, 73–75 (*See also*
        hazardous waste)
  industrial waste and, 256, 260–61
  mixed household waste and, 10, **10**, 11,
        256–57
  open system method in, 171–72
  programs for, 66–73, 80
  sewage sludge and, 115–16, 257–59,
        273–74
  solid waste disposal crisis and, 7, 65
  windrows (*See* windrows)
  yard waste in, 65–69, 256
municipal solid waste (MSW). *See*
        municipal composting

mushrooms (mycoremediation), 74–75,
        259
mycorrhizal fungi, 16, 17, 89

National Organic Program (NOP), 6,
        243
  approved commercial composting
        farms and processors, 279–80
  biodegradable plastic ruling, 262
  compost requirements, 151–52
  compost tea regulations, 240–41
  organic farm requirements, 276–77
  organic foods industry and, 245
  private recyclers and, 243–44
  sewage sludge regulations, 259
  vermicompost requirements, 276–77
nematodes (eelworms), 33, 36, **39**,
        41, 60
night crawlers, 183, **184**, **186**. *See also*
        earthworms
nitrates, fertilizers and, 12, 25
nitrogen, 29, 53–54, 107, 146
  as activator, 88–90, 164–65
  in chemical fertilizers, 7, 12, 19,
        24–25
  cycle, 31, **31**
  sources of, 123–25, 127–32, 137, 146
no-heat Indore composting, 185
"no-work" mulching (Ruth Stout),
        174–75
nursery crops, compost mixes
        for, 60
nutrients, 18–20, 28, 49–50, 53–58

odors, 30, 68, 163, 164, 180, 210,
        253, 274
olive waste, 109
organic foods industry, 245
organic land management systems,
        6–7, 11
organic matter, sources of, 122–23,
        137
organic movement, 5–7
oxygen, 17, 30, 47, 48, **48**. *See also* air

"Pain mound" technique, 75, 76
paper, as mulch, 109–10
passively aerated windrow systems
      (PAWS), 266
pathogens, 59–61, 79, 150, 273–74
peat moss, 110
pea wastes, 110
pens, 144, 196, 206–8, **206**, **207**
pesticides, 68, 86
pet tanks, 42–43, **42**, **43**
pet wastes, 85–86, 111, 140
pH, 23, 32, 107, 108, 258
phosphate, 12, 87, 111, 125, 137
phosphate rock, 54, 87, 111–12
phosphoric acid, 127–32
phosphorus, 25, 54, 107, 112, 118
photosynthesis, 48, **48**
pine needles, 112
pits, 169, 186–89, **187**, **188**, **189**,
      208–10
   worm composting and, 140, 186–91,
      187, **188**, **189**, **190**, 209
plants
   diseases of, 59–61, 62, 238, 240
   growth of, 24, 45–47
   nutrition and, 20, 53–58, **57**
plant starter solutions, 237–38, 238
plant wastes. *See* yard waste
plastics, 262
pollution. *See* water, pollution
polybrominated biphenyls (PBBs),
      258–59
polychlorinated biphenyls (PCBs), 74,
      258–59
posthole composting, 177–78
potash, 118, 125–27, 127–32, 137
potassium, 25, 54–55, 107
potato wastes, 112
potworms (white worms), **39**
pressed cocoa cake, 95
proteins, in composting process, 28
protozoa, 33, 35, 36, **39**
pseudoscorpions, 36, **38**
public health

   in large-scale composting, 258, 272–74
   sewage sludge and, 258, 273–74

recycling, 10–11, **10–11**, 12–13
red worms (red wigglers), 23, 182, 184,
      184, 186, **186**
   protecting in winter, 189–91, **190**
regulations, government, 243, 270–75.
      See also National Organic
      Program
respiration, 47–48, 48, **48**
rice hulls, 112–13
rock phosphates, 54, 87, 111–12
Rodale, J. I., 5, **5**, 178–79
"rolling method" of composting, 253
roots, **21**, 46, 47, **48**, 49
rotifers, 33, 36, 39, 41
roundworms, 86

safety, shredders and, 222–23, **223**
sawdust, 113–14
scalping, 186
seaweed (kelp), 87, 114
seeds
   germination of, **20**, 237
   starter mix for, 232
   starter solutions for, 237–38, 238
seed-starting mixes, 96, 237
sewage sludge, 22, 115–16, 257–59
   microplastics in, 262
   municipal composting and, 257–59,
      273–74
   NOP regulations and, 259
   public health and, 258, 273–74
   static-pile systems and, 259, 265–66
   toxic contaminants in, 258–59
sheet composting, 172–77, 226
shredders, 214–24, **216**, **218**, **219**, **220**,
      223
shrubs, applying compost to, 235, **236**
side-dressing, **229**
slag, composition of, 91–92, **92**
slugs and snails, 33, 37, **39**
sodium nitrate, 147

soil, 21
  aeration of, 17–18
  aggregates, 13, 14–16
  air in, 17–18, 47, 48, **48**
  in composting, 116
  erosion of, 16–17, **18**, **19**
  health of and plant diseases, 59–61
  improving, 15–16, 26–27, 134–36, 137
  microorganisms in (*See*
      microorganisms)
  moisture in, 16
  pH of, 23, 108, 258
  structure of, **12**, 13, 14–16
  temperature of and plant growth,
      45–47
  toxin neutralization in, 22–23
some-work mulching method,
    175–77
sow bugs, 33, 37
spiders, 33, 37
springtails, 33, 36, 37, **38**
starter solutions, 237–38, 238
static-pile systems, 76–77, 259, 265–66
step-by-step composting method,
    168–69
straw, 116–17, 118
sugar wastes, 117
sulfur, 56, 118
superphosphate, 111

tanbark, 117–18
tankage, 118
tea grounds, 118–19
temperature, 153
  in composting process, 32, 152
  decomposers and, 32, 33, **33**, 151–52
  effect of on bacteria, 34–35, 147–48
  effect of on fungi, 34–35
  monitoring, 150, 158
  NOP requirements for, 151–52
  plant growth and, 45–47
thermophilic microorganisms, 32, 34,
    150

tillers, 226–27
tobacco wastes, 119
toilets, composting, 77–79
top-dressing, 232, 235
toxic waste, 73–75, 86, 115, 258–59,
    278–79
tractors, 226
trash can composting, 210–12, 211,
    211
trees, applying compost to, 235, **236**
trench composting, 177–78
troubleshooting, 181, 181
tumblers, 144, 165–66
turning, 144, 147, 150, 157, 159

urea, 147
urine, 79, 134, 137, 164

vegetable gardens, **229**, 232, 233
vermicomposting, 152, 276–77. *See also*
    earthworms
vivarium, 42–43, **42–43**

"wandering" compost pile, 147–48,
    148
water
  in pet tanks, **42**, 43, **43**
  plant growth and, 46, 48–49
  pollution of, 25, 54, 65, 112, 136, 243,
      275
water hyacinths, 87, 119
weeds, 32, 119–20
  seeds of, 137–38, 150, 151, 153, 161, 162,
      167, 177
white worms (potworms), **39**
windrows, 171–72
  California method, 156–57, **156**, **159**
  farm composting and, 171–72, 250–54,
      251, **252**
  for municipal composting, 171–72,
      261
  passively aerated windrow system,
      266

winter composting
  indoors, 191–94, **193**
  outdoors, 147, 189–91, **190**, 205, 208–10
wood ashes, 87, 120
wood chips, 120–21
wool wastes (shoddy), 121
worm composting, 152, 276–77. *See also*
  earthworms; worms

worms. *See also* earthworms
  flatworms, 33, 36, **39**, 41
  potworms (white
    worms), **39**

yard waste, 65–66, 67

zinc, 58